Springer Texts in Education

D1823875

More information about this series at http://www.springer.com/series/13812

Stacia C. Miller · Suzanne F. Lindt
Editors

Moving INTO the Classroom

A Handbook for Movement Integration
in the Elementary Classroom

 Springer

Editors
Stacia C. Miller
Midwestern State University
Wichita Falls, TX
USA

Suzanne F. Lindt
Midwestern State University
Wichita Falls, TX
USA

ISSN 2366-7672   ISSN 2366-7680   (electronic)
Springer Texts in Education
ISBN 978-981-10-6423-4   ISBN 978-981-10-6424-1   (eBook)
DOI 10.1007/978-981-10-6424-1

Library of Congress Control Number: 2017951171

© Springer Nature Singapore Pte Ltd. 2018
This work is subject to copyright. All rights are reserved by the Publisher, whether the whole or part of the material is concerned, specifically the rights of translation, reprinting, reuse of illustrations, recitation, broadcasting, reproduction on microfilms or in any other physical way, and transmission or information storage and retrieval, electronic adaptation, computer software, or by similar or dissimilar methodology now known or hereafter developed.
The use of general descriptive names, registered names, trademarks, service marks, etc. in this publication does not imply, even in the absence of a specific statement, that such names are exempt from the relevant protective laws and regulations and therefore free for general use.
The publisher, the authors and the editors are safe to assume that the advice and information in this book are believed to be true and accurate at the date of publication. Neither the publisher nor the authors or the editors give a warranty, express or implied, with respect to the material contained herein or for any errors or omissions that may have been made. The publisher remains neutral with regard to jurisdictional claims in published maps and institutional affiliations.

This Springer imprint is published by Springer Nature
The registered company is Springer Nature Singapore Pte Ltd.
The registered company address is: 152 Beach Road, #21-01/04 Gateway East, Singapore 189721, Singapore

Preface

This book details integrating movement activities into the content areas. The book is designed with research-based strategies for pre-service and certified teachers to assist with effective ways to integrate movement activities into lessons. The textbook includes an introductory chapter that focuses on research in movement integration, the benefits of physical activity in the classroom, and the importance of movement to the whole child; while the second chapter addresses barriers to movement in the classroom, offering insightful tips for navigating a more kinesthetic setting. The third chapter of the text offers a guide that explains how to use the lesson plan template seen throughout the text, with descriptions of the components of the plan and examples of classroom management techniques for using movement in the classroom. The eight remaining chapters provide research regarding movement in English language arts, mathematics, science, and social studies and include activities and lesson plans for the lower and upper elementary classrooms. The text makes few assumptions regarding prior knowledge in these fields, though previous classes in the four disciplines would benefit the reader of the textbook. Though the textbook specifically targets the elementary grade levels, secondary teachers and pre-service teachers would likely be able to modify the activities to fit secondary lessons.

Having interacted with in-service and pre-service teachers alike, the editors realize the interest in integrating movement into the classroom, but there is a need for quality resources to use as exemplars. This practical textbook will benefit both pre-service and current teachers. This text will provide pre-service teachers with a resource they can use during their coursework and is one that will continue to be a resource in their own classrooms. Current classroom teachers will also benefit from this text, which includes lessons and handouts that can be used immediately in their classrooms.

The textbook has several unique and outstanding features, including content from experts in the field, subsections to address each component of each core subject, and sample lesson plans appropriate for lower and upper elementary movement integration. First and foremost, content experts have written the literature reviews, created the sample activities, and crafted the lesson plans. These content experts include faculty members with extensive k-12 classroom experience and pre-service teachers from the content areas. There are four content chapters in the text, and each chapter has a literature review, supporting the integration of movement for that specific content area; at least five sample activities, one per strand; one sample lesson plan for lower elementary, and one sample lesson plan for upper elementary.

In addition to the lesson plans and detailed activities, the text includes supplements to assist the reader with movement integration. Included in the activities are pictures of students participating in the lessons, tables to provide examples, and an appendix with printable handouts and assessment tools.

This book offers meaningful activities and lessons aimed at improving engagement and learning in the elementary classroom. This book will become instrumental for educators interested in integrating movement into the classroom for the purposes of engaging students and increased learning.

Wichita Falls, TX, USA   Sincerely,
                                                              Stacia C. Miller Ph.D.
                                                              Suzanne F. Lindt Ph.D.

Acknowledgements

We are greatly indebted to the countless authors, educators, reviewers, parents, and students who helped us in putting together each chapter of this textbook. We are especially grateful for the EURECA program at Midwestern State University for giving us funding that allowed us to begin this project with undergraduate students. This project would not have been possible without the ongoing support from family, friends, and colleagues.

Contents

Chapter 1
Movement Integration: What Is It and Why Should We Do It?

Mary Brady, Stacia C. Miller and Suzanne F. Lindt

Abstract This chapter offers an introduction to movement integration, including a definition of movement integration, reasons for integrating movement into the classroom, benefits of physical activity in the classroom, and the importance of movement to the whole child. Knowing more about movement integration will provide classroom teachers with the confidence to begin using activities and lessons that will benefit both the teacher and the students.

A Case for Movement Integration

Michelle taught the concept of lines, rays, and angles to her 3rd grade math class. During one of the lessons, Michelle told the students that in order to have a better understanding of the differences between lines, rays, and angles, they were going to sing a song to the tune of Frère Jacque (Wright, Wright, & Willbanks, 2010). She asked the students to sing the following words with her:

> Line, ray, angle.
>
> Line, ray, angle.
>
> Which is which?
>
> Which is which?
>
> Lines are never ending.
>
> Rays are one way sending.
>
> Angles bend. Angles bend.

M. Brady · S.C. Miller (✉) · S.F. Lindt
Midwestern State University, Wichita Falls, TX, USA
e-mail: stacia.miller@mwsu.edu

M. Brady
e-mail: marybrdy@gmail.com

S.F. Lindt
e-mail: suzanne.lindt@mwsu.edu

© Springer Nature Singapore Pte Ltd. 2018
S.C. Miller and S.F. Lindt (eds.), *Moving INTO the Classroom*,
Springer Texts in Education, DOI 10.1007/978-981-10-6424-1_1

After the students had an understanding of the song, she split them into groups of two–three and asked them to come up with movements for the song using their hands, feet, arms, and legs. She suggested that they use their bodies to represent lines, rays, and angles to make up a dance. Then she had groups of students demonstrate their dances for the class.

This example of incorporating dance and song into math helped to enhance student memory of lines, rays, and angles. Even students in Michelle's class with special education modifications were able to distinguish the differences between the angles. Specifically, one student with autism actively participated in the class and worked well with peers to create his song. Because Michelle integrated movement into her lesson to reinforce the differences between lines, rays, and angles, her students gained a more thorough understanding of these concepts, while also increasing their physical activity. Though Michelle teaches all types of lessons, students seem to enjoy and participate in her movement-integrated lessons the most. As a result, Michelle's students gain a more thorough understanding of concepts taught in her 3rd grade mathematics class.

Defining Movement Integration

Although physical education, physical activity, and recess are an important part of the curriculum, some elementary schools have reduced physical education and recess to spend more time studying English language arts and mathematics as they strive to meet the requirements of the No Child Left Behind Act (NCLB) (Center on Education Policy, 2008). The Center on Education Policy (2008) conducted a survey of 349 school districts, reflecting the majority of schools in the nation. This survey showed that 9% of all the school districts surveyed decreased physical education in elementary school by an average of 40 min each week, and 20% of all the school districts surveyed decreased recess in elementary schools by an average of 50 min every week (Center on Education Policy, 2008). There is no federal law protecting physical education requirements and mandates, which only amplifies the decrease in physical education (NASPE & American Heart Association [AHA], 2012).

Since many states do not require schools to provide students with adequate time for physical education and physical activity (NASPE & AHA, 2012), schools are using physical activity programs to benefit students' health by helping them reach the nationally recommended 60 min of physical activity each day (American Alliance for Health, Physical Education, Recreation and Dance [AAHPERD], 2013; Centers for Disease Control and Prevention [CDC], 2013). These physical activity programs include physical activities before, during, and after school to help students stay active throughout the school day (AAHPERD, 2013; CDC, 2013). For example, before and after each school day, students may be in sports programs or in programs where the students ride a bike or walk to and from school. During school, the physical activity programs recommend providing recess, physical activity breaks during school time, and integrated movement lessons.

Two of the more widely accepted physical activity programs include a Comprehensive School Physical Activity Program (CSPAP) (AAHPERD, 2013; CDC, 2013) and *Let's Move!* Active Schools (www.letsmoveschools.org). The goals for CSPAP, *Let's Move!* Active Schools, and other similar programs are to provide students with at least 60 min of physical activity daily and to meet the physical education goal of advancing students' skills, knowledge, and confidence to continue participating in physical activity throughout their lifespan. The different physical activity programs have proposed unique and diverse strategies to assist schools and communities in increasing physical activity opportunities for the children. Per the focus of this text, classroom teachers have an opportunity to participate as an integral part of these programs by providing physical activity in the classroom. Through a variety of movement activities, teachers can help their students receive the recommended amount of physical activity each day (AAHPERD, 2013; CDC, 2013).

Despite the fact that many teachers are striving to change the decreasing trends in physical activity by integrating physical activities in the classroom to help students reach the daily goal of 60 min of physical activity, many barriers may hinder teachers from using physical activity and movement in the classroom setting. While many elementary classroom teachers are trained and certified as generalists, often taking courses designed to educate them to teach a range of content including physical education, we are not suggesting that classroom teachers become physical educators. As discussed in Chap. 2, there are many barriers and difficulties associated with providing classroom physical activity. Therefore the focus of this text is "movement integration", meaning that classroom teachers' lessons remain focused on the current curriculum and learning outcomes. Also, the activities in this text have been written by former classroom teachers, who have extensive experience in the classroom, and who focused on the best approach to integrating movement into the different content areas. In addition, the activities were selected for the simplicity and manageability for the classroom teachers.

The term movement integration has generally been used in the literature to refer to any level of physical activity infused into normal classroom time, including academic lessons incorporating physical activity, short physical activity breaks, and physical activity during transition periods (Webster, Russ, Vazou, Goh, & Erwin, 2015). Movement integration is unlike kinesthetic learning, as proposed by Gardner (1983), which describes bodily movement as an intelligence. Instead, movement integration is proposed as a benefit for all students both as a means to improve physical fitness and as a means to improve student learning. For the purpose of this text, we considered previous areas of educational research that support the blending of two separate content areas into one cohesive context; which facilitated our use of the term movement integration. Curriculum integration, defined by Hall-Kenyon and Smith (2013), combines objectives from at least two content areas into one lesson. Along with curriculum integration, interdisciplinarity integrates subject content from at least two disciplines of knowledge that are typically taught separately (Holley, 2009). Most importantly when using movement integration, the core subject content and the physical activity content must both be valid lessons individually, and when integrated, they must facilitate students' achievement of goals in each content area (Brophy & Alleman, 1991). Therefore, we define movement integration as an interdisciplinary method of teaching, which incorporates physical activity into core content areas, for the purpose of improving student understanding and learning outcomes. To comprehend the definition of movement integration, it is imperative to understand the difference between physical activity and physical education (Beighle & Morrow, 2014). Movement integration uses physical activity to help students stay active in the classroom, but educators should be cautious not to substitute the term "physical activity" for the term "physical education" because these two terms have distinct definitions (Beighle & Morrow, 2014). Physical activity is movement by the body that facilitates people's health (U. S. Department of Health and Human Services [USDHHS], 2008); while physical education strives to promote and create individuals who are physically educated and who possess the skills, knowledge, and confidence to remain physically active throughout their lives (National Association for Sport and Physical Education [NASPE], 2011). Physical education includes physical activity, and the USDHHS recommends that during a physical education class period, a minimum of 50% of the class time should be spent in moderate to vigorous physical activity (MVPA) (USDHHS, 2010). In addition to providing students with physical activity, physical education also incorporates health (NASPE, 2011), fitness, skill techniques, and the importance of physical activity (Beighle & Morrow, 2014). While knowing the differences between physical activity and physical education is necessary to understanding movement integration, understanding the current state of physical education and physical activity remains salient to classroom teachers' motivation and purpose for integrating movement into the classroom.

Current State of Physical Education, Physical Activity, and Recess

In an effort to circumvent the diminishing state of physical education, several national organizations have set recommendations for physical education, physical activity, and recess (NASPE & AHA, 2012; USDHHS, 2008). Even though the federal government does not require schools to provide physical education, the USDHHS and NASPE, which has been renamed to the Society of Health and Physical Educators (SHAPE America), provide recommendations for physical activity (USDHHS, 2008), physical education, and recess (NASPE & AHA, 2012). The USDHHS recommends at least an hour a day of exercise for 6–17-year old children and adolescents (USDHHS, 2008), but the National Health and Nutrition Examination Survey (NHANES) measured physical activity with accelerometers in students aged 6–11 years old and found that only 42% of these children meet the recommended 60 min of physical activity each day (Troiano et al., 2008). Therefore, many school-aged children do not receive enough daily physical activity to maintain healthy lives.

SHAPE America recommends that schools help students reach the daily goal of physical activity by providing them with at least 150 min of physical education each week (NASPE & AHA, 2012), and that physical education classes in elementary schools should not exceed 25 students to one teacher (NASPE, 2006b). This class size limit helps the teacher provide a safe and successful environment where students can receive adequate individualized instruction and sufficient opportunities to learn (NASPE, 2006a).

In addition to physical education, SHAPE America recommends that elementary students receive at least one recess period for a minimum of 20 min each day (NASPE, 2006b). SHAPE America also advises that recess and physical education both be provided during school hours because recess offers an opportunity for students to engage in physical activity through unstructured play, while physical education helps develop students' movement concepts, motor skills, and fitness through progressive instruction (NASPE, 2006b). Both recess and physical education are beneficial and one should not replace the other (NASPE, 2006b). Although organizations have set recommendations for physical education, physical activity, and recess, very few states meet these recommendations (NASPE & AHA, 2012).

Since the federal government does not require states to provide physical education during school hours, some states have set their own physical education criteria; however, the responsibility of fulfilling each state's requirements is given to the school districts (NASPE & AHA, 2012). Forty-three states require elementary schools to provide physical education. However, only 16 states require schools to provide a minimum amount of physical education per week or per day. Some states follow the recommended 150 min of physical education for elementary school students each week, while other states do not meet these recommendations. Louisiana, New Jersey, and Florida are the only states that require the recommended 150 min or more of physical education a week.

In addition to their failure to meet the weekly physical education recommendations in most states, many physical education classes exceed the recommended ratio of 25 students to one teacher. Some physical educators have 40 or more students per class. These large class sizes can lead to management problems, disruptive behavior and safety issues, inadequate amounts of space and supplies, less individualized instruction, and fewer practice opportunities. Large class sizes can negatively affect the physical education environment by decreasing the amount of physical activity in which students can engage. With fewer opportunities to participate in physical activity in large physical education classes, students may develop their skills and knowledge at a slower pace (NASPE, 2006a).

In addition to many states not meeting the national recommendations for physical education, many states do not require schools to provide recess (NASPE & AHA, 2012). Elementary schools in only nine states are required to provide students with recess every day. This lack of offered recess demonstrates another example of how students are not provided the recommended amount of physical activity during school every day. The previous section provides a review of the requirements and recommendations for physical education, physical activity, and recess throughout the states, and due to the lack of physical activity provided to students during school hours, schools and teachers are striving to change this trend by implementing physical activity programs into other parts of the school day. This proposed change may help students reach the daily goal of 60 min of physical activity.

Context for the Textbook

Classrooms are characteristically sedentary environments, requiring that children spend a great deal of time sitting (Holt, Bartee, & Heelan, 2013). Additionally, society has become more sedentary as children spend much of their time with technology. There is evidence that physical activity may help improve students' academic achievements, while using physically active lessons may also positively impact children's daily physical activity levels (Norris, Shelton, Dunsmuir, Duke-Williams, & Stamatakis, 2015). Given the increased academic pressure in schools, including the demands of high-stakes testing, classroom teachers may not have a strong commitment to physical education (Prosser & Jiang, 2008). Consequently, teachers may be reluctant to utilize movement in the classroom to help students reach the daily goal of 60 min of physical activity.

Research has found mixed results about classroom teachers' feelings toward the integration of physical activity in the classroom setting, suggesting that teachers have varying preferences (Webster et al., 2015). Much of the research establishes that while classroom teachers support classroom physical activity for students, many see a lack of time as a major barrier (Cothran, Kulinna, & Garn, 2010; Howie, Newman-Norlund, & Pate, 2014). Other studies highlight barriers such as behavior concerns (Howie et al., 2014; Nicksic, 2015) and perceived competence (Vazou & Skrade, 2014). As existing research on classroom teacher self-efficacy for teaching physical education demonstrates, some classroom teachers may feel unprepared to teach physical education (Fletcher, Mandigo, & Kosnik, 2013; Miller, Lindt, & McIntyre, 2014). While evidence suggests that teachers perceive many barriers to integrating movement, realistic expectations and opportunities must be provided for sustainability. For example, emerging evidence shows teachers prefer activities that are connected to academic content (McMullen, Kulinna, & Cothran, 2014) and that are compatible with their teaching skills (Webster et al., 2013). As such, the aims of the lessons in this text are to provide teachers with activities designed specifically for the classroom environment, that connect directly to academic content and learning outcomes for each discipline. Although the goal of movement integration has traditionally been to increase physical activity in children; more recent attention has been given to the connections to improving children's academic performance. There is a growing body of evidence indicating that physical activity in the classroom can benefit both the health and academic performance of children (Norris et al., 2015), with a focus on the whole child.

Benefits for the Child

Whole Child

A holistic form of educating the whole child has been promoted in schools to help students align their health with their cognitive, social, and emotional development. A whole child education aims to develop the student physically, cognitively, socially, and emotionally (Slade & Griffith, 2013). The following sections describe the benefits of movement integration to students' physical, cognitive, social, and emotional well-being.

Physical. One of the most obvious ways that movement integration can benefit the whole child is through physical improvements. Movement in the classroom can expand physical activity by increasing the number of steps a child takes in a day (Adams-Blair & Oliver, 2011; Erwin, Abel, Beighle, & Beets, 2011a; Erwin, Beighle, Morgan, & Noland, 2011b; Mahar et al., 2006). For example, Erwin et al. (2011a, b) monitored the physical activity of 106 students from 3rd to 5th grade and found that the teachers who integrated physical activity into their classrooms at least once a day increased students' daily steps by one-third. Also, Adams-Blair and Oliver (2011) measured elementary students' steps on days when students did not have physical education but engaged in movement integration lessons for 30 min throughout the day and found that students averaged about 1500 more steps each day.

In addition to increasing the number of steps students take, physical activity in the classroom can benefit students' bone mass and strength (Macdonald et al., 2008). Macdonald et al. (2008) studied 410 children aged nine to eleven from ten schools in British Columbia, Canada with 293 children in the intervention group and 117 children in the control group. The teachers in the intervention group implemented Action Schools! BC and Bounce at the Bell physical activity programs for 15 min throughout each day. Students in the intervention group participated in high-impact jumping activities three times each day for 4 days every week as part of the Bounce at the Bell program. These researchers found that boys in the intervention group had improved bone mass in both total body and in the lumbar spine, and girls, who had teachers that had an 80% or higher compliancy rating with the intervention, had increased bone strength and mass at the femoral neck (Macdonald et al., 2008).

Besides providing an improvement to students' bone mass and strength, movement integration can help decrease Body Mass Index (BMI) percentiles (Hollar et al., 2010a, b), decrease weight z-scores, and decrease blood pressure (Hollar et al., 2010b). Hollar et al. (2010a, b) studied students in four intervention elementary schools and one control elementary school in Florida for 2 years. The intervention schools participated in the Healthier Options for Public Schoolchildren (HOPS) obesity prevention program which included movement integration lessons during the second year of the study. The researchers reported that significantly more intervention students (vs. control students) remained in the normal BMI percentile range and girls in the intervention group decreased their overall BMI z-scores (Hollar et al., 2010a). In Hollar et al. (2010b), the researchers found that in comparison to the control group, the intervention girls had a significant decrease in diastolic blood pressure for both years and a significant decrease in systolic blood pressure during the first year of the study. Also, the intervention girls' body mass index and weight z-scores decreased significantly when compared with the control group. The results from these studies indicate that integrating physical activity into the classroom can lead to greater physical benefits for students.

Cognitive. In addition to physical benefits, movement integration and physical activity provide the whole child with cognitive benefits, such as increased brain function and academic performance. Hall (2007) explains the impact movement integration lessons can have on cognition. When students use more muscles during movement integration lessons than during traditional desk work lessons, more sensory fibers are recruited, and they transport impulses from the muscles to the brain which helps the students' learning become more concrete. When students exercise, the cardiovascular system sends an increased amount of blood flow through the body to the brain. The brain benefits from physical activity because the increased blood flow brings more oxygen and glucose to the brain, which increases the brain's function. In a study involving 29 3rd grade students with 16 intervention students and 13 control students for 20 weeks, the intervention teacher provided movement integration lessons using the students' math and reading content for at least 20 min each day, while the control teacher did not use movement integration lessons (Erwin, Fedewa, & Ahn, 2013). Results offer that the intervention students scored higher in mathematics and reading fluency than the students who did not receive the movement integration intervention, further emphasizing the benefits of movement integration in the classroom. In addition to fluency, students' planning ability may be positively related to the amount of physical activity in which they participate. Davis et al. (2007) conducted a study that included 94 overweight students aged 7–11. Students were placed randomly in a 20 min a day physical activity group, a 40 min a day physical activity group, and a control group that received no extra physical activity. The intervention groups participated in physical activity for 5 days a week for 15 weeks. All of the students in this study completed a Cognitive Assessment System (CAS) test before and after the intervention, which assessed four cognitive processes, one of which included planning. The researchers found that the children who engaged in high-intensity physical activity outperformed the control group students, who participated in no physical activity in the CAS for planning, a measure of executive functioning. This study provides further evidence that students who exercise vigorously can improve their executive functioning (Davis et al., 2007), leading to greater brain activity and learning.

Academic Performance. Cognitive benefits, such as academic performance in content scores may also occur as students engage in movement activities (Adams-Blair & Oliver, 2011). Mullender-Wijnsma et al. (2015) followed 2nd and 3rd grade students for a year after their participation in movement integrated math and reading lessons and found that those participating in the movement lessons attained higher grades than those who had not participated in the movement lessons.

Results support that participating in physically active classroom lessons may improve students' understanding of classroom content to assist students in long-term retention. In addition to long-term gains in academic achievement, integrating movement may help students who struggle with academic content. Incorporating movement into the classroom may also help students who perform in the lower 20% increase their academic scores on national exams (McClelland, Pitt, & Stein, 2015). Researchers reported the greatest effect sizes with these students to suggest that movement integration may serve as an intervention for students struggling with academic content.

Specific programs may also be implemented into schools and the classroom to benefit test scores and academic achievement by students. Physical Activity Across the Curriculum (PAAC) is a program in which the intervention teachers were asked to provide 90 min of moderate to vigorous movement integration lessons per week. In a 3-year study, fourteen schools received the intervention and ten schools were in the control group with traditional lessons instead of movement integration lessons (Donnelly et al., 2009). This study revealed significant academic achievement improvements in the intervention group in reading, composite, spelling, and math scores. Further evidence of the benefit of integrating movement into the classroom is supported in a study in California, which evaluated students' Physical Fitness Tests and California Standards Tests. Results suggested a positive relationship between physical fitness and standardized test scores (California Department of Education, 2005). Though research supports the benefit of increased physical activity to developing the cognitive process of planning, studies have also found that increasing the amount of physical activity in the classroom does not hinder academic success or classroom behavior (CDC, 2010). In a review of the literature, the CDC reported that eight out of nine studies that researched physical activity in the classroom suggested that a positive relationship may exist between physical activity and academic success, academic behavior, cognitive skills, and cognitive attitudes. None of these studies found a negative relationship. Caterino and Polak (1999) found similar results as to what the CDC reported. They discovered that 4th grade students who participated in 15 min of physical activity before a concentration test performed significantly better than the 4th grade control group that received no physical activity. However, they also found that 2nd and 3rd grade students who engaged in 15 min of physical activity before the concentration test did not perform any better than the control group who received no physical activity. These results demonstrate that an increased amount of physical activity during the school day does not decrease cognition on a concentration test and therefore does not detract from academic success in the classroom. These studies further support that integrating movement into the classroom can benefit students' cognition and learning.

Social and Emotional. Though physical activity may benefit children physically and cognitively, children may also benefit socially and emotionally from physical activity. When students engage in small-group movement integration lessons, the students develop social skills such as problem solving, settling disagreements, and taking turns (Skoning, 2010). These students learn to succeed by establishing goals and working together as a group to meet the goals. In a case study, Skoning (2010) describes a 4th grade boy with an emotional behavioral disorder and an English language learner. Before the teacher introduced movement into the classroom, this student was seldomly engaged in class when doing group work. However, when small-group movement integration activities, which focused on academic concepts and social skills, were incorporated into the class period, the student became more engaged in the lesson and started to make friends with his classmates (Skoning, 2010). Integrating movement may also benefit students who experience difficulty typically socializing with other students, even those on the autism spectrum (Miller & Lindt, 2016).

In addition to the example from Skoning (2010), a child's self-esteem can be positively influenced by the indirect teaching method of physical activity, which Theodorakou and Zervas (2003) call the creative movement teaching method. This creative movement method of teaching is classified as pupil-centered and indirect, and this teaching method uses experimentation, improvisation, discovery, exploration, and problem solving to enhance learning. In the creative movement method of teaching, the teacher establishes parameters, and the students create their own movements within the parameters. Theodorakou and Zervas (2003) studied 107 5th and 6th grade students from a public school in Athens, Greece. The intervention group received the creative movement instruction, and the control group received traditional instruction in physical education for 45 min two times a week for 3 months. In the traditional teaching method, the teacher commands, demonstrates, and makes the decisions for the students. Therefore, creative movement instruction may positively influence students' self-esteem because students have an opportunity to make their own decisions about activities in which to engage. In addition, Theodorakou and Zervas (2003) concluded that the creative movement method of teaching benefitted all of the aspects of self-esteem, including: social acceptance, behavioral conduct, physical appearance, academic ability, athletic ability, and global self-worth. Therefore, movement taught in integrated lessons through the creative, indirect teaching style may have a positive relationship with students' self-esteem. In addition, increasing moderate physical activity for children is positively related to overall emotional well-being as well as risk-taking (Ward, Duncan, Jarden, & Stewart, 2016). These benefits to a child's emotional health are likely to be seen in a classroom with integrated movement. As teachers consider integrating movement into their classrooms, they should not only realize the benefits of movement to their students' development, but they should also consider possible positive benefits to the classroom.

Benefits to the Classroom Environment

Though the implementation of movement integration provides a direct benefit to students, movement integration lessons also provide benefits for the classroom. Participating in movement integration lessons may lead to an increase in students' motivation and engagement levels during class, while also increasing students' on-task behavior.

Motivation and Engagement

Bybee et al. (2006) proposed the 5E Instructional Model for instructional design, in which "engage" is listed as the first element in lesson-planning. They suggest that by engaging students in a lesson, students will be more likely to experience curiosity and make connections between prior and new knowledge. Engagement may also serve as a form of formative assessment for the classroom teacher to determine students' prior knowledge and to assist him or her in designing appropriate lessons for the unit. Movement integration, as a novel activity, may be used at the beginning of a unit to assess students' prior knowledge and to provide an introduction to a task. However, movement integration may also be used in the middle or end of a unit to help students engage and organize information from previous lessons. By providing students with differentiated activities within an instructional unit, they may be more likely to engage in learning.

Movement in the classroom may also help students become excited about the content. Vazou, Gavrilou, Mamalaki, Papanastasiou, and Sioumala (2012) studied 147 students in 4th, 5th, and 6th grades in Crete, Greece. The students participated in six lessons for 2 weeks, and were assigned to movement integration lessons (treatment) or traditional lessons (control). The first two lessons were taught in the traditional teaching method, the third and fifth lessons were taught using movement integration, and the fourth and sixth lessons were taught using the traditional teaching method. Before each lesson ended, students completed the Intrinsic Motivation Inventory, which measured students' Interest/Enjoyment, Effort, Pressure/Tension, Perceived Competence, and Value/Usefulness. The researchers found that the students' interest and enjoyment (intrinsic motivation), effort, and perceived competence increased significantly when teachers integrated physical activity into the classroom. Results also revealed that the movement integration lessons did not increase students' awareness of pressure and did not detract from the value of the lesson. The students reported greater enjoyment while participating in the movement integration lessons and felt the movement integration lessons were more interesting than traditional lessons. Therefore, students who enjoy the lessons and feel proficient in the content are more inclined to put greater effort into the lessons, and they are less inclined to feel that the lessons are meaningless or encounter pressure (Vazou et al., 2012).

Additional reasons exist for using movement integration during class to help improve students' motivation and engagement levels. Hruska and Clancy (2008) recognize that many students' motivation and focus to learn can increase when teachers change the lesson format. Research in technology (Light & Pierson, 2014) and music (Roberts, 2015) suggest a positive relationship between the inclusion of novel tasks that elicit differentiated instruction and spark interest from students to student engagement in their classes. Teachers suggest that by using movement activities along with their regular lessons, students are interested and engaged and experience greater learning (Lindt & Miller, 2017). By bringing movement into the classroom, teachers can create a new lesson format that may help students increase their motivation and their focus on the content.

Movement integration may also serve as a way to enhance students' interest, which may lead to greater sustained attention in the classroom (Ainley, Hidi, & Berndorff, 2002). Hidi and Renninger (2006) describe interest as a four-phase model through which learners move: triggered situational interest, maintained situational interest, emerging individual interest, and well-developed individual interest. Triggered situational interest can be generated from surprising information that causes short-term changes in affective and cognitive processing (Hidi & Baird 1986, 1988; Mitchell, 1993) and is usually a result of external stimulation (Hidi & Renninger, 2006). Movement integration may act as a way to trigger students' situational interest because incorporating movement into core content areas is a fun, new stimulating way for students to learn in the classroom (Mitchell, 1993; Vazou et al., 2012). Mitchell (1993) suggests that to create situational interest, teachers should provide lessons that stimulate the students. Lessons which incorporate group work, computers, and puzzles help stimulate and capture students' attention because they offer variety in the classroom (Mitchell, 1993). While catching students' attention is important, providing lessons that maintain students' situational interest impact students more than those that do not and lead students into phases of personal interest (Hidi & Renninger, 2006). In order to hold students' situational interest, teachers should provide lessons that empower the student (Mitchell, 1993). Teachers can empower their students by providing lessons that are meaningful and relevant to their lives and hold students' interest by involving the students in the lessons. Providing students with novel, stimulating, meaningful, and involving lessons by integrating movement into the core content areas may lead to greater student interest than sitting and lecturing to students when teaching new content (Mitchell, 1993). One of the many benefits of movement for elementary students is for the purpose of increasing students' engagement while reducing problems and off task behaviors. Benes, Finn, Sullivan, & Yan (2016) concluded that students involved in movement lessons in the classroom were more engaged in the lessons and even suggested that integrating movement between traditional lessons helped students to refocus on the content.

Behavior

In addition to increasing motivation and engagement, providing movement integration lessons can also increase students' on-task behavior when compared to students in classrooms with traditional non-movement lessons (Miller & Lindt, 2016; Mullender-Wijnsma et al., 2015). Students with movement as a regular part of the curriculum may be less likely to engage in problem behaviors significantly more than those without movement lessons (Käll, Malmgren, Olsen, Linden, & Nilsen, 2015). Mahar et al. (2006) studied students in kindergarten through fourth grade at an eastern North Carolina public school with three classes in each grade level. The researchers randomly assigned two classes from each grade level (except for 3rd grade who only had one class that was in the intervention group) to engage in the intervention. The intervention included one 10-min movement integration activity each day for 12 weeks, described as an Energizer. Thirty minutes before and after the Energizers, the researchers evaluated on-task behavior for 62 3rd and 4th grade students. The results demonstrated that this movement integration intervention significantly increased all students' on-task behavior by over 8%. Furthermore, students who were on-task less than half the time before the Energizers, increased their on-task behavior by 20% after they finished the Energizers activities (Mahar et al., 2006).

In addition to increasing on-task behavior, previous research also suggests that incorporating movement into the classroom may reduce noise and increase concentration levels (Norlander, Moås, & Archer, 2005). In a study of 84 students in a primary and secondary school in Sweden, researchers measured five of the classrooms' noise levels before and after the intervention for 4 weeks, and they measured the noise levels of one class that served as the control group, which did not receive the intervention. The intervention included 2, 5–10 min stretching and relaxation exercises each day; one intervention exercise was performed after the morning break, and the second intervention was provided after lunch. This study found that the five classes that received the intervention significantly reduced their noise levels from 63.24 decibels (dB) to 50.50 dB. The teachers also rated their students' concentration levels before and after each intervention and found that the students were able to concentrate more after the intervention (Norlander et al., 2005). These studies show that movement integration can help increase conducive behavior for the classroom setting.

Conclusion

As mentioned in this chapter, many students do not receive the physical activity that they need during school hours. Teachers can help students receive physical activity in their own classrooms by integrating movement into the core content areas. By integrating movement, teachers not only allow students to receive beneficial physical activity, but teachers also provide their students the opportunity to increase cognitive, social, and emotional health. Teachers may also benefit from integrating movement into their classrooms, as increased physical activity has been linked to greater student motivation, engagement, and constructive behavior. Although movement integration can provide students many benefits, some perceived barriers of movement integration may hinder teachers from using this method of teaching in their own classrooms. The perceived barriers to movement integration have been addressed in the following chapter. Furthermore, the lesson-planning format discussed in detail in Chap. 3 was designed specifically to address the perceived barriers in the planning stages. Finally, activity ideas have been presented for the various strands within the different content areas to provide more ideas for integrating movement. The lesson plan template has been used throughout the text, for the content areas of math, science, history, and English, to provide teachers with useful examples of lesson plans that implement movement into the classroom.

References

Adams-Blair, H., & Oliver, G. (2011). Daily classroom movement: Physical activity integration into the classroom. *International Journal of Health, Wellness and Society, 1*(3), 147–154.

Ainley, M. D., Hidi, S., & Berndorff, D. (2002). Interest, learning and the psychological processes that mediate their relationship. *Journal of Educational Psychology, 94*, 1–17.

American Alliance for Health, Physical Education, Recreation and Dance. (2013). *Comprehensive school physical activity programs: Helping students achieve 60 minutes of physical activity each day (position statement)*. Reston, VA: Author.

Beighle, A., & Morrow, J. R. (2014). Promoting physical activity: Addressing barriers and moving forward. *JOPERD: The Journal of Physical Education, Recreation and Dance, 85*(7), 23. doi:10.1080/07303084.2014.937190.

Benes, S., Finn, K. E., Sullivan, E. C., & Yon, Z. (2016). Teachers' perceptions of using movement in the classroom. *Physical Educator, 73*(1), 110–135. doi:10.18666/TPE-2016-V73-I1-5316.

Brophy, J., & Alleman, J. (1991). A caveat: Curriculum integration isn't always a good idea. *Educational Leadership, 49*(2), 66.

Bybee, R., Taylor, J. A., Gardner, A., Van Scotter, P., Carlson, J., Westbrook, A., et al. (2006). *The BSCS 5E instructional model: Origins and effectiveness*. Colorado Springs, CO: BSCS.

California Department of Education. (2005). *California physical fitness test: A study of the relationship between physical fitness and academic achievement in California using 2004 test results*. Sacramento, CA: Author.

Caterino, M., & Polak, E. (1999). Effects of two types of activity on the performance of second-, third-, and fourth-grade students on a test of concentration. *Perceptual and Motor Skills, 89*(1), 245–248.

Center on Education Policy. (2008). Instructional time in elementary schools: A closer look at changes for specific subjects. *Arts Education Policy Review, 109*(6), 23–28.

Centers for Disease Control and Prevention. (2010). *The association between school based physical activity, including physical education, and academic performance*. Atlanta, GA: U.S. Department of Health and Human Services.

Centers for Disease Control and Prevention (CDC). (2013). *Comprehensive physical activity programs: A guide for schools*. Atlanta, GA: U.S. Department of Health and Human Services.

Cothran, D. J., Kulinna, P. H., & Garn, A. C. (2010). Classroom teachers and physical activity integration. *Teaching and Teacher Education, 26*(7), 1381–1388.

Davis, C. L., Tomporowski, P. D., Boyle, C. A., Wailer, J. L., Miller, P. H., Naglieri, J. A., et al. (2007). Effects of aerobic exercise on overweight children's cognitive functioning: A randomized controlled trial. *Research Quarterly for Exercise and Sport, 78*(5), 510–519.

Donnelly, J. E., Greene, J. L., Gibson, C. A., Smith, B. K., Washburn, R. A., Sullivan, D. K., et al. (2009). Physical activity across the curriculum (PAAC): A randomized controlled trial to promote physical activity and diminish overweight and obesity in elementary school children. *Preventive Medicine: An International Journal Devoted to Practice And Theory, 49*(4), 336–341. doi:10.1016/j.ypmed.2009.07.022.

Erwin, H., Fedewa, A., & Ahn, S. (2013). Student academic performance outcomes of a classroom physical activity intervention: A pilot study. *International Electronic Journal of Elementary Education, 5*(2), 109–124.

Erwin, H. E., Abel, M. G., Beighle, A., & Beets, M. W. (2011a). Promoting children's health through physically active math classes: A pilot study. *Health Promotion Practice, 12*(2), 244–251. doi:10.1177/1524839909331911.

Erwin, H. E., Beighle, A., Morgan, C. F., & Noland, M. (2011b). Effect of a low-cost, teacher-directed classroom intervention on elementary students' physical activity. *Journal of School Health, 81*(8), 455–461. doi:10.1111/j.1746-1561.2011.00614.x.

Fletcher, T., Mandigo, J., & Kosnik, C. (2013). Elementary classroom teachers and physical education: Change in teacher-related factors during pre-service teacher education. *Physical Education and Sport Pedagogy, 18*(2), 169–183.

Gardner, H. (1983). *Frames of mind: The theory of multiple intelligences.* New York: Basic Books.

Hall, E. M. (2007). Integration: Helping to get our kids moving and learning. *Physical Educator, 64*(3), 123–128.

Hall-Kenyon, K., & Smith, L. (2013). Negotiating a shared definition of curriculum integration: A self-study of two teacher educators from different disciplines. *Teacher Education Quarterly, 40*(2), 89–108.

Hidi, S., & Baird, W. (1986). Interestingness—A neglected variable in discourse processing. *Cognitive Science, 10,* 179–194.

Hidi, S., & Baird, W. (1988). Strategies for increasing text-based interest and students' recall of expository texts. *Reading Research Quarterly, 23,* 465–483.

Hidi, S., & Renninger, K. A. (2006). The four-phase model of interest development. *Educational Psychologist, 41*(2), 111–127.

Hollar, D., Messiah, S. E., Lopez-Mitnik, G., Hollar, T. L., Almon, M., & Agatston, A. S. (2010a). Effect of a two-year obesity prevention intervention on percentile changes in body mass index and academic performance in low-income elementary school children. *American Journal of Public Health, 100*(4), 646–653.

Hollar, D., Messiah, S. E., Lopez-Mitnik, G., Hollar, T. L., Almon, M., & Agatston, A. S. (2010b). Healthier options for public schoolchildren program improves weight and blood pressure in 6-to 13-year-olds. *Journal of the American Dietetic Association, 110*(2), 261–267. doi:10.1016/j.jada.2009.10.029.

Holley, K. A. (2009). Special issue: Understanding interdisciplinary challenges and opportunities in higher education. *ASHE Higher Education Report, 35*(2), 1–131.

Holt, E., Bartee, T., & Heelan, K. (2013). Evaluation of a policy to integrate physical activity into the school day. *Journal of Physical Activity and Health, 10*(4), 480–487.

Howie, E. K., Newman-Norlund, R. D., & Pate, R. R. (2014). Smiles count but minutes matter: Responses to classroom exercise breaks. *American Journal of Health Behavior, 38*(5), 681–689. doi:10.5993/AJHB.38.3.3.

Hruska, B., & Clancy, M. E. (2008). Integrating movement and learning in elementary and middle school. *Strategies A Journal for Physical and Sport Educators, 21*(5), 13–20.

Käll, L. B., Malmgren, H., Olsson, E., Lindén, T., & Nilsson, M. (2015). Effects of a curricular physical activity intervention on children's school performance, wellness, and brain development. *Journal of School Health, 85*(10), 704–713.

Light, D., & Pierson, E. (2014). Increasing student engagement in math: The use of khan academy in Chilean classrooms. *International Journal of Education and Development Using Information and Communication Technology, 10*(2), 103–119.

Lindt, S. F., & Miller, S. C. (2017). Using movement to teach: Instructional methods to increase student interest. *Phi Delta Kappan,* April 2017, 34–37.

Macdonald, H. M., Kontulainen, S. A., Petit, M. A., Beck, T. J., Khan, K. M., & McKay, H. A. (2008). Does a novel school-based physical activity model benefit femoral neck bone strength in pre- and early pubertal children? *Osteoporosis International, 19*(10), 1445–1456. doi:10.1007/s00198-008-0589-z.

Mahar, M. T., Murphy, S. K., Rowe, D. A., Golden, J., Shields, A. T., & Raedeke, T. D. (2006). Effects of a classroom-based program on physical activity and on-task behavior. *Medicine and Science in Sports and Exercise, 38*(12), 2086–2094.

McClelland, E., Pitt, A., & Stein, J. (2015). Enhanced academic performance using a novel classroom physical activity intervention to increase awareness, attention and self-control: Putting embodied cognition into practice. *Improving Schools, 18*(1), 83–100.

McMullen, J., Kulinna, P., & Cothran, D. (2014). Physical activity opportunities during the school day: Classroom teachers' perceptions of using activity breaks in the classroom. *Journal of Teaching in Physical Education, 33*(4), 511–527.

Miller, S. C., & Lindt, S. F. (2016). *Engaging students through movement integration: A mixed method study to understand interest and concept retention.* Poster presented at the annual meeting of the American Educational Research Association, Washington, DC.

Miller, S. C., Lindt, S. F., & McIntyre, C. J. (2014). Methods for improving pre-service teacher efficacy to integrate movement in the classroom. *The Texas Forum of Teacher Education, 4,* 105–120.

Mitchell, M. (1993). Situational interest: Its multifaceted structure in the secondary school mathematics classroom. *Journal of Educational Psychology, 85*(3), 424–436.

Mullender-Wijnsma, M. J., Hartman, E., de Greeff, J. W., Bosker, R. J., Doolaard, S., & Visscher, C. (2015). Improving academic performance of school-age children by physical activity in the classroom: 1-year program evaluation. *Journal of School Health, 85*(6), 365–371. doi:10.1111/josh.12259.

National Association for Sport and Physical Education. (2006a). *Teaching large class sizes in physical education: Guidelines and strategies [Guidance document].* Reston, VA: Author.

National Association for Sport and Physical Education. (2006b). *Recess for elementary school students [Position statement].* Reston, VA: Author.

National Association for Sport and Physical Education. (2011). *Physical education is critical to educating the whole child [Position statement].* Reston, VA: American Alliance for Health, Physical Education, Recreation, and Dance.

National Association for Sport and Physical Education, & American Heart Association. (2012). *2012 shape of the nation report: Status of physical education in the USA.* Reston, VA: American Alliance for Health, Physical Education, Recreation and Dance.

Nicksic, H. (2015). *Classroom physical activity: Evaluating elementary teacher preparedness for adoption and implementation.* Unpublished doctoral dissertation. The University of Texas at Austin, Austin, TX.

Norlander, T., Moås, L., & Archer, T. (2005). Noise and stress in primary and secondary school children: Noise reduction and increased concentration ability through a short but regular exercise and relaxation program. *School Effectiveness and School Improvement, 16*(1), 91–99. doi:10.1080/09243450500114173.

Norris, E., Shelton, N., Dunsmuir, S., Duke-Williams, O., & Stamatakis, E. (2015). Physically active lessons as physical activity and educational interventions: A systematic review of methods and results. *Preventive Medicine, 72,* 116–125.

Prosser, L., & Jiang, X. (2008). Relationship between school physical activity and academic performance of children. *International Journal of Learning, 15*(3), 11–16.

Roberts, J. C. (2015). Situational interest of fourth-grade children in music at school. *Journal of Research in Music Education, 63*(2), 180–197.

Skoning, S. (2010). Dancing the curriculum. *Kappa Delta Pi Record, 46*(4), 170–174.

Slade, S. S., & Griffith, D. (2013). A whole child approach to student success. *KEDI Journal of Educational Policy,10*(3), 21–35.

Theodorakou, K., & Zervas, Y. (2003). The effects of the creative movement teaching method and the traditional teaching method on elementary school children's self-esteem. *Sport, Education and Society, 8*(1), 91–104.

Troiano, R. P., Berrigan, D., Dodd, K. W., Masse, L. C., Tilert, T., & McDowell, M. (2008). Physical activity in the united states measured by accelerometer. *Medicine and Science in Sports and Exercise, 40*(1), 181–188. doi:10.1249/mss.0b013e31815a51b3.

U.S. Department of Health and Human Services. (2008). *2008 physical activity guidelines for Americans*. Washington, DC: Author.

U.S. Department of Health and Human Services. (2010). Strategies to improve the quality of physical education.

Vazou, S., Gavrilou, P., Mamalaki, E., Papanastasiou, A., & Sioumala, N. (2012). Does integrating physical activity in the elementary school classroom influence academic motivation? *International Journal of Sport and Exercise Psychology, 10*(4), 251–263. doi:10.1080/1612197X.2012.682368.

Vazou, S., & Skrade, M. (2014). Teachers' reflections from integrating physical activity in the academic classroom. *Research Quarterly for Exercise and Sport, 85*(S1), A38–A39.

Ward, J. S., Duncan, J. S., Jarden, A., & Stewart, T. (2016). The impact of children's exposure to greenspace on physical activity, cognitive development, emotional wellbeing, and ability to appraise risk. *Health and Place*. doi:10.1016/j.healthplace.2016.04.015.

Webster, C. A., Caputi, P., Perrault, M., Doan, R., Doutis, P., & Weaver, R. G. (2013). Elementary classroom teachers' adoption of physical activity promotion in the context of a statewide policy: An innovation diffusion and socio-ecologic perspective. *Journal of Teaching in Physical Education, 32,* 419–440.

Webster, C. A., Russ, L., Vazou, S., Goh, T. L., & Erwin, H. (2015). Integrating movement in academic classrooms: Understanding, applying and advancing the knowledge base. *Obesity Reviews, 16*(8), 691–701. doi:10.1111/obr.12285.

Wright, B., Wright, P., & Willbanks, A. (2010). Math dance (line, ray, angle). *PE central: Lesson plans for physical education*. Retrieved May 23, 2015 from http://www.pecentral.org/lessonideas/ViewLesson.asp?ID=9891#.V-Qy2ZMrJBy.

Chapter 2
Decreasing Perceived Barriers and Enhancing Facilitators of Movement Integration

Hildi M. Nicksic

Abstract This chapter deals with the idea that classroom teachers may not be prepared to facilitate physical activity within the academic setting. Perceived barriers are addressed with practical suggestions for decreasing barriers and steps are given to facilitate classroom physical activity.

Given the benefits of physical activity on both health and academic performance, and the prevalence of school-aged children who are not achieving the recommended levels of daily physical activity, an increase in opportunities for students to be active during the school day is necessary. Models and initiatives, such as the Comprehensive School Physical Activity Program (CSPAP; see Fig. 2.1) and *Let's Move! Active Schools* (see http://letsmoveschools.org), identify physical activity within the classroom as a necessary component in this whole-of-school approach (Kohl & Cook, 2013). Content-area teachers, as the individuals with the most contact time with students, must be prepared to facilitate physical activity within the academic setting.

When considering the likelihood of any behavior change, understanding an individual's perception of potential barriers to and facilitators of taking action is paramount to promoting successful change. Curricular change, although generally viewed as an overhaul or revision of current lesson plans, materials, and standards at a policy-level, refers to any change to current practices within the classroom. Implementation of new or different classroom practice is largely dependent upon the classroom teacher, as the planner and facilitator of lesson plans. The success of implementation is dependent upon educators accepting change (Zimmerman, 2006), and changes in classroom practices ultimately rely on teachers (Borko, 2004; Spillane, 1999). Accordingly, it stands to reason that teachers are instrumental in the success, or failure, of adding or increasing physical activity into the general education classroom. Specifically, Martin and Murtagh (2015) propose that teacher attitude toward movement integration is linked with the level of activity among

H.M. Nicksic (✉)
Texas A&M University, College Station, TX, USA
e-mail: hnicksic@tamu.edu

© Springer Nature Singapore Pte Ltd. 2018   19
S.C. Miller and S.F. Lindt (eds.), *Moving INTO the Classroom*,
Springer Texts in Education, DOI 10.1007/978-981-10-6424-1_2

Fig. 2.1 Comprehensive School Physical Activity Program (CSPAP) model. Image adapted from SHAPE America (see http://www.shapeamerica.org/cspap/what.cfm). Note *Asterisk* distinct from during school physical education

students, further demonstrating the impact of the teacher on the effectiveness of classroom physical activity practices.

There is evidence to support that teachers acknowledge the need for classroom physical activity, but that barriers exist to limit implementation. When these barriers are perceived by the teacher as greater than the benefits, teachers are less likely to integrate movement into curricula. However, there are also evidenced facilitators of classroom physical activity that are correlated with the number of movement opportunities that teachers offer. Gaining an understanding of both perceived barriers and facilitators to movement integration is critical to promotion efforts. This understanding enables teachers and supporters to proactively diminish barriers and enhance facilitators, thereby increasing the likelihood of successful integration of movement within the classroom.

Perceived Barriers to Classroom Physical Activity

Research in multiple disciplines offers insight into common barriers to movement integration as perceived by classroom teachers. Research in organizational change has identified failure to recognize the need for change, fear of the unknown, and habit as three individual barriers to initiating action (Greenberg & Baron, 2000). If teachers are unaware of the need for the addition or increase of classroom physical activity, or do not support this change, implementation is improbable. In addition, a sense of comfort and security can be derived from maintaining familiar lesson plans, such that change that causes a disruption to current patterns may not be well-received by teachers. Classroom teachers have a great amount of responsibility and may be less inclined to offer curriculum they feel unprepared to teach (Hall,

Little, & Heidorn, 2011). Similarly, with the pressures of state testing and the lack of accountability for classroom physical activity implementation, teachers may feel their planning time should focus on core subjects (Hall et al., 2011) and less on the implementation of other non-core areas. Adopting new practices in the classroom may also be contingent upon relationships with colleagues and the level of support within the school (Opfer & Pedder, 2010). Administrative support is important (Parks, Solmon, & Lee, 2007), as teachers feel that school change is often contingent upon the principal (Till, Ferkins, & Handcock, 2011). As a more proximal barrier, teachers may also be constrained by lack of support from fellow teachers who disapprove of pedagogical strategies that integrate movement.

As further support of time as a barrier, in a qualitative assessment of classroom teachers' thoughts about offering physical activity, Cothran, Kulinna, and Garn (2010) determined a key factor of implementation was scheduling. Finding time within the school day for classroom physical activity was difficult for the interviewed teachers, and teachers felt available class time should be spent on academics (Cothran et al., 2010). This finding was replicated in a similar study by Howie, Newman-Norlund, and Pate (2014) where classroom teachers revealed, via focus groups, that physical activity breaks were difficult to implement given the lack of time within the daily routine. As part of a 5-week intervention targeting classroom physical activity, teachers in this sample also reported an initial fear that students would not be able to settle down after activity, but found instead that students demonstrated an improvement in learning and behavior following exercise breaks (Howie et al. 2014). This finding suggests that teachers will include student behavior as a barrier to classroom physical activity, but that following implementation, teachers may feel differently. In a quantitative study, prioritization of core subjects, lack of planning time, habit, lack of materials, and behavior concerns were the highest rated barriers to classroom physical activity implementation among classroom teachers (Nicksic, 2015).

Several studies have assessed classroom teachers' perceptions of providing physical education lessons to students. Although teaching a traditional physical education lesson in a gymnasium is not equivalent to providing classroom physical activity, this research may be relevant in further hypothesizing classroom teachers' perceived barriers to classroom physical activity implementation. In an early qualitative study that offered future researchers a foundation of knowledge, Faucette and Patterson (1989) found that classroom teachers tasked with providing physical education lessons reported only negative perceptions. Teachers felt that teaching physical education was not a valuable use of their time, that it required too much energy, and that academic subjects took precedence. Furthermore, all teachers felt unprepared to facilitate physical education and cited their lack of expertise in the area, along with a lack of materials and resources, as a barrier to teaching physical education lessons (Faucette & Patterson, 1989). Morgan and Hansen (2008) interviewed classroom teachers about barriers to delivering physical education programs and found a range of individual and institutional obstacles. Teachers reported a lack of confidence, lack of knowledge, and lack of expertise for teaching physical education. Personal attitudes about and experience in physical education were also influential, as was individual perception about the value of physical education. Teachers felt that physical education was not a teaching priority and that successful implementation was constrained by class size and lack of materials, resources, and administrative support, with the primary barrier being lack of time (Morgan & Hansen, 2008). These results were corroborated in a larger sample of teachers who believed insufficient time was a major barrier to providing physical education lessons and listed insufficient training, lack of experience, and lack of facilities as other inhibitors (Morgan, 2008).

Taking Action to Decrease Barriers

Together, these data provide an overview of perceived barriers to classroom physical activity implementation among classroom teachers (see Fig. 2.2). Many of the highly ranked barriers may be managed through an increase in knowledge, including provision of materials. Knowledge is a multi-faceted component for diminishing

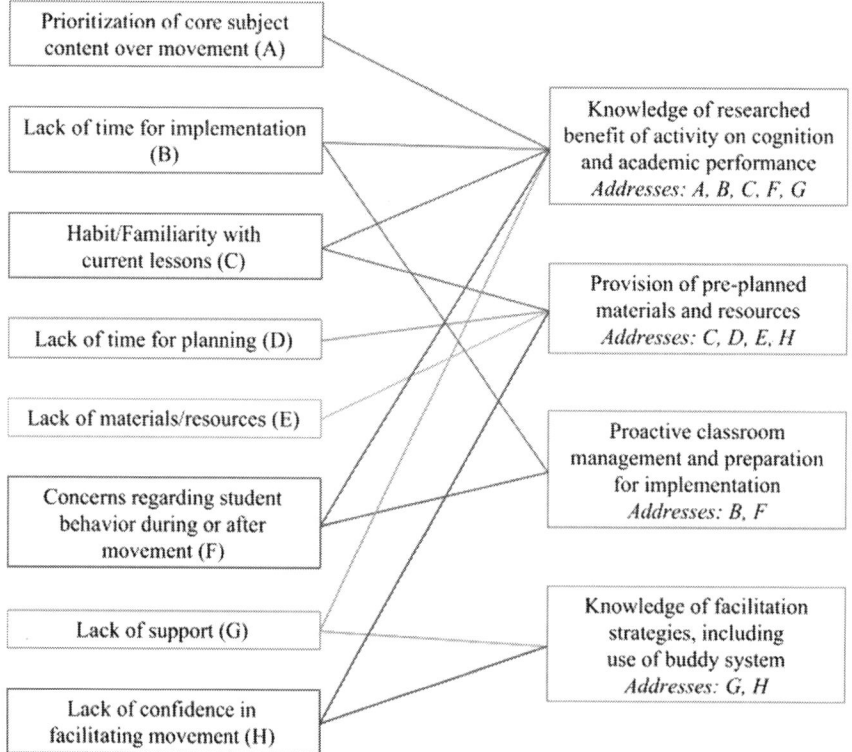

Fig. 2.2 Common barriers to classroom physical activity as perceived by classroom teachers and strategies to diminish or overcome perceived barriers

barriers, as it can refer to knowledge of the benefit of movement integration, knowledge of available materials, and knowledge of effective methods and strategies for implementation and facilitation. Evidence to support the health and academic benefits of classroom physical activity is critical. This knowledge is necessary both to alter the teacher's perception of the barriers-benefits ratio, and to generate support from teaching colleagues and school administration. Further, being knowledgeable of the research that supports a positive or neutral impact of movement integration on academic achievement targets the barrier of class time utilization.

A knowledge of materials that offer activity ideas and lesson plans removes the barriers to movement integration attributable to lack of materials and lack of planning time. Access to both preexisting materials and resources that provide tips and tricks for implementation can also address lack of confidence for facilitation of movement in the classroom. This knowledge about how to prepare for and offer movement integration to students is pivotal for initial adoption of classroom physical activity and for movement integration to become habitual.

Facilitators of Classroom Physical Activity

While identifying perceived barriers is an important step in exploring approaches for incorporating more physical activity into the classroom setting, equally important is the need to identify factors that may facilitate, or enable, organizational and classroom change, including adoption of new behaviors by the teacher to offer physical activity opportunities. Behavior theories, such as the Diffusion of Innovations, suggest that initial adoption of classroom physical activity is more likely if teachers feel implementation is compatible with their current teaching practices and easy to do, and that continued use of movement integration is more likely if teachers see positive results of implementation. Teachers who are more innovative may also offer physical activity in their classroom sooner and more willingly than teachers who are less innovative. Other behavioral theories address additional factors associated with an individual teacher's likelihood to engage in curricular change, such as perceived barriers, perceived benefits, and behavior-specific self-efficacy, or perceived competence to perform the behavior (Rosenstock, Strecher, & Becker, 1988). When applied to the implementation of classroom physical activity, these theories would suggest that facilitators to integrating movement into the classroom include perceived compatibility of movement, innovativeness, high-perceived benefits, and low-perceived barriers of implementation, and high personal confidence to offer opportunities.

Teachers who feel they are likely to adopt new educational teaching practices or be among the first to try different classroom practices can be identified as innovative. In a study of classroom teachers' implementation of classroom physical activity, Webster et al. (2013) found that teacher innovativeness was predictive of integrated physical activity opportunities in the classroom. A belief that classroom physical activity would fit well into current teaching practices was also related to offered opportunities for movement, as was a belief that activity would produce results observable by school administration (Webster et al., 2013). An indirect relationship between promotion of activity and perceived school support (Webster et al., 2013) further suggests that while lack of support at the school level is a barrier to implementation, existence of support is a facilitating factor.

Perceived confidence in one's ability to successfully engage in a behavior, or self-efficacy, is an important factor assessing the likelihood that action will occur (Rosenstock et al., 1988). Teachers with higher levels of self-efficacy are more open to professional learning and engagement in new classroom practice than teachers with lower self-efficacy (Scribner, 1999). A teacher's decision to adopt new practices and the level of adoption are both impacted by self-efficacy (Fritz, Miller-Heyl, Kreutzer, & Macphee, 1995; Posnanski, 2002). In addition, self-efficacy in linked to maintaining the teaching practice over time, and to persistence when confronted with barriers (Posnanski, 2002).

When assessing implementation rates of content-based physically active lessons, Bartholomew and Jowers (2011) found a link with teacher self-efficacy regarding classroom management during physical activity. Self-efficacy specific to planning and offering activity in the classroom is also related to implementation (Nicksic, 2015). In a review of studies specific to teaching science, Posnanski (2002) presents evidence that self-efficacy is associated with content knowledge, such that teachers who report greater levels of science knowledge similarly report higher levels of science teaching self-efficacy beliefs, and that when teachers gain content and pedagogical knowledge, self-efficacy increases. These data support that self-efficacy beliefs regarding the provision of classroom physical activity opportunities can be positively impacted by providing teachers with knowledge about classroom physical activity, and that self-efficacy is associated with implementation.

One large-scale study with a sample of 314 elementary teachers and 38 elementary principals assessed willingness to implement classroom physical activity using a collective efficacy perspective (Parks et al., 2007). In this context, collective efficacy, an extension of self-efficacy, is a shared belief held by teachers within a school that they, as a collective entity, can positively affect student achievement. Several enabling factors were revealed in findings, with six items associated with highest likelihood of offering integrated movement. Participants reported they would be influenced by a campus-wide goal of classroom physical activity implementation, encouragement from administration, successful experience, and personal participation with classroom physical activity implementation, access to external demonstrations of successful implementation, and ability to observe peers successfully offering classroom physical activity. Furthermore, results indicated that 77% of teachers and principals felt physical activity was very important and that over 80% would be willing to incorporate engagement opportunities on at least 2 days per week. Interestingly, the majority of the sample (44%) felt math would be the subject most conducive to movement integration, followed by language arts (23%), science (21%), and reading (12%; Parks et al., 2007). As such, it may be beneficial to target math as the first subject in which to try classroom physical activity, as initial success leads to continued implementation.

Facilitator	Method of Enhancement
Compatibility of movement with current or habitual lessons plans	Increased knowledge of researched benefits of movement; access to materials that offer activities by subject or topic to aid in connectivity
Teacher innovativeness	Innovativeness is a stable character trait, but increased knowledge of researched benefits of movement may increase likelihood to initially attempt classroom physical activity
School-wide support for movement	Administrative and colleague awareness of researched benefits of movement, especially on academic achievement and learning preparedness
Low perceived barriers, high perceived benefits	Increased knowledge of researched benefits of movement; access to implementation and facilitation materials and resources
Teacher self-efficacy	Self-efficacy is a character trait that can be increased through successful trials of movement integration; observing colleagues' implementation; increased knowledge of implementation and facilitation strategies

Fig. 2.3 Potential methods for enhancing facilitators of movement integration

Taking Action to Enhance Facilitators

Research suggests that teachers will be more likely to adopt and maintain classroom physical activity practices if perceived barriers are low, and facilitating factors are present. Enhancing these facilitators, such as knowledge, self-efficacy, and connectivity to current practice, and decreasing barriers can be concurrently addressed through the provision of materials, resources, and information about integrating movement into the academic curriculum (see Fig. 2.3).

Strategies to Successfully Integrate Movement into Core Content

Step 1: Learn About, and Teach, the Benefits of Classroom Physical Activity

Perhaps the first step to overcoming barriers to classroom physical activity is to educate teachers about physical activity, the impact, and implementation strategies, as there is a strong correlation between increased knowledge and skills and a change in teaching practice (Garet, Porter, Desimone, Birman, & Yoon, 2001). As revealed in chapter one, integrating movement into the classroom can enhance learning preparedness through an improvement in attention, concentration, on-task behavior, and cognitive performance. In addition, school-based physical activity is either positively related to academic performance or there is not a significant relationship (Honas et al., 2016; Rasberry et al., 2011), supporting the use of class time for movement integration as a mechanism to impact academics.

Having a personal knowledge of the impact of physical activity on academic outcomes is necessary for implementation by the teacher, but educating others on these benefits is also crucial to implementation success. To set the foundation for classroom physical activity as an expected component of the academic school day, teachers should share information with students about the purpose and potential impact of physical activity engagement. Providing students with the intent for classroom physical activity will increase the likelihood of appropriate participation in movement integration (Eccles & Wigfield, 2002). Furthermore, sharing data with fellow teachers and with administration may engender necessary support for classroom movement. The known association between physical fitness and stan-dardized test scores (Castelli, Hillman, Buck, & Erwin, 2007; Chomitz et al., 2009; Grissom, 2005; Van Dusen, Kelder, Kohl, Ranjit, & Perry, 2011) may encourage administrative support, while peers may be inclined to support, or even adopt, physical activity practices based upon associations with learning preparedness and behavior (Centers for Disease Control and Prevention, 2010; Goh, Hannon, Webster, Podlog, & Newton, 2016; Herman, Beer, & Morton, 2013; Mahar et al., 2006).

Step 2: Adopt Appropriate Classroom Management

Garnering support for classroom physical activity through an increase in knowledge of its benefits, among both colleagues and principals, diminishes a primary barrier to implementation. Yet increasing knowledge of implementation strategies among teachers is equally critical. Incorporation of appropriate procedures for activity facilitation is a necessary foundation for classroom movement. This could include anything from arranging the furniture in the classroom to be most conducive to movement patterns to establishing start/stop cues to effective transition back to seated work methods. Strategies to increase the likelihood of successful movement integration facilitation are discussed further in chapter three of this text.

Setting expectations for movement integration is fundamental to managing student behavior during and after activity. Effective implementation of clearly set guidelines for acceptable behavior decreases disruptions and the need for disciplinary action (Marzano, 2003). As Boynton and Boynton (2005) note, teachers must invest the time to formally educate students on these guidelines and the expectations and parameters for behavior. For special situations, events, or locations, such as movement integration, Marzano (2003) proposes the provision of specific rules of conduct. To encourage students' ownership of these rules, teachers can facilitate the creation of a Code of Conduct specific to physical activity in the classroom (see Fig. 2.4).

To create a student-driven, movement-specific code of conduct

- Students brainstorm ideas for appropriate guidelines
- Teacher, as the scribe of each suggestion, encourages students to rephrase ideas as positive statements (ex: "walk" in place of "don't run")
- Students vote on the most important or influential guidelines until the list is narrowed down to no more than eight points

Fig. 2.4 Sample code of conduct for classroom physical activity. Copyright 2015 by Classrooms in Motion, LLC

Mrs. Smith's Class

Code of Conduct

for Classroom Physical Activity

We, the students of room 100, agree to…

…listen and follow directions.

…focus on doing the movement correctly.

…keep our bodies under control.

…try our best.

…be safe.

…stay in our own space bubbles.

…return to seated work quietly.

…have fun!

©2015 Classrooms in Motion, LLC

- When the code is completed, each student signs his/her name indicating s/he will abide by the rules of the contract.

Proactively addressing classroom management can decrease the likelihood that students will exhibit disruptive behavior during or after movement opportunities. In addition, properly setting up the expectations for classroom physical activity, and maintaining these expectations, will enable movement to be more seamlessly integrated into the school day, thereby ensuring best use of available time. As mentioned in step one, sharing the purpose and intentions of activity with students is also critical to managing behavior. Students should view physical activity within the classroom as just another component of the academic school day that is intended to assist them in achieving learning outcomes.

Step 3: Utilize Available Materials and Resources

As demonstrated by the upsurge in research about classroom physical activity over the past decade (Castelli et al., 2014), the concept of integrating movement into school settings is increasingly recognized and supported. This awareness has facilitated the creation of a multitude of materials and resources to aid educators with implementation. One of the purposes of this textbook, for example, is to provide the classroom teacher with ready-to-implement lesson plans that incorporate activity into academic content. To supplement these ideas, online sources like Active Academics offers a searchable database of lesson plans categorized by grade level and content area (see http://www.activeacademics.org). In addition, free programs such as Fuel Up to Play 60 (see https://www.fueluptoplay60.com) and GoNoodle (see https://www.gonoodle.com) offer teachers simple physical activities for the classroom that require little to no planning; initial use of these activities may enable teachers to increase self-efficacy for movement facilitation before delving into the integration of activity into academic content.

The availability of materials and helpful resources reduces or removes several perceived barriers, including, of course, lack of materials. In addition, access to preexisting lesson plans addresses lack of planning time as an inhibitor to adoption of movement integration. Lack of confidence in facilitating movement may also be diminished as teachers will likely feel more confident with the provision of a lesson plan that provides step-by-step instructions.

Step 4: Start Small and Create a Peer Support System
if Possible

When implementing curricular change, as with any attempted behavior change, it is important to start small and have realistic expectations for execution. Prior to making the attempt to add or increase the level of movement within the classroom, teachers should assess the classroom environment and the students to determine an appropriate goal. Depending upon the outcome of the assessment, that goal may range from offering 3 to 5 min of structured physical activity several times per week to presenting a daily content-based, physically active lesson like those outlined in this textbook. Minor changes should be implemented first to allow both teachers and students to become familiar with the modifications. Again, expectations should be based upon current practices. If a teacher has previously offered multiple physically active academic lessons, a realistic expectation may be to offer one per day, while a teacher who is hesitant about implementation should begin with short opportunities for movement using a tool like GoNoodle.

Making small, realistic changes allows teachers to try new teaching practices and monitor results. This trialability is important as research reveals that perceptions and expectations of outcome change following implementation. Prior to a 5-week period of integrating physical activity into the classroom, teachers anticipated that students would be overstimulated after activity; after the intervention, these same teachers reported that classroom physical activity actually limited disruptive behavior (Howie et al., 2014). In trialing movement integration and monitoring results, teachers can assess what does or does not work in his/her specific classroom and plan accordingly for future implementation efforts.

Having a peer or team of support when trialing any new teaching practice is also beneficial, as it enables individual teachers to share lesson plans and success stories, gain external insight, and brainstorm resolution and future action after any negative implementation. This partner or team can also provide support, encouragement, and motivation to maintain classroom physical activity practices over a sustained period. Research suggests that forming a new habit takes an average of 66 days (Lally & Gardner, 2013), and having external support and accountability increases the chances that a teacher will continue to integrate movement into the classroom until it becomes habitual.

Step 5: Create a Culture of Movement in the Classroom

Classroom physical activity, as a concept, can be thought of as three components: procedural physical activity, structured physical activity, and content physical activity (see Fig. 2.5; Nicksic, 2015). Content physical activity, the movement integration promoted in this text, is the pinnacle of classroom physical activity as it enables activity to fit seamlessly into the learning process, enhancing the academic curriculum. That said, creating a classroom culture that embraces activity by including all three forms has the potential to diminish lingering barriers to movement integration.

Procedural physical activity is task-oriented movement. This would constitute opportunities for students to move about the classroom for a specific purpose, such as submitting an assignment or sharpening a pencil. Modifying simple classroom

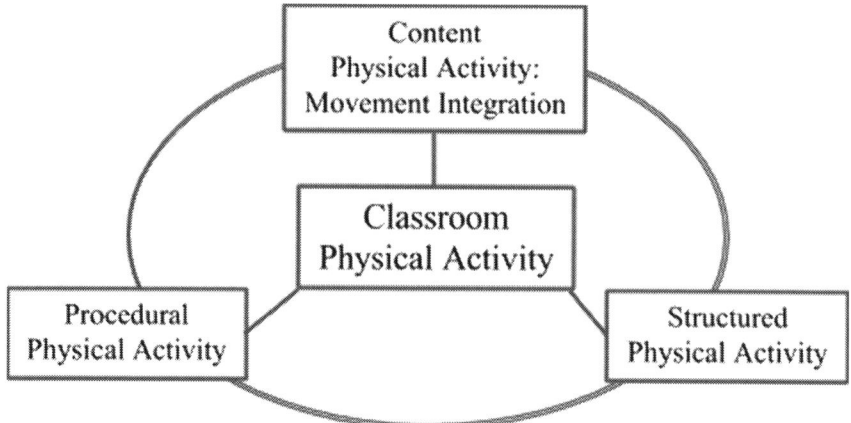

Fig. 2.5 Classroom physical activity triad

procedures to allow students to leave their seats makes physical activity a normal and expected component of the school day. For example, have a turn-in basket in one location of the classroom where students walk to place completed work, rather than having one individual collect work from seated students. If a student requires a new pencil, establish a procedure where he/she walks to a pencil cup to deposit the dull pencil and select a sharp one. Adopting procedural physical activity removes the novelty of being able to stand and move around the classroom while enables students to practice body control (Fig. 2.4).

Structured physical activity is movement within the classroom that is unrelated to academic content. This form of movement may be referred to as a brain break, although research that supports the impact of activity on cognition suggests that movement should not be considered a "break". Depending upon the length of the activity, structured physical activity may also constitute an attentional reset, allowing students to "reset" their attention to the academic task at hand. Teachers who may feel overwhelmed by the prospect of movement integration may be more comfortable offering structured physical activity first, which will likely facilitate an increase in self-efficacy while solidifying activity-specific classroom management techniques.

Finally, content physical activity, the movement integration into content curriculum, completes the triad to create a classroom culture of activity and movement for learning enhancement. To initiate this practice, teachers should first review their current units and activities and assess how movement can enhance preexisting plans. For example, perhaps a previous lesson had students estimate, and then use a ruler to measure, the length of objects pictured in the math textbook. As an alternative plan that integrates movement, students could use items around the room, first estimating and then measuring while they walk. For those teachers who feel comfortable and want to extend the activity, students could perform a different locomotion between items—tiptoe, giant step, bunny hop. By connecting movement to lessons that teachers already feel comfortable teaching, a further increase in self-efficacy is likely to occur.

By adopting a culture that promotes and supports movement, teachers can enhance the educational experience of students in their classrooms. Engaging students in multiple opportunities for activity throughout the school day, via both procedure and core content, enables them to reap the health and academic benefits of classroom physical activity.

Chapter Takeaways

- There are barriers, perceived and real, to impede the successful implementation of movement into the classroom. Knowledge of these impediments is critical in devising a plan to address specific barriers.
- Barriers to classroom physical activity can be diminished with effective preparation and application of knowledge and materials.
- Proactively addressing barriers to classroom physical activity while enhancing facilitators increases the likelihood of successful implementation, thus enabling both teacher and students to reap the benefits of movement integration.

References

Bartholomew, J. B., & Jowers, E. M. (2011). Physically active academic lessons in elementary children. *Preventive Medicine, 52*(Supplement), S51–S54. doi:10.1016/j.ypmed.2011.01.017.

Borko, H. (2004). Professional development and teacher learning: Mapping the terrain. *Educational Researcher, 33*(8), 3–15.

Boynton, M., & Boynton, C. (2005). *The educator's guide to preventing and solving discipline problems*. Alexandria, VA: Association for Supervision and Curriculum Development.

Castelli, D. M., Centeio, E. E., Hwang, J., Barcelona, J. M., Glowacki, E. M., Calvert, H. G., et al. (2014). VII. The history of physical activity and academic performance research: Informing the future. *Monographs of the Society for Research in Child Development, 79*(4), 119–148. doi:10.1111/mono.12133.

Castelli, D. M., Hillman, C. H., Buck, S. M., & Erwin, H. E. (2007). Physical fitness and academic achievement in third- and fifth-grade students. *Journal of Sport and Exercise Psychology, 29* (2), 239–252.

Centers for Disease Control and Prevention. (2010). *The association between school-based physical activity, including physical education, and academic performance*. Atlanta, GA: U.S. Department of Health and Human Services.

Chomitz, V. R., Dawson, G. F., Hacker, K. A., McGowan, R. J., Mitchell, S. E., & Slining, M. M. (2009). Is there a relationship between physical fitness and academic achievement? Positive results from public school children in the Northeastern United States. *Journal of School, 79*(1), 30–37.

Cothran, D. J., Kulinna, P. H., & Garn, A. C. (2010). Classroom teachers and physical activity integration. *Teaching and Teacher Education, 26*(7), 1381–1388. doi:10.1016/j.tate.2010.04.003.

Eccles, J. S., & Wigfield, A. (2002). Motivational beliefs, values, and goals. *Annual Review of Psychology, 53,* 109–132. doi:10.1146/annurev.psych.53.100901.135153.

Faucette, N., & Patterson, P. (1989). Classroom teachers and physical education: What they are doing and how they feel about it. *Education, 110*(1), 108.

Fritz, J. J., Miller-Heyl, J., Kreutzer, J. C., & Macphee, D. (1995). Fostering personal teaching efficacy through staff development and classroom activities. *The Journal of Educational Research, 88*(4), 200–208. doi:10.1080/00220671.1995.9941301.

Garet, M. S., Porter, A. C., Desimone, L., Birman, B. F., & Yoon, K. S. (2001). What makes professional development effective? Results from a national sample of teachers. *American Educational Research Journal, 38*(4), 915–945. doi:10.3102/00028312038004915.

Goh, T. L., Hannon, J., Webster, C., Podlog, L., & Newton, M. (2016). Effects of a TAKE 10! classroom-based physical activity intervention on third- to fifth-grade children's on-task behavior. *Journal of Physical Activity and Health, 13*(7), 712–718. doi:10.1123/jpah.2015-0238.

Greenberg, J., & Baron, R. A. (2000). *Behavior in organizations: Understanding and managing the human side of work* (7th ed.). Upper Saddle River, NJ: Prentice Hall.

Grissom, J. B. (2005). Physical fitness and academic achievement. *Journal of Exercise Physiology Online, 8*(1), 11–25.

Hall, T. J., Little, S., & Heidorn, B. D. (2011). Preparing classroom teachers to meet students' physical activity needs. *Journal of Physical Education, Recreation and Dance, 82*(3), 40–52. doi:10.1080/07303084.2011.10598596.

Herman, W., Beer, C., & Morton, D. (2013). The impact of a physical activity session on year two students' subsequent classroom behaviour. *TEACH Journal of Christian Education, 7*(1), 9.

Honas, J. J., Willis, E. A., Herrmann, S. D., Greene, J. L., Washburn, R. A., & Donnelly, J. E. (2016). Energy expenditure and intensity of classroom physical activity in elementary school children. *Journal of Physical Activity and Health, 13*(6 Suppl 1), S53–S56. doi:10.1123/jpah.2015-0717.

Howie, E. K., Newman-Norlund, R. D., & Pate, R. R. (2014). Smiles count but minutes matter: Responses to classroom exercise breaks. *American Journal of Health Behavior, 38*(5), 681–689. doi:10.5993/AJHB.38.5.5.

Kohl, H. W., III, & Cook, H. D. (Eds.). (2013). *Educating the student body: Taking physical activity and physical education to school.* Washington, DC: The National Academies Press.

Lally, P., & Gardner, B. (2013). Promoting habit formation. *Health Psychology Review, 7*(sup1), S137–S158. doi:10.1080/17437199.2011.603640.

Mahar, M. T., Murphy, S. K., Rowe, D. A., Golden, J., Shields, A. T., & Raedeke, T. D. (2006). Effects of a classroom-based program on physical activity and on-task behavior. *Medicine and Science in Sports and Exercise, 38,* 2086–2094.

Martin, R., & Murtagh, E. M. (2015). An intervention to improve the physical activity levels of children: Design and rationale of the "Active Classrooms" cluster randomised controlled trial. *Contemporary Clinical Trials, 41,* 180–191. doi:10.1016/j.cct.2015.01.019.

Marzano, R. J. (2003). *What works in schools: Translating research into action.* Alexandria, VA: Association for Supervision and Curriculum Development.

Morgan, P. J. (2008). Teacher perceptions of physical education in the primary school: Attitudes, values and curriculum preferences. *Physical Educator, 65*(1), 46–56.

Morgan, P. J., & Hansen, V. (2008). Classroom teachers' perceptions of the impact of barriers to teaching physical education on the quality of physical education programs. *Research Quarterly for Exercise and Sport, 79*(4), 506–516. doi:10.1080/02701367.2008.10599517.

Nicksic, H. (2015). *Classroom physical activity: Evaluating elementary teacher preparedness for adoption and implementation.* Unpublished doctoral dissertation. The University of Texas at Austin, Austin, TX.

Opfer, V. D., & Pedder, D. (2010). Benefits, status and effectiveness of continuous professional development for teachers in England. *Curriculum Journal, 21*(4), 413–431. doi:10.1080/09585176.2010.529651.

Parks, M., Solmon, M., & Lee, A. (2007). Understanding classroom teachers' perceptions of integrating physical activity: A collective efficacy perspective. *Journal of Research in Childhood Education, 21*(3), 316–328. doi:10.1080/02568540709594597.

Posnanski, T. J. (2002). Professional development programs for elementary science teachers: An analysis of teacher self-efficacy beliefs and a professional development model. *Journal of Science Teacher Education, 13*(3), 189–220. doi:10.1023/A:1016517100186.

Rasberry, C. N., Lee, S. M., Robin, L., Laris, B. A., Russell, L. A., Coyle, K. K., & Nihiser, A. J. (2011). The association between school-based physical activity, including physical education, and academic performance: A systematic review of the literature. *Preventive Medicine, 52*, Supplement, S10–S20. doi:10.1016/j.ypmed.2011.01.027

Rosenstock, I. M., Stretcher, V. J., & Becker, M. H. (1988). Social learning theory and the health belief model. *Health Education Quarterly, 15*(2), 175–183.

Scribner, J. (1999). Teacher efficacy and teacher professional learning: Implications for school leaders. *Journal of School Leadership, 9*, 209–234. ISSN-1052-6846

Spillane, J. P. (1999). External reform initiatives and teachers' efforts to reconstruct their practice: The mediating role of teachers' zones of enactment. *Journal of Curriculum Studies, 31*(2), 143–175. doi:10.1080/002202799183205.

Till, J., Ferkins, L., & Handcock, P. (2011). Physical activity based professional development for teachers: The importance of whole school involvement. *Health Education Journal, 70*(2), 225–235. doi:10.1177/0017896910396218.

Van Dusen, D. P., Kelder, S. H., Kohl, H. W., Ranjit, N., & Perry, C. L. (2011). Associations of physical fitness and academic performance among schoolchildren. *Journal of School Health, 81*(12), 733–740. doi:10.1111/j.1746-1561.2011.00652.x.

Webster, C. A., Caputi, P., Perreault, M., Doan, R., Doutis, P., & Weaver, R. G. (2013). Elementary classroom teachers' adoption of physical activity promotion in the context of a statewide policy: An innovation diffusion and socio-ecologic perspective. *Journal of Teaching in Physical Education, 32*, 419–440. https://doi.org/10.1123/jtpe.32.4.419.

Zimmerman, J. (2006). Why some teachers resist change and what principals can do about it. *NASSP Bulletin, 90*(3), 238–249. doi:10.1177/0192636506291521.

Chapter 3
Using This Textbook to Effectively Plan for Movement Integration

Suzanne F. Lindt, Stacia C. Miller and Hildi M. Nicksic

Abstract This chapter serves as a guide to explain how to use the lesson plan template in the text, as seen throughout the following chapters. Descriptions are provided for the different components of the lesson plan, and examples of classroom management techniques are described.

As mentioned in Chap. 2, barriers exist for implementing movement into the classroom. If teachers are aware of the barriers and anticipate classroom management needs, they will be better able to overcome barriers and to offer physical activity opportunities designed to enhance students' physical, cognitive, and socioemotional growth. The purpose of this textbook is to provide research on movement in content areas, quick and ready to use movement activities for various content area strands, and detailed lesson plans for upper and lower elementary grades. The provided lessons offer practicing and pre-service teachers with specific plans for movement integration in the content areas of English Language Arts, Mathematics, Science, and Social Studies.

This chapter offers an overview of classroom management followed by an explanation for using the lesson plan format included in the content chapters (see Fig. 3.1). Though some aspects of the lesson plan will be familiar to classroom teachers, all components of this lesson plan template have been explicitly explained in this chapter to ensure effective use of this textbook.

S.F. Lindt · S.C. Miller (✉)
Midwestern State University, Wichita Falls, TX, USA
e-mail: stacia.miller@mwsu.edu

S.F. Lindt
e-mail: suzanne.lindt@mwsu.edu

H.M. Nicksic (✉)
Texas A&M University, College Station, TX, USA
e-mail: hnicksic@tamu.edu

© Springer Nature Singapore Pte Ltd. 2018
S.C. Miller and S.F. Lindt (eds.), *Moving INTO the Classroom*,
Springer Texts in Education, DOI 10.1007/978-981-10-6424-1_3

Lesson Plan Title
Suggested Grade Level:

Lesson Overview:

National Content Standards	*Copy and paste all the Standards that apply to the lesson.*
Goals	*Each standard needs an overall goal.*
Objectives	*Each standard needs a specific objective. Objectives tell what the student will learn, not what they will do.*

Description of Activity

Outline a specific, detailed step-by-step description of your plan to deliver instruction. This description should enable another person (such as a substitute teacher) to follow it without needing any additional information. Include components of a quality lesson such as engagement, transitions, introduction to new material, guided practice, independent practice, extension and lesson closure.

Suggested Time Frame	*Approximately how long will the activity last?*
Equipment/ Technology	*What equipment and or technology is needed?*
Start/Stop Signals	*What signals will you use to start and stop the activity? For example: ringing a bell or clapping your hands.*
Verbal Skill Cues	*What skill cues are needed to reinforce students' movements?*

Fig. 3.1 Lesson plan template for movement integration. Adapted from "West College of Education—lesson plan format," by the Midwestern State University West College of Education, 2009, Unpublished, West College of Education, Midwestern State University, Wichita Falls, Texas

Verbal Safety Cues	*What safety cues should be included to provide a safe environment?*
Teaching Style	*Command, Practice, Peer Teaching, Self-check, Choice, Guided Discovery, Convergent, or Divergent*
Assessment	*Summative or Formative*
Format of Assessment	*Observation, Paper/Pencil Tests, etc.*
Transition Activity	*This is an activity that brings students back to the focus of the lesson.*

Modifications/Accommodations:

How will you address the needs of students who are "at risk" or who have disabilities? What are some general simplifications or extensions of the lesson to meet the students' individual needs?

Reflection Assessment:

Did the lesson progress as intended? Explain.

What could be changed to enhance the lesson?

Add any other comments or information.

Fig. 3.1 (continued)

Classroom Management

Classroom management describes students' consistent engagement in classroom activities with little interruption. In an extensive literature review, Wang, Haertl, and Walberg (1993) provided researchers and educators clear evidence of the importance of classroom management. Among all variables considered, such as student cognitive processes and student/teacher interactions, classroom management had the greatest effect on student achievement (Wang et al., 1993), which is the primary goal of education. Therefore, maintaining a classroom with consistent routines to increase student engagement and on task behavior is critical to consider when integrating movement into the classroom. In addition, teachers who establish classroom routines provide students with greater on task behavior (Emmer, Evertson, & Worsham, 2003). Marzano and Marzano (2003) suggest the importance of establishing rules and procedures for the classroom to help students understand what behavior is appropriate and what is inappropriate. Teacher strategies, such as cueing, may be effective in providing students with a signal to stop off-task behavior or during transition, helping them to increase on-task behavior when teachers switch from one task to another. While education literature offers numerous strategies for effectively managing a classroom, teachers should establish their own management techniques to ensure classroom learning goals are met (Marzano, 2011). Though this chapter offers an explanation of the lesson plan used in this textbook, teachers may find additional strategies to increase effectiveness with their specific students or classroom environment.

The activities in this textbook were designed to maximize student participation, thus addressing the classroom environment and content learning goals. In other words, to effectively integrate movement, teachers should minimize students' wait time and increase individual student engagement. Because students may be more likely to display disruptive behavior when they complete any classroom task or assignment and feel bored, providing students with continuous activity may help maintain an effective learning environment. In addition, using signals and transition activities to manage movement lessons may increase the effectiveness of movement integration into the classroom, enabling students to experience the benefits of integrated movement.

Understanding the Lesson Plan Template

In order to assist classroom teachers in effectively using the movement integrated activities in this textbook, the lesson plan template (see Fig. 3.1) used throughout the text is explained in detail below. The lesson plan format was created to enhance the movement experience in the classroom with a focus on reputable classroom management strategies.

Suggested Time Frame

The need to allot an appropriate amount of time for the planned lesson is common among curriculum design. More experienced teachers may have a better concept of how long a proposed lesson will be, but timing of presenting a lesson is often not fully determined until after teaching the lesson once or twice. Timing is often dictated by a daily schedule, and limited by the need to transition to a new subject, lunch, or special class. However, it is important to recognize that integrating movement into a lesson may alter the duration of the lesson, and should be considered when estimating how long the activity will last. Furthermore, more time may need to be allocated to a movement integration lesson when the practice is being introduced, while less time may be needed once routines are well established.

Equipment and Technology

Movement integration does not require equipment or technology, but including equipment or technology may enhance an activity depending upon the lesson plan. When using equipment or technology, teachers should ensure they are prepared in advance of the lesson for implementation, and that students understand the rules and expectations for use of either.

Equipment. Equipment is important to the design and management of any physically active lesson. Some of the lessons in this textbook include equipment that many elementary teachers already have, such as: rulers, tape, note cards, etc. However, some equipment may need to be borrowed from the school's physical education teacher, who may also be a great resource for lesson planning and implementation. The following are suggestions for planning and using equipment:

Plan for plenty of equipment. Having enough equipment maximizes participation and ensures that each child has the opportunity to actively engage. Equipment is also a key factor for providing individualized instruction, so teachers should make sure each student is using equipment appropriately for his or her ability level.

Tips for maximizing participation:

- If possible, provide enough equipment for all students to participate at the same time.
- When facilitating groups, keep numbers small, such as: three to four students, to enhance engagement and participation.
- Offer a variety of equipment (i.e. sizes, weights, textures) when possible so that students have choices.

Managing equipment. The organization and distribution of equipment can either enhance or hinder classroom management, so teachers should plan ahead. Prior to instruction, decide how much and what type of equipment is needed, determine how to organize the equipment in the classroom space, and create a plan for distributing the equipment. Teachers should ensure that students will have enough space to use the equipment safely and should discuss equipment safety with students prior to the beginning of the lesson. Equipment will be distributed in a variety of ways, depending upon the flow of the lesson. Management will be more effective when teachers use appropriate strategies for distributing the equipment.

Tips for Distributing and Managing Equipment:

- Set the expectation for how to handle equipment BEFORE activities begin.
- Put the equipment out at the desks or stations where students will be working, so it is ready to use when needed.
- Make students responsible for getting and returning equipment, for their group/table/row. Consider assigning a student as the equipment manager for the lesson. For example, have the student with the closest birthday be equipment manager that day.

Borrowing or making equipment. Physical education programs often have a variety of equipment that classroom teachers can borrow for the different movement lessons. Also, teachers should consider seeking advice from the physical educators on their campus about movement integration, as physical educators can offer suggestions for equipment use and activity ideas. In some lessons, teachers may be able to make equipment using things from home, found at school, or by requesting students to bring items from their homes. For example, teachers can easily make weights with repurposed water or soda bottles, or use items such as disposable plates for Frisbees or mouse pads for floor spot/markers. More ideas on homemade equipment can be found at: www.pecentral.org.

Safety first when using equipment. Finally, teachers should check equipment before and after activities to ensure that the equipment is safe for student use. Equipment can become degraded over time from improper storage or from regular use. Students should not use equipment that is broken, unsafe, or worn out. After the movement activities, have students discard any broken, tattered or unusable equipment.

Technology. In addition to physical education equipment, teachers may also find that technology resources are beneficial to movement. As stated in Chap. 2, various classroom physical activity resources can be found on the Internet to assist teachers with ideas. In addition, technology, such as projectors, music devices and speakers, or activity tracing devices, may be needed to enhance implementation.

Start/Stop Signals

Physically active settings may be louder and may seem more chaotic than many classroom teachers are accustomed to experiencing; therefore, start/stop signals will be helpful to keep students on task and responsive. Start/stop signals are regularly used in the physical education setting to let students know when to begin an activity, when to stop an activity, and what to do at the end of the activity (i.e. put equipment down, kneel, no talking). By using a practical signal, teachers can establish a routine for the class to better manage time and student behaviors.

A variety of start/stop signals that have been used successfully in the physical education setting that might also be adequate for the classroom. An effective signal should quickly draw students' attention to the teacher. Many teachers start activities by simply saying, "Go". Some ideas have been listed below and start/signals have been included for each activity in the text.

Examples of start/stop signals:

- Music: When the music begins, students start the activity; when the music stops, students stop the activity, put the equipment down, and look to the teacher.
- Sayings/Phrases: When the teacher states the phrase, students stop the activity, put the equipment down, and look to the teacher.

  - "1, 2, 3, eyes on me" or "1, 2, 3, take a knee"
  - Use your school mascot. For example, "Hawks halt".

- Call and Response: The teacher makes a call, students stop the activity, put down the equipment and respond.

  - Teacher says, "1, 2" and students reply, "eyes on you".
  - Teacher says, "Ice" and students reply, "freeze".

- Clapping: Teachers can clap a rhythm to begin the activity and clap another rhythm to stop the activity; when students hear the rhythm they can repeat it. For example, the teacher claps twice and students begin activity; when the students hear five claps they stop the activity, put equipment down, and repeat the five claps while looking to the teacher.

Tips for Using Start/Stop Signals:

- Keep signals simple, positive, and fun.
- Inform students of the start/stop signals before the activity begins by teaching them the behavioral expectations. For example, "when you hear/see the signal, you will put equipment down, stop talking, and make eye contact with me".
- Practice using start/stop signals so students know the expectations.
- Repeat the signal until all students are paying attention.

Verbal Skill and Safety Cues

Research suggests that verbal cues can improve meaningfulness and can also be used to improve memory (Haibach, Reid, & Collier, 2011). Verbal information can provide information about a new skill, ideas about movement patterns, and expectations for movement patterns (Schmidt & Wrisberg, 2008). Furthermore, verbal skill cueing can enhance students' focus and attention to help them detect and correct errors. By suggesting to students what they need to think about during the activity, teachers can emphasize specific movement concepts, focus on critical information for the lesson, and remind students about safe play. Verbal cues, kept brief to not exceed students attention capacity (Magill, 2007), are typically a few words or brief phrases that describe or communicate something about a concept or skill for safety. For example, a teacher may say "squash your knees" to remind students to bend their knees when jumping or "hop on one foot" to remind students how to hop correctly.

Verbal cueing can also be used by teachers to create a safe environment. Anytime children are physically active, teachers should think proactively about providing a safe environment. Many accidents can be prevented by planning ahead, identifying foreseeable risks, and providing appropriate safety cues to minimize the risks. Before beginning activities, teachers should establish sufficient safety by teaching the procedures and rules to the students, using appropriate language for students' cognitive levels. Safety procedures and rules should be reinforced throughout the lesson through verbal safety cues. Safety cues are similar to skill cues, except that they focus on safety aspects of the activity.

Tips for Using Verbal Cues:

- Create meaningful cues that provide a mental image or relate to a familiar movement for children. For example, a physical education teacher may use metaphor by telling students to "reach into the cookie jar" when teaching the follow through for shooting a basketball.
- Keep cues short-no more than three words.
- Cue only the most critical components of the skill or safety risks, so students are not overwhelmed.

Teaching Style

When creating lesson plans, teachers should consider the specific teaching style that will be utilized in presenting the lesson. The Lesson Plan Template suggests a variety of teaching styles that offer multiple examples for teachers to consider when integrating movement, such as: Practice, Peer Teaching, Self-check, Choice, Convergent, or Divergent. In peer teaching, the lessons suggest that students work in partners or small groups to teach one another. This particular teaching style increases student motivation and engagement in the classroom. Self-check allows students to participate in movement while checking their understanding of the content. This style may serve as a type of formative assessment for the student. Choice style may allow students an opportunity to choose the type of movement they want, such as choosing a particular style of dance. Finally, convergent or divergent teaching styles encourage students to learn through creativity by encouraging them to bring ideas together or break them apart. Though the lessons in this textbook suggest specific teaching styles be used, alternative styles may be considered by the teacher, depending on the learning goal of the lesson.

Assessment and Format of Assessment

To ensure students achieved the learning objective of the movement integration activity, formative or summative evaluations should be included in lesson planning. Assessments are built into the teaching-learning process, and criteria for assessment should be selected prior to the lesson. Assessment criteria can be linked to objectives and the lesson content, and should be appropriate for the age/grade level of the children.

Formative evaluations occur during the learning process, to enable modification mid-way through an activity, while summative evaluations occur at the completion of the learning process. These assessments may be formal or informal. Teacher observation or a class discussion, which are informal assessments, can give students immediate feedback, and be used throughout the lesson, or at the end. Formal assessments may require students to produce a product to be assessed or to complete a quiz or test. These summative evaluations are used to determine students' progress towards the objectives and areas where they need more practice.

Transition Activity

Including a transition activity at the end of the movement lesson will assist classroom teachers in maintaining a well-managed classroom. At the conclusion of the movement lesson, students may need to transition from being active, excited, and energetic to quiet, calm and participating in seat work. Appropriate transition also allows for students to calm down after the activity, especially if the heart rate is increased. Physical activity does not always raise the heart rate, but when students get excited and adrenaline and endorphins increase, they may be more excitable than usual. Transitioning from one content area or activity to another often provides a challenge for classroom teachers, so teachers should ensure students have clear instructions on what to do next and provide students with tasks to keep them engaged.

By planning a transition activity, teachers can easily refocus students in order to maintain lesson flow and time management. Transition activities may include a calming exercise, such as stretches or breathing, or a task that relates to the lesson activities, such as a worksheet, peer teaching, or journaling. Students may need time to become familiar with transition activities, but as it becomes a regular practice in the classroom, students will get better at transitioning. If for some reason students have difficulty transitioning, teachers can use stop signals, as mentioned above, to gain students' attention.

Modifications and Accommodations

For the purpose of this component of the lesson plan template, modifications and accommodations can be considered synonymous as methods or strategies' that alter what the student is doing or how it is being done. Depending upon the activity and the participating students, modifications and accommodations are critical to ensure that all students are able to participate in the lesson. Movement lessons can be successfully modified to include all students, regardless of ability level or special needs.

One way to modify activities is to provide student-choice in directions, such as number of repetitions or movement form. For example, if students are supposed to engage in chair dips after a discussion about a social studies prompt, teachers could provide the option to do 5, or 10, or 15 dips. Using the chair dip example, another option for students would be to complete the dip with straight legs or bent legs.

Teachers can also make modifications to equipment or directions to match students' capabilities and developmental levels. For example, for activities that include targets, use different sized targets and mark different distances from the targets. Some students may need modified rules, changes in the task or actions, smaller play areas, or more attempts at the activity. For example, students with limited mobility may require a striking implement (i.e. pool noodle) in activities that require using feet to kick or pass so that they can push or stop an object. There are free online resources for providing tips and best practices for adapting physical activities, such as PE Central (see http://www.pecentral.org/adapted/adaptedactivities.html), the New PE (see https://www.thenewpe.com/adapted/adapted.htm), and American Printing House for the Blind (see http://www.aph.org/physical-education/articles/). North Carolina public schools has compiled a useful list of bullets that offer tips and suggestions for teaching students with some form of disability (http://www.ncpublicschools.org/docs/curriculum/healthfulliving/resources/instructional/bestpractices/inclusivepe.pdf). Though modifications to lessons to accommodate students may be specific to each lesson, many of the suggested accommodations can be used across several lessons. In this textbook, chapter authors provide suggested accommodations for each created lesson, but the classroom teacher may need additional modifications for his or her students.

Conclusion

By adopting the lesson plans offered in this textbook, teachers can more effectively integrate movement into their classrooms while maintaining a well-managed classroom environment. As suggested by Marzano and Marzano (2003), students are more likely to remain on task throughout a lesson when teachers include lesson components that allow for smooth transitions and establish classroom routines. Through appropriate movement integration, teachers may enhance their classroom environment and improve the learning preparedness and engagement of students, while enabling students to gain the physical, cognitive, and socioemotional benefits of activity. The following chapters will provide the classroom teacher with information to effectively integrate movement into the four selected content areas.

References

Emmer, E. T., Evertson, C. M., & Worsham, M. E. (2003). *Classroom management for secondary teachers* (6th ed.). Boston: Allyn and Bacon.

Haibach, P. S., Reid, G., & Collier, D. H. (2011). *Motor learning and development*. Champaign, IL: Human Kinetics.

Magill, R. A. (2007). *Motor learning and control: Concepts and applications* (8th ed.). New York, NY: McGraw-Hill.

Marzano, R. J. (2011). Classroom management: Whose job is it? *Educational Leadership, 69*(2), 85–86.

Marzano, R. J., & Marzano, J. S. (2003). The key to classroom management. *Educational Leadership, 61*(1), 6–13.

Schmidt, R. A., & Wrisberg, C. A. (2008). *Motor learning and performance: A situation-based learning approach* (4th ed.). Champaign, IL: Human Kinetics.

Wang, M. C., Haertel, G. D., & Walberg, H. J. (1993). Toward a knowledge base for school learning. *Review of Educational Research, 63*(3), 249–294.

Chapter 4
Integrating Movement in the Language Arts

**Krysta Woods, Christina Janise McIntyre, Emily Reeves
and Pamela Whitehouse**

Abstract This chapter includes some of the benefits of incorporating movement into the language arts curriculum. The authors offer several activities aligned to the five significant language arts areas or strands represented in both the National Council of Teachers of English (NCTE) national standards and Common Core Standards that effectively integrate movement into language arts to benefit both student learning and physical activity. The language arts strands included in this chapter are: reading, writing, oral and written conventions, research, and listening and speaking.

As was discussed in the general introduction to this textbook, the responsibility has fallen to elementary school educators to encourage student movement in the classroom to help students achieve the daily-recommended amount of physical activity. This chapter will outline some of the benefits of incorporating movement into the language arts curriculum and then offer suggestions for activities and lesson plans that effectively integrate movement into language arts to benefit both student learning and physical activity.

Previous research suggests the biological basis of movement integration, and a strong connection has been found among movement, learning, and brain development in children (Brewer, Damico, & Rinkevich, 2012). According to Piaget, movement is inherent in children, causing them to interact with their environments, and this interaction, facilitated by movement, increases cognitive development (Gellens, 2005; Greenfader & Brouillette, 2013; Kalyn, 2006). Movement may also

K. Woods · C.J. McIntyre (✉) · E. Reeves · P. Whitehouse
Midwestern State University, Wichita Falls, TX, USA
e-mail: Christina.mcintyre@mwsu.edu

K. Woods
e-mail: turtlegirl2333@yahoo.com

E. Reeves
e-mail: emily.graves@mwsu.edu

P. Whitehouse
e-mail: Plwhiteh@gmail.com

© Springer Nature Singapore Pte Ltd. 2018
S.C. Miller and S.F. Lindt (eds.), *Moving INTO the Classroom*,
Springer Texts in Education, DOI 10.1007/978-981-10-6424-1_4

increase memory, cognition, and attention (Brewer et al., 2012; Reed et al., 2010). Collins, Miller, and Yates (2005), discuss how movement affects the release of neurotransmitters in the brain, which "prime" students to learn. Additionally, integrating movement into the classroom may increase cognitive skills, fluid intelligence, academic achievement, and intrinsic motivation (Collins et al., 2005; Reed et al., 2010; Vazou, Gavrilou, Mamalaki, Papanastasiou, & Sioumala, 2012). In a study by Trost, Fees and Dzewaltowski (2008) implemented a "Move and Learn" program for 3–5 year olds. The program included different content areas: math, language arts, social studies, science, and nutrition education. At the end of the study, the teachers involved reported that students were "enthusiastic, attentive, and persistent in their learning tasks" (Trost et al., 2008, p. 99). This finding is encouraging as it highlights the benefits of a movement-rich environment. Overall, a number of research studies have shown that movement in general is beneficial to the cognitive development and motivation of students and can be linked to academic achievement; therefore, integrating movement into language arts may lead to students' attainment of increased cognitive abilities and greater academic success.

For language arts, specifically, research suggests that movement is beneficial to student learning. Kercood and Banda (2012) tested the effects of gross motor movement on listening comprehension; their results offer that gross motor movement not only improved listening comprehension but also improved student attention. Movement in language arts has been shown to aid in literacy development as well (Brewer et al., 2012; Callcott, Hammond, & Hill, 2015). Movement that can be used to increase literacy includes conveying meaning of words through movement (e.g., acting out action words) and using sports to show how to choose appropriate words and sentence structures for certain purposes (Brewer et al., 2012). Additionally, Callcott et al. (2015) conducted a study in which they evaluated the effectiveness of teaching specific early literacy skills, such as phonological awareness, in combination with a 15-min movement program. The researchers found that children who received the early literacy instruction alongside the movement program scored significantly higher on measures of spelling and phonological awareness than children who received only early instruction (Callcott et al., 2015). A number of authors have suggested that acting out literature and drama can promote literacy development by (a) allowing the students to develop their own interpretations of the text, (b) helping the students put a context around decontextualized words that they may not understand within texts, (c) teaching the students about plot, character, and theme, and (d) introducing novelty into the classroom, which can increase student engagement and participation (Brewer et al., 2012; Bernath & Masi, 2005; Greenfader & Brouillette, 2013). In Pica's (2010) *Linking Literacy and Movement* article, she discusses the benefits of movement in language arts. She suggests that language and movement are both means by which people can communicate with others and express themselves, and she notes that both movement and words have a rhythm. Because of this, movement easily lends itself to the instruction of language arts. Pica offers suggestions of activities that incorporate movement into language arts including (a) having students use their bodies to form the curves and straight lines of letters that they find confusing, so they can feel the difference between them; (b) having children tap in rhythm with the rhythm of poetry, so students can feel the beats in the poems; and (c) having students do sequences of actions together, so they will understand how words are strung together to create sentences.

Language arts is typically seen as a fairly sedentary subject with little gross motor movement involved. If teachers take the initiative and seek ways to incorporate movement into language arts, students may benefit greatly, both physically and cognitively. The remaining part of this chapter contains several activities that incorporate movement into the language arts. The following are activities that correspond with five significant language arts areas or strands represented in both the National Council of Teachers of English (NCTE) national standards and Common Core Standards as well: Reading, Writing, Oral and Written Conventions, Research, and Listening and Speaking.

Reading

Reading involves not only decoding, but also comprehending, yet the act of reading transcends these two activities as it can be a means for not only knowledge acquisition but also for connecting to the experiences of others and to help us make sense of ourselves and the world around us. The National Council of Teachers of English (NCTE) Standards for reading ask that students read a wide range of print and non-print texts, employing strategies to build an understanding of texts, themselves, and the world around them. The standards also ask that students read literature representing various genres and time periods in order to build an appreciation for literature and an understanding of the human experience (http://www. ncte.org/standards/ncte-ira). The Common Core State Standards for reading ask that students read stories, literature, and complex texts that provide facts and background knowledge in various disciplines that stress critical thinking and problem solving (http://www.corestandards.org/ELA-Literacy). Development of literacy skills is integral to academic development and achievement and this development can be supported by movement.

Research suggests that teaching early literacy skills, such as phonological awareness, in combination with movement can lead to an increase in the development in literacy skills (Callcott et al., 2015). In a study conducted with 5-year-old children, researchers found that the children who were taught phonological awareness alongside a 15-min movement program scored significantly higher on measures of spelling and phonological awareness than did children who were taught phonological awareness skills without physical activity (Callcott et al., 2015).

Brewer et al. (2012) discuss the importance of developing literacy skills and the biological basis of brain development as it relates to the development of literacy skills. They offer that children have an innate desire to move and suggest strong connections among movement, learning, and brain development in children. Specifically, stimulation of the inner-ear and cerebellar system and the reticular activating system during movement help children develop understanding of texts, reading comprehension, and writing (Brewer et al., 2012). Some specific examples of movement activities that can help the development of literacy are as follows: (1) Conveying meaning of words through movement can aid in vocabulary development, which will increase reading comprehension; (2) Acting out stories and plays can help students show their own interpretations of literature, which, again, aids in reading comprehension; and (3) Using sports to show how to use words in appropriate contexts and how to choose appropriate words and sentence structures for certain purposes increases vocabulary (Brewer et al., 2012).

Activity Name: It Is Not Greek to Me

Suggested Grade Level: 4/5

NCTE Standards: 3: Students apply a wide range of strategies to comprehend, interpret, evaluate, and appreciate texts. They draw on their prior experience, their interactions with other readers and writers, their knowledge of word meaning and of other texts, their word identification strategies, and their understanding of textual features (e.g., sound-letter correspondence, sentence structure, context, graphics).
Common Core State Standards: CCSS.ELA-LITERACY.L.5.4.B: Use common, grade-appropriate Greek and Latin affixes and roots as clues to the meaning of a word (e.g., *photograph, photosynthesis*).
Goals: Students will use non-locomotors movement to learn the meanings of Greek and Latin root words.
Objectives: The students will perform a series of movements to demonstrate an understanding of words comprised of Greek and Latin roots.

Suggested time frame	30–40 min
Equipment/technology	Computer, projector with slideshow to display roots and definitions; card sort activity—20 cards for each group (five cards with roots and five definition cards; five cards with words made up of roots and five definition cards)
Start/stop signals	To start activity say "Start" To stop the activity when the teacher says "Alpha" have the students say "Omega" stop what they are doing, and look at the teacher for further instructions. This should be repeated until everyone is still and has eyes on the teacher for further instructions *Note: Try to make the signal fun by using Greek words*
Skill cues	Model for the students the various movements that correspond with the roots using the cues in Fig. 4.1. Exaggerate movements
Safety cues	Remind the students to be at least an arm's width away from walls, desks, chairs, and other people when they are doing their

(continued)

(continued)

	movements especially in their groups. Tell the students to be mindful of other students, so they do not bump into them
Teaching style	Direct instruction; practice; cooperative learning
Assessments of content through the activity	Observational checklist; anecdotal notes
Transition activity	Have the students stand by their chairs, do a big stretch toward the sky breathing deeply and then be seated

Description of Greek Root Words Activity

Introduction: Greek Roots

- Begin the activity by showing on the board a complex word like "autobiography" or "telegraph" with which students are unlikely to be familiar. Ask students if they know what the word means or how it is pronounced. The students will probably not know, but reassure them that learning how to say, spell, and understand complex words like this one is something they are capable of.
- Explain to the students that they will be learning about the "building blocks" for many words that we use today and that an understanding of what the "building blocks" mean gives us the ability to decode complex words such as "philanthropy." Visually demonstrate how this particular word can be broken down into parts called roots, prefixes, or suffixes as detailed below in the activity for Greek Roots Movement (i.e. "philo" = love; "sophos" = meaning of life).
  Note: Though not a focus of this lesson, it is helpful if students have a basic knowledge of prefixes and suffixes from previous grades to understand the terminology.
- Use a diagram, web, or graphic organizer and start with the root "graph." Model as students follow along. Show how roots can be parts of other words like "photograph" or "autograph." Explain the different words and meanings and have students fill in blanks on their own paper or graphic organizer. Then explain that there are hundreds of Greek and Latin roots, prefixes, and suffixes, but today they will learn the meaning of 10 roots that when combined in different ways create complex words.

Activity: Greek Roots Movements

- Explain to the students that in order to facilitate their learning and retention, they will be learning movements that represent the meanings of the roots. Refer to Fig. 4.1 with examples of roots and movements for the following activity. Refer to the pictures as well for further explanation of the roots and movements.
- The teacher should create a slide for each root to project onto the front board. Each root should have its own slide and another slide should be created with the

Fig. 4.1 Roots, their
definitions, and movements

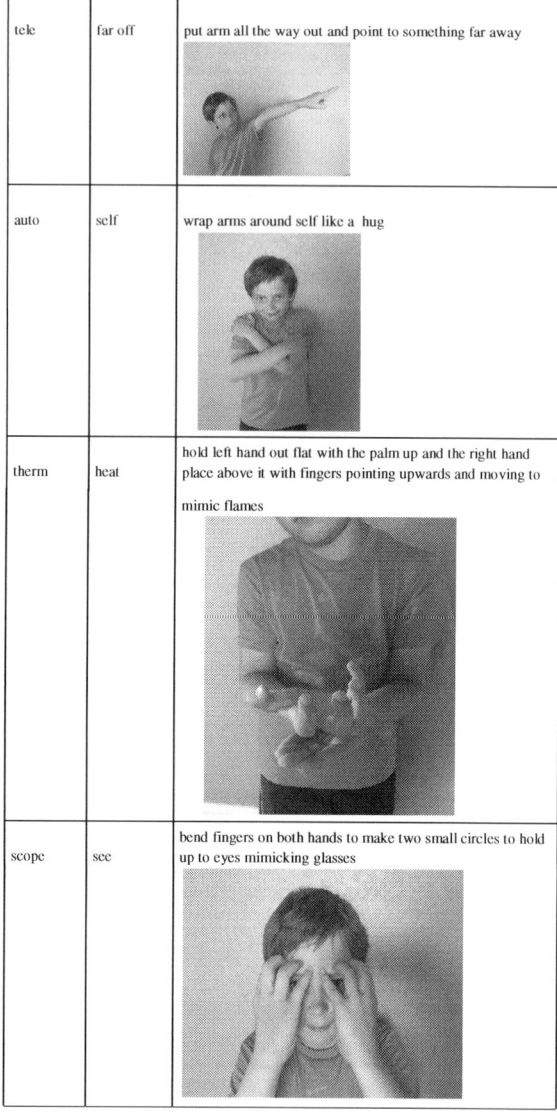

tele	far off	put arm all the way out and point to something far away
auto	self	wrap arms around self like a hug
therm	heat	hold left hand out flat with the palm up and the right hand place above it with fingers pointing upwards and moving to mimic flames
scope	see	bend fingers on both hands to make two small circles to hold up to eyes mimicking glasses

root and its definition. (The teacher could also make slides for each root and definition on a flip chart.) Show one root on the board and pronounce it for the class. Have the students pronounce the root as it is projected onto the front screen. Repeat if necessary. For example, explain that the root "tele" as in telephone means "far away". Explain to students and demonstrate that when you say the root word "tele", they will stand and point to something far away.

meter	measure	make the movement of pulling out a measuring tape and pretending to measure something in the air
		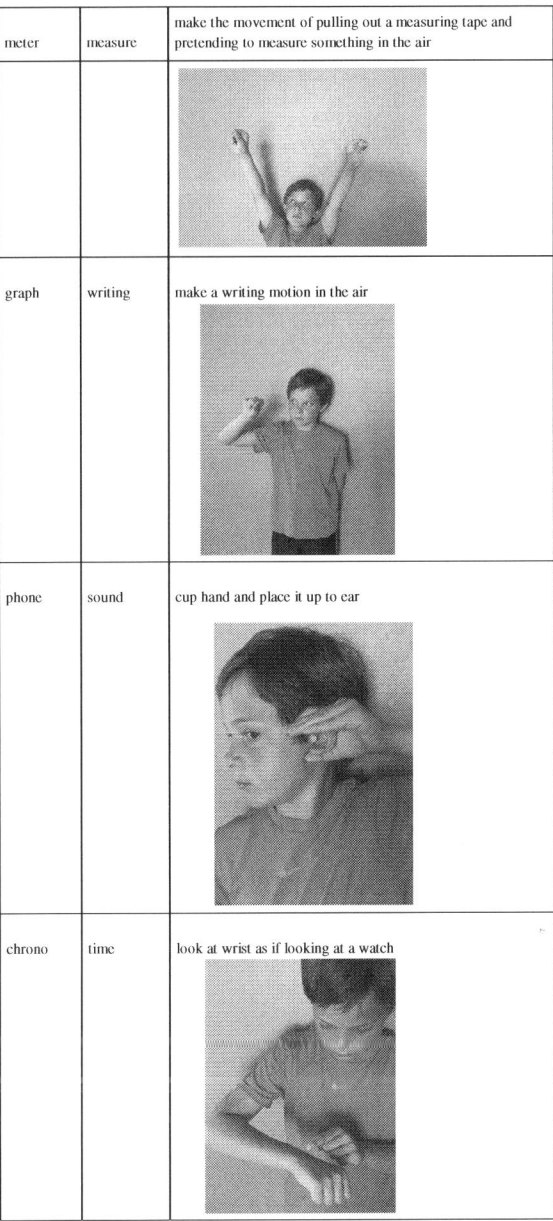
graph	writing	make a writing motion in the air
phone	sound	cup hand and place it up to ear
chrono	time	look at wrist as if looking at a watch

Fig. 4.1 (continued)

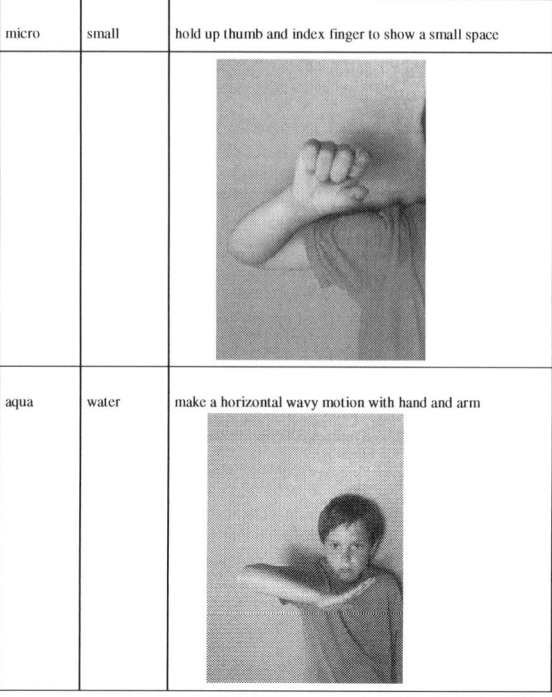

| micro | small | hold up thumb and index finger to show a small space |
| aqua | water | make a horizontal wavy motion with hand and arm |

Fig. 4.1 (continued)

- Show the root on the front board with the corresponding definition and say it aloud for the class. Model the corresponding movement and then have the students stand and perform the movement, say the word, and then say the definition. They may refer to the board during this time so keep the root and definition displayed. Go through each of the ten roots once, modeling and having students follow along.
  Note: Depending on grade and developmental level, it may be appropriate to feature only five roots at a time.
- Go back through the root and definition slides one at a time, showing both the root and definition on the board and have students attempt to perform the movements independently, prompting when needed. Do this as many times as necessary.
- Next, just show the root and have the students perform the movement and say the definition aloud. Do this as many times as necessary so that you can tell they are remembering the movement and connecting it to the definition.
- At this point they have been acting out movements for roots only. Now show a word made up of roots they can decipher. For example display the word "autograph." Have them create the movements in succession (to aid in recalling the meanings) and then say what they think the word means. (For "autograph", the

students would first wrap their arms around themselves like a hug and then make a writing motion in the air.) Do this for two or three different words and adjusting the literal root meanings to actual word definitions. This is important because sometimes the words are not a literal translation of the two roots but with the knowledge of the roots, generating a definition is much easier.

Cooperative Activity: Greek Root Word Card Sort With Movements

- Have the students get into groups of four to five to complete a card sort. Model the transition activity from the above chart and have students perform transition activity before being seated and teach the stop/start signal.
- Have roots printed on one set of cards and the root definitions printed on another set using the roots and definitions they learned above in whole class instruction. You can group students by color coding cards. Have students match the roots with the definitions and practice the movements. Adjust the number of cards for grade and developmental level.
- Next, have students set aside the root definition cards or take them up. Give each group cards with dictionary definitions to words made up of the root cards they already have. Using a definition card, have students arrange the root cards into the word that represents each definition card. Have students execute the movements for each word. They can also be asked to record these words and definitions on a worksheet or their own paper. Adjust the number of cards for grade and developmental level.

  Note: To modify for developmental level, give students both cards with the words made up of the roots they have learned movements for and cards with corresponding definitions. Have the students make the movements that comprise the words and then match them with the definition card.

The following are examples of roots, their definitions, and movements that can be used with them see Fig. 4.1. You may make up motions for as many others as you choose to teach throughout the year.

Extension: To extend this activity you may have students use the root cards in the first cooperative activity to explore creating different words by combining and rearranging the root cards, predicting and writing possible definitions, and then checking for accuracy with a dictionary, using a blank graphic organizer (see Fig. 4.2) like the one utilized during the introduction. Later, students can also create their own movements for new roots they are introduced to.

Modifications/Adaptations: For students with physical disabilities, the students may sit and perform the movements or they can be partnered with someone to assist them with the movements. The number of roots and complexity of words can be adjusted for developmental level as well, and suggestions for other modifications are listed above with the activity.

Fig. 4.2 Example of
extension activity to create
own words

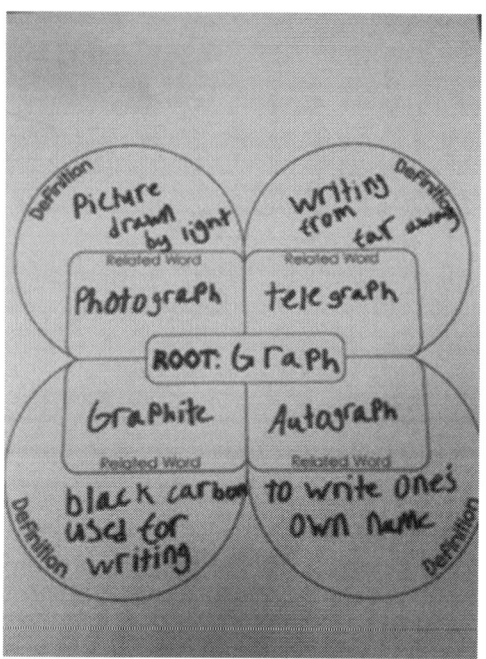

Writing

The NCTE language arts standards for writing ask that students are able to employ a
variety of strategies to write for a variety of purposes. Additionally, students should
utilize the writing process to draft and revise in order to communicate effectively in
writing (http://www.ncte.org/standards/ncte-ira). Common Core standards for
writing in elementary focus on the development of the sophisticated use of
vocabulary, syntax, and organization of written ideas (http://www.corestandards.
org/ELA-Literacy/W/introduction/).

Brewer et al. (2012) explain that conveying meaning of words through movement
can help students develop vocabulary, while using specific moves from different
sports can help students learn how to use words in appropriate contexts and understand
how to choose appropriate words and sentence structures for certain purposes. Pica
(2010) suggests having students use their bodies to form the curves and straight lines
of letters that they find confusing can help them feel the difference between the letters.
Movement can also be used to teach students the rhythm of words and sentences, since
movement itself can have rhythm. Incorporating movement into writing may seem
difficult, but when done well, it may increase students' literacy skills and understanding of sentence and essay structures.

Activity Name: Story Train

Suggested Grade Level: 1

NCTE Standards: 12: Students use spoken, written, and visual language to accomplish their own purposes (e.g., for learning, enjoyment, persuasion, and the exchange of information).

Common Core State Standards: CCSS.ELA-LITERACY.W.1.3: Write narratives in which they recount two or more appropriately sequenced events, include some details regarding what happened, use temporal words to signal event order, and provide some sense of closure.

Goals: Students will learn to identify the beginning, middle, and end of a story.

Objectives: Students will understand the importance of including the beginning, middle, and end of a story when writing by participating in a story train activity.

Suggested time frame	35–40 min
Equipment/technology	Various equipment for free play, such as a playground equipment, sport balls, jump ropes, hula hoops, and rackets. Train cards—engine, cars, caboose
Start/stop signals	Use the whistle as a start/stop signal during free play. One whistle to start or change the activity, two whistles to stop the activity and get the students attention To start the activity say "Move to your train station" To end the activity say "Quietly move back to your seats"
Skill cues	At the playground, remind students "eyes up, heads up", "squash your knees when landing", and "eyes on the ball"
Safety cues	At the playground, remind students to be mindful of others, to share the equipment, and to pace themselves in the activities In the classroom, remind the students to be mindful of others and the desks and chairs when they are moving about the room, so they do not run into anything or anyone
Teaching style	Guided discovery; cooperative learning
Assessments of content through the activity	Use a checklist throughout the activity. While students are finding their place on the train, make note of those who struggle. Also, actively monitor the discussion throughout the activity and make notes as needed
Transition activity	Have the students stand by their seats stretching tall to represent the beginning of the story, bending at the waist for the middle, and touching their toes for the end

Description of Story Train Activity

Introduction: Parts of a Story

- Introduce students to the three parts of a story by reading a very short story, such as "Goldilocks and the Three Bears". After reading this familiar story, the teacher should explain that in the beginning of the story, goldilocks goes into the bear's house when no one is home. In the middle of the story, goldilocks tries the bear's porridge, chairs, and beds to determine that the one of each is "just right", and at the end of the story, the bears come home to find Goldilocks asleep. She wakes up and runs away frightened, never to return.
  (Model the transition activity listed in the above chart to emphasize the story parts and teach the transition. The teacher may also add another story here to help students understand the parts of a story or use another story in place of "Goldilocks".)

Activity: Creating a Story Through Free Play

- After the introduction to the three parts of a story, take students outside for free play. Explain to the students that they will have 10 min to play however they would like (i.e. different equipment, with various classmates), but they should listen for the teacher's whistle while they are playing.
- At the sound of the whistle, students should change what they are doing by either playing a new game, changing equipment, or changing the people in their playgroup. Also, remind students to be aware of the sequence of events while they are playing because they will later be asked to recall their activities during free play (if needed, students can take a notebook to journal when the teacher blows the whistle).
- After the 10-min free play period, take students back to the class where they will be asked to construct a story of their playtime.
- Have students return to their desks and perform the transition activity listed in the above chart before being seated. Give each student three cards to represent the parts of the story (beginning, middle, and end) and have them write about what happened during the playtime.

Cooperative Activity: Story Train Car Movements

- Explain to the students that they will be practicing arranging the engine (beginning), cars (middle), and caboose (end) of a train (story) using the stories their peers wrote about playtime.
- Collect all of the students' cards, then shuffle them up, then redistribute them randomly throughout the class. Actively discuss that the engine represents the beginning, the cars represent the middle, and the caboose represents the end of a story. Each section of the train plays an important part in the story.
  Note: Have a designated space in the classroom for the engine, cars and caboose of the train (taped on the wall or on the floor).

Fig. 4.3 Students standing by one of the middle cars during the story train activity

- Tell the students that they will be deciding what part of the story they have, and will move to the engine, cars or caboose depending on what they think. Once all students have a card, have the entire class navigate their way across the classroom to their section of the train by saying "move to your train station." See Fig. 4.3.
- Once all students are in place, have the engine stand up and the cars and caboose sit down. Talk about the function of the beginning of a story when writing and ask students for examples from the stories their peers wrote.
- Next, have the engine cards sit down and the cars cards stand up, repeating the conversation with a focus on the middle of a story.
- Finally, have the engine and cars cards sit while the caboose cards stand up again repeating the narrative about importance and examples with a focus on the end of a story. Finish by telling students that when writing, they should always think about the beginning, middle, and end of their story so their writing is complete.

Extension: Post the train cards on the wall and refer students to them during writing workshop.

Modifications/Adaptations: Provide a variety of equipment during the playtime to ensure that all students can be actively engaged in physical activity. Pair students who may need encouragement during playtime. Be sure that there is enough room around the desks for any students with physical disabilities to move about the room unimpeded. If necessary, push the desks to the sides of the room.

Fig. 4.4 Forward bend

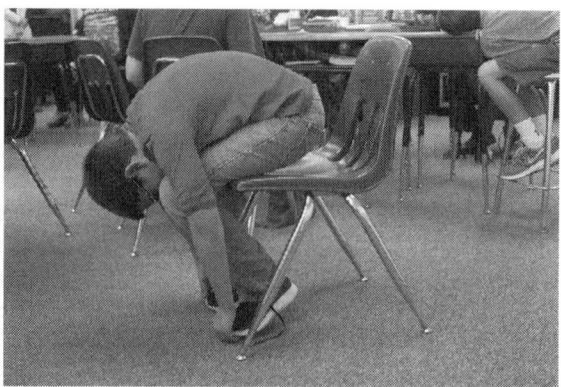

Fig. 4.5 Leg lift

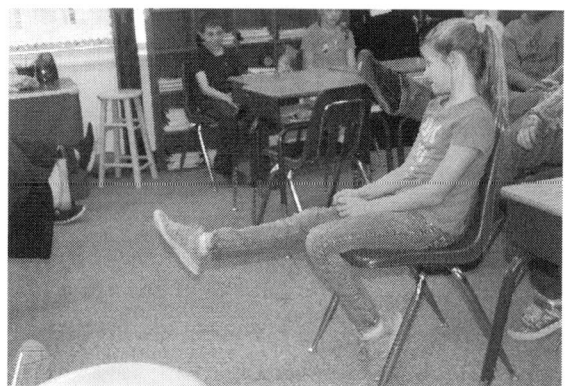

Oral and Written Conventions

NCTE standards ask that students apply knowledge of language structure and language conventions such as spelling and punctuation to communicate effectively (http://www.ncte.org/standards/ncte-ira). More specifically in the Common Core standards, these conventions include grammar, mechanics, and knowledge of parts of speech to create simple, compound, and complex sentences. This encompasses skills such as subject verb agreement and pronoun antecedent agreement to communicate effectively. Conventions also include recognition of and the various uses of punctuation marks in the English language (http://www.corestandards.org/ELA-Literacy/W/1). Students are expected to use the different conventions appropriately for both writing and speaking.

According to Collins et al. (2005), movement can facilitate the learning of language. They also note that some research has suggested that physical activity is the medium through which most young children want to learn. Because movement has been shown, in neurological studies, to increase memory and cognition (Reed et al., 2010), connecting English language conventions with physical activity may be an advantageous method to facilitate students' memory of these conventions.

Activity Name: Preposition Hula Hoop

Suggested Grade Level: 1/2

NCTE Standards: 6: Students apply knowledge of language structure, language conventions (e.g., spelling and punctuation), media techniques, figurative language, and genre to create, critique, and discuss print and non-print texts.
Common Core State Standards: CCSS.ELA-LITERACY.L.1.1.I: Use frequently occurring prepositions (e.g., *during, beyond, toward*).
Goals: Students will recognize and understand the function of prepositions and prepositional phrases.
Objectives: Students will perform actions using a hula hoop to demonstrate their understanding of prepositions and prepositional phrases.

Suggested time frame	20–30 min
Equipment/technology	Visual media for demonstration at the beginning. 10–15 hula hoops
Start/stop signals	During cooperative pairs activity, teacher plays music lightly in the background. Instruct students to begin partner work when the music starts. Instruct students to stop moving, place the hoop on the floor, place one foot inside the hoop and look to the teacher when the music stops
Skill cues	Move the hoop all around your body—demonstrate to students the different movements that are possible with a hula hoop Personal space—remind students to keep their hoop in their own space
Safety cues	Tell students to only use the hula hoop to demonstrate the movements. Make sure student pairs are spaced so that they do not hit each other with the hoops. Remind pairs to be far enough away from each other not to collide
Teaching style	Direct instruction; cooperative learning
Assessments of content through the activity	Observational checklist
Transition activity	Return quietly to desks, be seated and do three chair exercises, such as forward bend, leg lift and spinal twist. See Figs. 4.4, 4.5, and 4.6 for examples

Fig. 4.6 Spinal twist

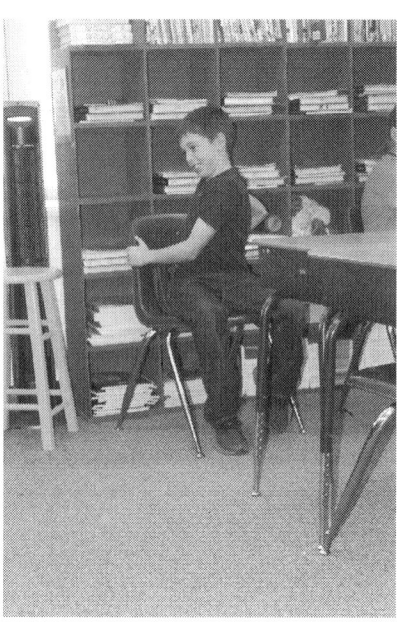

Description of Preposition Hula Hoop Activity

Introduction: Prepositions

- Briefly explain what a preposition is and show the word "Preposition" up on the board. Circle the root "position" and tell them that prepositions often deal with where things are in relation to other things… their position. Show several prepositions. Read them aloud and have students read/repeat them aloud as you go. Ask students if they have ever heard these words before.
- To assist with the understanding of prepositions, give them a visual. You may show something like a picture of a tree and use a monkey graphic to demonstrate the concept of position by moving the monkey around and saying prepositions like "under," "in," "by." Have them come up with some additional prepositions by you moving the monkey and having them supply an appropriate preposition.
- Tell the students that the best way to understand some types of prepositions is to demonstrate them instead of just reading about them and they will be doing movements with hula hoops to demonstrate prepositions.

Activity: Preposition Hula Hoop Movements

- For this activity, there needs to be enough space for the hula hoop and two people to work together. You may need to move desks or chairs in the room to create an open space.
- Place hula hoops on the floor around the room appropriately spaced apart. Play music and tell students to walk around the hoops not stepping inside a hoop until

the music stops. As soon as the music stops, tell them to step inside a hoop but only two people are allowed inside each hoop. If someone cannot find a hoop or is standing alone in a hoop have them raise their hand to find a partner. This will get them paired up.

- Instruct students to leave the hoop on the floor and to each put one foot outside the hula hoop. Stand quietly and wait for further instruction.
- Show a preposition on the board like "inside." Model with a hula hoop the preposition "inside" by placing a hoop on the floor and stepping one foot inside the hoop. Say my foot is inside the hoop and your foot is inside the hoop too.
- Then show the preposition "outside." Have students move their foot to the outside of the hoop with both feet now placed outside of the hoop and read aloud the word "outside."
- Then show at least two more prepositions such as "beside" or "under" on the board, one at a time. Then demonstrate the preposition using the hula hoop while saying the word with both students following your movements and having students repeat the word.
- Instruct students to place the hoop on the floor and to each put one foot inside the hoop, and stand quietly to wait for further instruction. You may choose to have students sit on the floor near their partner and hoop before the next part of the lesson.

Cooperative Pairs Activity: Prepositions with Hula Hoop Movements

- Part 1—State that prepositions are usually parts of a group of words called prepositional phrases which tell where things are in reference to one another like your foot and the hoop in the last activity. Refer back to the visual of the monkey and tree, described in the introduction to the activity. Place the monkey above the tree. Ask students what a good preposition would be to describe where the monkey is. Next, explain what a prepositional phrase is and say the phrase "above the tree." Move the monkey in different locations and have students say a corresponding prepositional phrase. *If developmentally appropriate, introduce object of the preposition at this time.*
- Then show the prepositional phrase "above my head" on the board and explain how the preposition word makes up the phrase by showing where the hula hoop is in relation to something else—your head. Hold the hula hoop above your head and say, "above my head." Then demonstrate a couple of other phrases by saying "below my waist" and "beside my foot." Have students follow along in pairs both taking turns using the hoop and saying the phrases aloud.
- Part 2—Show a series of prepositional phrases one at a time that you say aloud. Have students repeat the phrase aloud. Have the pairs use the hoop to take turns acting out the phrase. Refer to Fig. 4.7 for examples.
- Part 3—Show several prepositions on the board and have students say the preposition aloud and then taking turns with their partner verbally create a prepositional phrase from the word displayed and demonstrate the action with the hoop.

Fig. 4.7 Examples of
prepositions and
corresponding phrases to use

Through	Through the hoop
In	In the hoop
Behind	Behind the hoop
Between	Between my arms
Above	Above my head
Under	Under the hoop
On	On the floor
Over	Over my head/ Over your head
Beside	Beside the hoop
Into	Into the hoop
Around	I swung the hoop around my hips.

- Part 4—Have students return to their desks be seated and perform the transition activity from the above chart.
  Note: Teacher will need to teach transition, predetermine where students will return the hoops, and how desks will be arranged to original layout following the activity.
- Display a picture of an object on the wall such as a tree. Give all students a die cut shape with a preposition word printed on it to place on the tree in the appropriate location. (You will need to tape as they are called forward). See Fig. 4.8.
  Note: If developmentally appropriate, display the list of prepositions you used at the beginning of the lesson and have students pick one, write it on the die cut shape, and place it on the picture.

Extension: Depending on the students' understanding and developmental level, guide them in generating and writing prepositional phrases. Additionally, have students write one to two sentences that include prepositional phrases. They may also complete a color sheet with objects to color and label with preposition words.

Fig. 4.8 Picture of die cut prepositions in relation to the tree

Modifications/Adaptations: For students who may not be able to use a hula hoop, teachers may substitute a jump rope, string, or a noodle. Students may need a partner for certain movements, such as holding the hoop above their head. Other modification suggestions are made in the above activity.

Research

NCTE standards ask that students conduct research on issues and interests by generating ideas and questions and by posing problems in which they gather, evaluate, and synthesize data from a variety of sources to communicate their discoveries for a specific audience (http://www.ncte.org/standards/ncte-ira). Common Core standards ask that students learn a range of research skills, including how to find reputable sources of information. Students also discover how to assess the relevancy and accuracy of the information they find. Students are also expected to organize this information in a logical manner so that they can present it to an audience (http://www.corestandards.org/ELA-Literacy/W/6). As movement integration into content lessons has been shown to enhance student intrinsic motivation (Vazou et al., 2012), integrating movement into lessons within the scope of research may make the content more interesting to students, actively engaging them more in the content and better communicating that research is an active process that can be interesting and appealing. Additionally, using movement in teaching the research process, such as in collecting data and hypothesis testing, students are better able to envision research as relevant and applicable to their lives.

Activity Name: Leaf Walk

Suggested Grade Level: Grade 2

NCTE Standards: 7: Students conduct research on issues and interests by generating ideas and questions, and by posing problems. They gather, evaluate, and synthesize data from a variety of sources (e.g., print and non-print texts, artifacts, people) to communicate their discoveries in ways that suit their purpose and audience.

Common Core State Standards: CCSS.ELA-LITERACY.W.2.8: Recall information from experiences or gather information from provided sources to answer a question.

Goals: Students will gather and display leaves by shape, size, and color.

Objectives: Students will gather leaves on a nature walk and create a visual display of findings organized by shape, size, and color.

Suggested time frame	25 min
Equipment/technology	Small poster board or large paper, glue, and markers or crayons
Start/stop signals	When we are outside, please listen for the following start/stop signals: When you hear one whistle, you can begin the activity When you hear three whistles, you should freeze wherever you are, find the teacher with your eyes and listen for instructions
Skill cues	Walk quickly to find your leaves Remember your personal space when grabbing leaves (Remind students to be considerate of each other when selecting their leaves. Students should adhere to standard procedures for being outside during class. This is not a competitive activity and everyone will get to select leaves.)
Safety cues	Remind students to walk and safely pick up leaves. This is not play time but a specific activity
Teaching style	Guided practice
Assessments of content through the activity	Observe and actively discuss with students throughout the activity. Then, use their display to check for understanding
Transition activity	When returning from collecting leaves, have students place their leaves on their desk and stand behind their chairs. Once everyone is back in place, tell them to take three deep breaths and then have a seat so you can move on to the next part of the activity

Fig. 4.9 Examples of
different types of leaves found
on a leaf walk

Description of Leaf Walk Activity

Introduction: Leaf Collection Walk to Gather Data

- Begin by telling students "we are going to go on a walk searching for different shapes, sizes, and colors of leaves." Ask students to predict what colors and shapes they might find. See Fig. 4.9 for examples of types of leaves that can be found on the walk.
- Next, have students line up and take a nature walk on school grounds. Students should each find at least five different leaves to bring back to the classroom with them. When the class reaches the end of the walk remind students to check to make sure they have at least five leaves and return to the room.

Activity: Organizing and Displaying Data

- Once back in the classroom, explain to students that they are going to sort their leaves by shape, size, and color into different groups. As students are organizing their leaves, actively monitor and discuss with students the difference in the leaves they picked up during the walk. While walking around the room and monitoring students, pass out glue sticks and large paper.

- After students have organized their leaves, students should glue their leaves in place on the large paper. If time permits, students may use markers or crayons to write words that describe their leaves on the display and discuss how their earlier predictions turned out.
- Finally, display student work to reference later for extension activities such as writing about their experience or comparison discussions.

Extension: Have students complete the sentence, "I sorted by _____ on their display."

Variation: If a nature walk is not a possibility, the teacher could bring leaves or paper leaves prepared in advance and place them throughout the school to create an indoor nature walk.

Modifications/Adaptations: The movements in this activity can be modified for students with physical disabilities. For example, if students cannot move around to gather leaves, the teacher can place objects in proximity so that the student has to reach and extend in order to pick the leaves from above their head or off the ground. The teacher can give the student some kind of tool for reaching or grabbing, such as a butterfly net.

Listening and Speaking

Both NCTE and Common Core standards include the listening and speaking strand of English language arts that involves students listening and responding to the ideas of others while contributing their own ideas in conversations and in groups in an appropriate manner. Listening and speaking entails more than simply sitting and listening to others' ideas but also offering their own ideas, so students work together to co-construct knowledge. It encompasses attentiveness and comprehension skills so that students can offer responses to information presented in diverse formats including visual and oral media. Studies support movement for increasing attentiveness. Trost, Fees, and Dzewaltowski (2008) implemented a move and learn program for 3–5 year olds, and they found that students were "enthusiastic, attentive, and persistent in their learning tasks" (p. 99). Alertness is essential for student success during movement activities in the classroom. Students must pay close attention to the teacher's instructions in order to perform the physical tasks correctly and to learn the content that is connected to the movement. Additionally, movement activities frequently require students to attend closely to what their peers are saying and doing. For instance, in movement integration activities in which students are instructed to interact with each other, both good listening and good speaking skills are vital to the success of the activity and the acquisition of the content. The more students interact with each other and with their teacher in movement integration activities, the more listening and speaking skills they will develop.

Activity Name: Paired Maze

Suggested Grade Level: Grade 5

NCTE Standards: 12: Students adjust their use of spoken, written, and visual language (e.g., conventions, style, vocabulary) to communicate effectively with a variety of audiences and for different purposes.

Common Core State Standards: CCSS.ELA-LITERACY.SL.5.2: Summarize a written text read aloud or information presented in diverse media and formats, including visually, quantitatively, and orally.

Goals: Students will practice writing, receiving, and giving oral instructions.

Objectives: Students will write, follow, and give oral instructions that include multiple action steps in a maze.

Suggested time frame	20–25 min
Equipment/technology	Paper, pens, blindfold, and one example of instructions
Start/stop signals	Start the activity by saying "Begin" End the activity by the teacher saying "Simon Sez" and students repeating "Stop." This should be repeated until everyone is still and has eyes on the teacher for further instructions
Skill cues	Bend—forward at the waist or at the knees Hop—stay on the same foot, use the arms to reach Crawl—on hands and knees
Safety cues	Remind students to move intentionally and listen carefully so they do not run into each other or classroom furniture. Stop someone who is about to run into another person or object. No running during this activity. Do not put on blindfold until the student is at the start place. Must use quiet voices so students can hear their partner's commands
Teaching style	Cooperative learning
Assessments of content through the activity	While the students are doing the activity, move about the room and observe them. Look at their instructions and provide assistance then necessary. Then, actively monitor while students are using their instructions to walk each other through the maze. Make note of students who struggle and why
Transition activity	As students finish up, have them return to their seats and write down how they felt as the person giving the instructions and as the person receiving the instructions while blindfolded. Have them make a bulleted list that they can share out with the class

Description of Paired Maze Activity

Introduction: Writing and Following Instructions

- Students will be paired and told to work together to write instructions in order to retrieve/locate an item. The purpose is to write clear instructions and to listen carefully to follow oral instructions.
- Prepare an example and have one student follow your commands to model the activity and expectations. For example, Take four steps and stop. Hop in place three times. Take one step back and then turn your body to the right. Bend over and touch your toes then take six steps forward. Reach your hands up and touch the object in front of you.
- Instructions should include that the directions they write are limited to only five commands but should involve navigating through the classroom. The environment should not be manipulated; students should maneuver around existing structures and not create obstacles. Two of the three movements listed above (crawl, hop, bend) should be included. The partners should stay together and the person giving commands should talk softly and watch for any problems. See Fig. 4.10 for a photo of students writing directions.
- Once they have the instructions, they will take turns giving instructions to their partner to navigate through the room to locate/retrieve a specific item.
- Give pairs 5–10 min to write the instructions they will use. Have them begin by choosing the item they will locate/retrieve.

Fig. 4.10 Students writing directions for their maze movement

Fig. 4.11 Students walking blindfolded through the maze

Activity: Cooperative Pairs Movement Maze

- Once students have written their instructions with their partner, they will practice giving oral instructions and listening to oral instructions by walking each other through the classroom blindfolded to retrieve said item. See Fig. 4.11.
- Each person should have a chance to give the instructions to their blindfolded partner and also be the blindfolded person. Use the start/stop signal from the above chart. This can be done with partners switching and using the same commands or pairing up with a new person to listen to new commands.

Extension: Have students reflect on the experience. For example, were the instructions easy to follow? What could be changed to make directions more clearly written and understood?

Modifications/Adaptations: If any students have physical disabilities, help their group write instructions that they are able to perform. For students who regularly have difficulty following instructions, allow them to complete the activity in a quieter space with fewer distractions and remind partners to repeat instructions multiple times. If time permits, this activity can be expanded by using the hall, the school library, or playground.

References

Bernath, C., & Masi, W. (2005). Movin' and groovin': Integrating movement throughout the curriculum. *Dimensions of Early Childhood, 33*(3), 22–26.

Brewer, H., Damico, J., & Rinkevich, J. (2012). Enhancing core skills outside of the traditional core curriculum: The biological, physical, and visual and what they mean to literacy. *National Teacher Education Journal, 5*(2), 5–14.

Callcott, D., Hammond, L., & Hill, S. (2015). The synergistic effect of teaching a combined explicit movement and phonological awareness program to preschool aged students. *Early Childhood Education Journal, 43*(3), 201–211. doi:10.1007/s10643-014-0652-7.

Collins, V. K., Miller, S. A., & Yates, H. M. (2005). The language arts get physical: Fun, fitness, and fundamentals. *Dimensions of Early Childhood, 33*(3), 33–40.

English Language Arts Standards. (n.d.). Retrieved September 28, 2016, from http://www.corestandards.org/ELA-Literacy/.

Gellens, S. (2005). Integrate movement to enhance children's brain development. *Dimensions of Early Childhood, 33*(3), 14–21.

Greenfader, C., & Brouillette, L. (2013). Boosting language skills of English learners through dramatization and movement. *Reading Teacher, 67*(3), 171–180.

Kalyn, B. (2006). Integration. *Teaching Elementary Physical Education, 16*(5), 32–36.

Kercood, S., & Banda, D. (2012). The effects of added physical activity on performance during a listening comprehension task for students with and without attention problems. *International Journal of Applied Educational Studies, 13*(1), 19–32.

NCTE/IRA Standards for the English Language Arts. (n.d.). Retrieved September 28, 2016, from http://www.ncte.org/standards/ncte-ira.

Pica, R. (2010). Linking literacy and movement. *YC: Young Children, 65*(6), 72–73.

Reed, J. A., Einstein, G., Hahn, E., Hooker, S. P., Gross, V. P., & Kravitz, J. (2010). Examining the impact of integrating physical activity on fluid intelligence and academic performance in an elementary school setting: A preliminary investigation. *Journal of Physical Activity & Health, 7*(3), 343–351.

Trost, S. G., Fees, B., & Dzewaltowski, D. (2008). Feasibility and efficacy of a 'Move and Learn' physical activity curriculum in preschool children. *Journal of Physical Activity & Health, 5*(1), 88–103.

Vazou, S., Gavrilou, P., Mamalaki, E., Papanastasiou, A., & Sioumala, N. (2012). Does integrating physical activity in the elementary school classroom influence academic motivation? *International Journal of Sport and Exercise Psychology, 10*(4), 251–263.

Chapter 5
Lesson Plans for Moving in the Language Arts Classroom

Christina Janise McIntyre and Emily Reeves

Abstract This chapter features seven full-length lesson plans designed to address the main areas of language arts represented in the National Council of Teachers of English (NCTE) and the Common Core State Standards (CCSS). As with any lesson plan, the activity can be adjusted in any number of ways to accommodate students' specific needs and developmental levels. Extension activities are provided that may extend the lesson beyond the estimated time allotment; however, these lessons may be modified or extended depending on the needs of your specific students.

Lesson Plan: Word Boundaries and Spaces

Suggested Grade Level: Kindergarten.
*Special Note: This lesson would be most useful near the end of the kindergarten year.

Lesson Overview

Engagement (10 min): Begin by reading short sentences aloud, such as: **The cat ran. The girl sings. A man sat**.
Transition: Tell the students that they will be doing an activity that involves walking and jumping, which will help them learn more about word boundaries and spaces between words in sentences.

C.J. McIntyre (✉) · E. Reeves
Midwestern State University, Wichita Falls, TX, USA
e-mail: Christina.mcintyre@mwsu.edu

E. Reeves
e-mail: emily.graves@mwsu.edu

© Springer Nature Singapore Pte Ltd. 2018
S.C. Miller and S.F. Lindt (eds.), *Moving INTO the Classroom*,
Springer Texts in Education, DOI 10.1007/978-981-10-6424-1_5

Word Jump Activity (15 min): Students will jump over spaces in words.

Transition: Move to the floor with pieces of paper to begin writing.

Cooperative Activity (8 min): Tell the students to work together to write down one of the sentences that they walked over in the activity.

Extension: (5 min) Have students practice writing a sentence from the board, making sure they leave sufficient space between words.

Closure (2 min): As you pick up the students' papers, ask: **What makes up sentences?** After receiving several responses, remind the students that sentences are made up of separate words with spaces in between.

NCTE	3: Students apply a wide range of strategies to comprehend, interpret, evaluate, and appreciate texts. They draw on their prior experience, their interactions with other readers and writers, their knowledge of word meaning and of other texts, their word identification strategies, and their understanding of textual features (e.g., sound-letter correspondence, sentence structure, context, graphics)
CCSS	CCSS.ELA-LITERACY.L.K.1.F: Produce and expand complete sentences in shared language activities
Goals	The students will use movement to learn that written words are separated by spaces
Objective	Students will recognize that sentences are comprised of words separated by spaces and demonstrate awareness of word boundaries in a movement activity involving jumping

Description of Word Boundaries and Spaces Activity

Engagement

- Begin by reading short sentences aloud, such as: **The cat ran. The girl sings. A man sat**. As you read, write the sentences on the whiteboard or write them on a piece of paper that is placed under the document camera.
- Circle the spaces in between the words. Ask the students: **What are the things that I circled?**
- After receiving several student responses, explain that the circled things are spaces between words. Explain that words have distinct endings and sentences are made up of separate words with spaces in between.

Transition

- Tell the students that they will be doing an activity that involves walking and jumping, which will help them learn more about word boundaries and spaces between words in sentences.

Word Jump Activity: Introduction

- Begin the lesson by explaining that words are put together to create sentences and there are spaces between words. Read and visually display a few short sentences aloud, such as *The cat ran, The man sat,* or *The girl sings*. Circle the spaces in between the words. Explain that words have distinct endings and sentences are made up of separate words with spaces in between.

- Explain to the students that they will be doing an activity that involves walking and jumping, which will help them learn more about word boundaries and spaces between words in sentences.

Activity Preparation

- You will need sentences that are separated into words and written on thick paper. (Each word from the sentence should be written on its own piece of paper).
- Lay one sentence on the floor making sure that there is sufficient space between the words and that the words are taped securely to the floor.

Activity Instructions

- Explain that the students will walk over each word and, if the students are able to read the words, say each word as they walk over them. When the students come to the end of each word, they jump over the space to reach the next word and continue on saying the words and jumping over the spaces.
- Choose a volunteer to help you demonstrate the activity. Once the volunteer student has demonstrated the activity, divide the students into three groups based on birth months, colors, or shirts, or regular class groups such as table groups and have students move to three different parts of the room, where sentences have already been taped to the floor. Tell the students in each group to line up at the word with the capital letter, which is the first word of the sentence.
- Use music to start and stop the activity. Tell the students that they can begin jumping one at a time when the music begins, and when the music stops, the students should freeze where they are and look to the teacher. The music should be played loud enough for the students to hear it but quiet enough that the students can hear themselves saying the words in the sentences.
- After each student has had the opportunity to walk and jump over the sentence at least three times, stop the music. If time permits, have groups rotate so the students have the opportunity to walk and jump over three different sentences.

Transition

Move to the floor with pieces of paper to begin writing.

Cooperative Activity

Once the students are seated on the floor in their groups, give each student a piece of paper. Tell the students to work together to write down one of the sentences that they walked over in the activity. The students should underline each word and circle the spaces between the words. Once the students are finished, they should make their way back to their seats with their papers.

Extension

Have students practice writing a sentence from the board, making sure they leave sufficient space between words.

Closure

As you pick up the students' papers, ask: **What makes up sentences?** After receiving several responses, remind the students that sentences are made up of separate words with spaces in between. Remind the students to look at word boundaries and the spaces between words when they are reading, and remind them to make sure they separate their words with spaces in between when they are writing sentences.

Suggested time frame	50 min
Equipment/technology	Visual media for demonstration at the beginning. At least three sentences with each word written on butcher paper. Speakers and music
Start/stop signals	Start the activity by starting music
	End the activity by stopping the music. Everyone should be still and has eyes on the teacher for further instructions
Skill cues	Remind the students that when they jump from one word to the next, they should keep both feet together and bend their knees when they land. Model correct form and have students practice
Safety cues	Remind the students to be aware of other students so they do not bump into them. Only one student should be allowed on the sentence at each time. Once a student has reached the end of the last word, the next student may begin. Additionally, the teacher should tape the words to the floor, so they do not slide when the students jump onto them
Teaching style	Practice; cooperative learning-small group
Assessment	Formative
Format of assessment	Observation during the activity and informal Q&A once the activity has ended
Transition activity	In order to transition, tell the students to stay in their groups and find a space on the floor that they can work together. After the activity, have students move to their desks

Modifications/Accommodations: If any of the students have a physical disability and are not able to jump, the activity can be modified as follows: Students that are unable to jump may clap and say "space" or walk over the taped words and say "space". Additionally, if they are able they can clap their hands when they say "space".

Lesson Plan: Hot Potato: Beginning, Middle, and End

Suggested Grade Level: 1

Lesson Overview

Engagement (10 min): Movement Activity: Hot Potato.

Transition: Tell students to move quietly to the carpet to sit down in their bubble (self-space) and start thinking about what happened while playing Hot Potato.

Shared Writing (15 min): Students will discuss and dictate a story about their experience playing Hot Potato as you write the story on large paper.

Whole Class Reading (5 min): When the story is written, read the story to the class and then have the class read the story together actively circling the beginning, middle, and end or the story.

Closure (2 min): Repeat and review the entire experience.

NCTE	3: Students employ a wide range of strategies as they write and use different writing process elements appropriately to communicate with different audiences for a variety of purposes
CCSS	CCSS.ELA-LITERACY.W.1.3: Write narratives in which they recount two or more appropriately sequenced events, include some details regarding what happened, use temporal words to signal event order, and provide some sense of closure
Goals	The students will use movement and shared writing to write a story and identify the beginning, middle, and end
Objectives	1. Students will write a brief story about a classroom experience
	2. Students will identify beginning, middle, and end in a brief story

Description of Hot Potato Activity

Engage

- Students will stand in a circle and underhand toss a small ball around to each other while music is playing. Encourage students to begin by using a two-handed catch during the activity. When the music beat changes, students should attempt tossing the small ball with their nondominant hand. When the music stops, the student with the ball take two steps back from the circle to make catching the small ball more challenging.
- Select music with varying beats and vary times the music stops. For example, 15, 30, and 20 s, etc.

- During the game, actively talk about what is happening using language like first, then, last and beginning, middle, end.
  - For example, **In the beginning of Hot Potato, _____ (student name) had to take two steps back. I wonder if he/she will still be able to catch the ball?**
  - **Now that we are in the middle of Hot Potato, I wonder who will be able to keep up with the different music beats and tossing the ball with their nondominant hand?**
  - **I wonder what will happen in the end of our game?**

Transition

- Tell students to move quietly to the carpet to sit down in their bubble (self-space) and start thinking about what happened while playing Hot Potato.
- Use signal words such as first, then, and last. **Today, we are going to write a story about playing Hot Potato. Let us start thinking about what happened in the beginning, middle, and end of Hot Potato**.

Shared Writing

- During this time, you should guide students through writing a story by actively discussing beginning, middle, and end. Use using signal words such as first, then, and last. Terminology should be reiterated throughout the writing process.
  - **Tell me about playing Hot Potato**.

    Listen to student dialogue as they brainstorm about their experience.

  - **Now we are going to write a story about playing Hot Potato. What did we do first?**

    Help student come up with one primary event. This is the first sentence of the story. Keep the sentence very basic.

  - **What happened in the middle of our game? Did anything stand out?**

    Again, guide students through a conversation that results in one basic sentence that represents the middle of the story.

  - **How did we end our game? What happened last?**

    Repeat the process used with the first and middle of the story. Focus on student ideas and reinforce that this is the end of the story.

Whole Class Reading

- When the story is written, read the story to the class and then have the class read the story together.
- Once the story has been written, read, and reread, use 3 different colors to circle/highlight the beginning, middle, and end of the story. Actively discuss these pieces and signal words to help students think about each part of the story.

- **Now we are going to review and identify the beginning, middle, and end of our story by circling each part in a different color.**
  - **Can anyone identify the beginning sentence of the story?**

- Have the class read the sentence and discuss why this is the beginning of the story. You or a student will circle the sentence in the first color.
  - **Now, who can identify the middle of our story?**
  - Actively discuss why the identified sentence is the middle of the story and read the sentence as a class. Then, you or a student will circle the sentence in the second color.
  - **Last but not least, what part of our story is the end?**

- Continue the discussion and read the last sentence of the story. Then, you or a student circle the sentence in the third color.

Closure

Repeat and review the entire experience highlighting the Hot Potato activity, writing about the Hot Potato activity story, and the beginning, middle, and end of their story.

Suggested time frame	45–60 min
Equipment/technology	Music device such as IPod, CD Player, or computer
	Small ball, preferably a foam ball or yarn ball (soft)
Start/stop signals	Start tossing the ball when the music starts
	When the music stops, students with the ball sit and all other students should freeze and look to the teacher
Skill cues	Face your target
	Step with your opposite foot towards the target (i.e., if throwing with right hand, step toward target with your left foot)
	Use a pendulum arm motion with the arm you are throwing with (i.e., like you are bowling)
	Follow through to the sky or ceiling with hand you are throwing with
Safety cues	Remind student to
	1. Make sure the person they are tossing to is making eye contact before they toss
	2. Pay attention to the ball so that it does not hit them when it is tossed their way
Teaching style	Guided practice
Assessment	Formative
Format of assessment	Observation during the activity and informal checklist during shared writing
Transition activity	Tell students to move quietly to the carpet to sit down in their bubble (self-space) and start thinking about what happened while playing Hot Potato

Modifications/Accommodations

For any students with physical limitations, making it difficult to catch or throw the ball, the activity can be modified as follows: The ball can be thrown into a basket placed in front of the student and the student can retrieve the ball to throw it. The student can use their feet to pass and trap the ball when it is their turn. The student can use equipment such as a pool noodle to pull the ball to them and to push the ball to another person in the circle. Encourage other students to roll the ball to the noodle.

For any students with hearing impairments, making it difficult to hear the music, the activity can be modified as follows: Students may work independently with a partner or teammate to catch the ball. You may use a hand or other sign (i.e., flashing light) to indicate when the music stops.

If working on a unit, this lesson plan can be used in conjunction with the Story Train activity in Chap. 4.

Lesson Plan: Alphabetize It

Suggested Grade Level: 3

Lesson Overview

Engagement (5 min): In small groups, have students individually write their first names on a die-cut shape. Seated in small groups and working together have students arrange the name shapes in alphabetical order. *Note: You may use shapes to group students.*

Instructional Input (5–10 min): Explanation of alphabetizing using up to the second letter in a word. Use board for visuals and refer to the engagement for further explanation if groups have students with names beginning with the same letter.

Cooperative Learning Small Group (5 min): Hand out word cards. Seated at their desks in groups, students will sort alphabet cards using up to second letter.

Cooperative Learning Whole Class (10–15 min): Have whole class stand up and move around with one word card to line up in alphabetical order using their cards.

Instructional Input (5 min): Explanation of alphabetizing using up to the third letter in a word. Use board for visuals and refer to the engagement for further explanation if groups have students with names beginning with the first two letters.

Cooperative Learning Small Group (5 min): Seated in their small groups, students will sort alphabet cards using up to third letter.

Cooperative Learning Whole Class (10 min): Have the whole class stand up and move around to line up in alphabetical order using their card.
Closure (2 min): Review alphabetizing.

NCTE	3: Students apply a wide range of strategies to comprehend, interpret, evaluate, and appreciate texts. They draw on their prior experience, their interactions with other readers and writers, their knowledge of word meaning and of other texts, their word identification strategies, and their understanding of textual features (e.g., sound-letter correspondence, sentence structure, context, graphics)
CCSS	CCSS.ELA-LITERACY.L.3.4.D
	Use glossaries or beginning dictionaries, both print and digital, to determine or clarify the precise meaning of keywords and phrases
Goals	Students will learn to alphabetize words using the first three letters of a word
Objective	In a whole group kinesthetic sorting activity, students will demonstrate understanding of alphabetizing by using up to the first three letters of a word

Special Note: Make sure students learned alphabetizing using the first letter in previous grades; adjust complexity of lesson accordingly.

Description of Alphabetize It Activity

Engage

- Seated in small groups, have students write their names on a piece of paper or a die-cut shape. *If you do not have the room arranged in small groups already, hand students shapes as they walk in and tell students with like shapes to group up in prearranged desks.* Tell them to arrange their shapes in their small groups by putting their names in alphabetical order using the first letter.
- Walk around and observe. If students in groups have names beginning with the same letter, tell them to try to solve the problem on their own. (You might arrange a situation in which this will occur). Do not answer questions at this point and have students try to solve the problem.
- Then, have them write their last names on the other side of the shape and arrange those as well.

Instructional Input

- Using the start/stop signal, get their attention and explain that they will be learning to alphabetize words in order to use a dictionary, organize items, etc.
- First, show an example on the board of how to alphabetize using the first letter only. Refer to the engagement when they arranged their names in alphabetical order. Ask if any of the groups had names beginning with the same letter. Refer to any of these situations in which students' names began with the same letter.
- Ask how they solved the problem and then explain how to alphabetize using the second letter of a word.

Part 1: Card Sort

- Give each group a stack of cards-one per student with one word printed on each side of the card. Mark the cards as side one and side two, or use dual colored cards. Make sure that there are no duplicate words in the whole class. Side one cards should have some words that must be alphabetized to the second letter.
- Have the students, still seated in their small groups, arrange side one words in alphabetical order. Walk around and observe using a checklist.

Part 2: Moving to Alphabetize

- Using the stop/start signal get their attention, have each student take one card each and stand up. Explain that they will line up alphabetically using the side one words.
- Model the marching technique and point out the cleared area where they will line up. Review safety cues. Have the whole class march around the room deciding how to line up and arrange themselves in alphabetical order using the side one words (see Fig. 5.1).
- Once lined up, have students step forward one at a time to say the words aloud and check to make sure they are in the correct order looking at the previous word and helping them make any adjustments. Explain that even if a word is difficult and they may not know how to say it or what it means, they can still alphabetize it.

Using the stop/start signal get their attention. Have students return with their cards to their desks, do a big stretch, and be seated.

Fig. 5.1 Students moving into alphabetical order

Part 3: Card Sort

- Ask students what to do if the first two letters are the same. Show some examples on the board. Tell students they will be using side two words to alphabetize using up to the third letter.
- Have the students, seated in their small groups, alphabetize the cards using up to the third letter. Walk around and assess the small groups' progress using a checklist.

Part 4: Moving to Alphabetize

- Using the stop/start signal, get their attention, have each student take one card each and have the whole class march around arranging themselves in alphabetical order using side two words.
- Once they have completed lining up, have them one by one step forward, say the word aloud, and check to make sure they are in the correct order by looking at the previous word (see Fig. 5.2). Help them make any adjustments.
- Using the stop/start signal get their attention. Have students return quietly to their desks and stand behind their chairs. Review alphabetizing by telling the students, **For this next activity, I am going to make a series of statements, and I want you to stretch your arms up high if you agree with the statement or I want you to reach down and touch your toes if you do not agree.**
- Make several true/false statements about alphabetizing, watching how the students answer. For example you might say, **When the first letters of two words are the same, I should alphabetize by using the 3rd letter** (Students should touch their toes).

Fig. 5.2 Students are lined up around the room in alphabetical order

Fig. 5.3 Adapted Frayer
Model graphic organizer

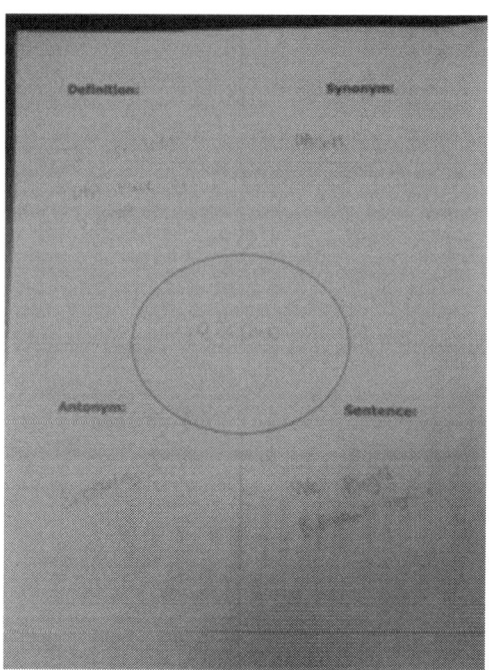

Extension:

Have students use a dictionary to locate and write the definition of the two words on their card. Students can use a thesaurus to locate and write synonyms and antonyms of their words. Students can also be provided with an adapted Frayer Model graphic organizer (see Fig. 5.3) for additional independent practice using a dictionary and/or thesaurus.

Closure:

Review alphabetizing. Ask students how to alphabetize words when the first three letters are the same to connect that the process is the same no matter how many letters.

Variation

If the class is too large or students need fewer words to sort, the class can be divided in half and two alphabetized lines can replace the whole class activity. The divided class can alphabetize in two separate lines first and then as a whole group for a culminating activity. If you choose to have the class divided up for the entire lesson, using duplicate cards for each half of the class is helpful as the two lines across from one another can be an additional way for them to peer check for the correct order.

Have the students move to line up in other ways besides marching. Call them out during the activity and change it up several times (i.e., tip-toe, baby steps, like a mouse).

Suggested time frame	45–55 min
Equipment/technology	Die-cut shapes for names. Visual media for demonstration at the beginning. Dual color note cards printed with words on each side to alphabetize for each group, adapter Frayer Model graphic organizer
Start/stop signals	Students start alphabetizing when the teacher claps twice
	Students stop alphabetizing, freeze where they are and look to the teacher when the teacher claps twice
	Note: you can create any clapping rhythm you would like to use
Skill cues	Stand tall
	Pull knees to chest
	Model for students the correct marching form so they can march around the room raising their knees while arranging themselves in alphabetical order
Safety cues	No touching classmates
	Give plenty of space to get in line
	Ask people to nicely let you in or move down in line
	Make sure the desks are arranged so that there is plenty of room to move around the room freely and an open area to line up without obstacles
	No running
Teaching style	Direct instruction/cooperative learning-small and large group
Assessment	Formative
Format of assessment	Observation during the activity and informal checklist during small groups or whole class line up. See Appendix A for a sample checklist
Transition activity	Stand by seat, big stretch, and be seated

Modifications/Accommodations: Make sure there is adequate room for students to maneuver around the room or allow students to sit in place while the other students organize around them.

If students need fewer words to sort, the class can be divided in half and two alphabetized lines can replace the whole class activity. Further explanation of this is detailed above in Variations.

Choose more challenging words to alphabetize for students, who grasp the concept easily or move on to the third letter.

Lesson Plan: Y and I Endings

Suggested Grade Level: 3/4

Lesson Overview

Engagement (5 min): Individually or in small groups, have students engage in a matching activity using manipulatives such as colored word and suffix cards at their desks to change out "y" and "i" word endings.

Instructional Input (5–10 min): Explanation of "y" and "i" ending spelling rules. Use board for visuals and refer to examples you noticed during the engagement.

Guided Practice (10 min): Students will use information and examples from instructional input to create words that indicate an understanding of "y" and "i" endings of words.

Independent Practice (15 min): Students will listen to words and sentences and will make the appropriate movement that you have modeled to indicate "y" and "i" endings. Check for understanding.

Extension: Using the *Y and I Endings* graphic organizer and the colored word stems and endings cards, students will create the correct form of the words and glue them in the appropriate place.

Closure (2 min): Recap the rules and remind students to use their graphic organizer for future help when deciding about word endings.

NCTE	3. Students apply a wide range of strategies to comprehend, interpret, evaluate, and appreciate texts. They draw on their prior experience, their interactions with other readers and writers, their knowledge of word meaning and of other texts, their word identification strategies, and their understanding of textual features (e.g., sound-letter correspondence, sentence structure, context, graphics)
CCSS	CCSS.ELA-LITERACY.RF.3.3.A
	Identify and know the meaning of the most common prefixes and derivational suffixes
Goals	Students will use non-locomotors movement to demonstrate their understanding "y" and "i" endings
Objective	The students will differentiate between "y" and "i" endings by arm and body movements

Description of Y and I Endings Activity

Engage

- Using their colored word and suffix cards (see explanation under equipment in the table below), tell students to create different possible words with "i" and "y" endings. While observing, do not make corrections at this point just allow students to make different combinations and explore the concept.
- Circulate and check their combinations. *Note: These can be premade, put in plastic bags, and handed out quickly; make word stems one color and endings another color.*

Instructional Input and Guided Practice

- Give students a copy of the *Y and I Endings* graphic organizer (in Appendix A) to use to reference during the instructional input. Students will also need their cards from the engagement activity above.
- Explain or review that "y" often concludes a word which has no other vowel such as "my" or "why". Show an example on the board. Have students apply that rule to their cards at their desks. Check for accuracy by walking around each student's desk. Examples: shy, try, dry. (See Appendix A for the Graphic Organizer.)
- Explain that "y" concludes words of more than one syllable such as "puppy". Show an example on the board. Have students apply that rule to their cards at their desks. Check for accuracy. Examples: happy, carry, mummy.
- Explain that "y" immediately follows another vowel such as "monkey". Show an example on the board. Have students apply that rule to their cards at their desks. Check for accuracy. Examples: honey, money, coney.
- *If students are ready, introduce plurals. Explain that if the word ends in a vowel (a, e, i, o, u) + y then just add s. Show an example on the board. Have students apply that rule to their cards at their desks. Check for accuracy. Examples: boy/boys, journey/journeys, key/keys, tray/trays.
- If the word ends in a consonant + y then y changes to -ies. Show an example on the board. Have students apply that rule to their cards at their desks. Check for accuracy. Examples: country/countries, goody/goodies.

Y and I Movement Activity

- After the engagement and instructional input, and once students understand the concept fairly well, explain that they will be listening to words and deciding if the words have "y" or "i" endings. They will indicate which by moving a certain way. Discuss safety cues.
- Have students stand up and then model for them holding arms up in a "y" shape to show a "y" ending (see Fig. 5.4). Have them hold their arms up in the y-shape and sway back and forth like a tree, bending at the waist a bit side to side.
- For an "i" position, model for them holding both arms straight up clasping hands for an "i" ending (see Fig. 5.5). When standing in the "i" position have them bend forward at the waist, roll upward straight and tall, bend back slightly for a

Fig. 5.4 Students demonstrating "y" endings

Fig. 5.5 Student demonstrating "i" endings

good stretch similar to the final position of the sun salutation with arms stretched high clasping hands for the "i".

- Make sure to connect that they are making a "y" shape with their arms apart for a "y" or with arms together for an "i" ending.

Movement Activity

- Read a few words that have both types of endings and have students say the word and then make the appropriate motion. Do a few together, then read words, and have students complete the movements independently, checking for understanding. Use increasingly difficult words as their understanding increases.
- The following examples range in complexity, so when you read a word like "worrying" you might get both motions, so stop, ask why, and discuss. See Fig. 5.6 for examples.

After reading several words, and when the students grasp the concept fairly well, read a series of sentences such as in the table below. Have them listen for the "i" and "y" words in the sentence, and repeat the word as they make the appropriate motion. See Fig. 5.7 for sample sentences.

Extension

Model and have students do the transition activity to stretch (referenced in chart below). Once seated, have them get their glue sticks out or pass them out and explain that they will be using their *Y and I Endings* graphic organizer with rules (see Fig. 5.8) from earlier in the lesson, and they will also use their colored word cards to glue an example for each of the rules discussed during the instructional input. Show an example. Use the start/stop signal to begin the activity.

Closure

Use the start/stop signal to end the activity. Recap the lesson and the rules before dismissal, and remind students to use their graphic organizer for future help when deciding about word endings.

baby babies	candy candies	dandy	money
handy	penny pennies	jelly jellies	bunny bunnies
lucky	mommy mommies	hungry	daddy daddies
party parties	worry worrying	happy happiness	carry carried
zombie	genie	veggie	pixie

Fig. 5.6 Examples of words ending in "i" and "y"

| The girl began to cry. |
| The mommy didn't want the dog to get wet. |
| It was rainy in the park that day. |
| The mommies all had their umbrellas. |
| The baby laughed because he got wet. |
| All of the daddies in the park decided to leave because it was raining. |

Fig. 5.7 Examples of sentences

Fig. 5.8 Examples of completed graphic organizer

Suggested time frame	45–55 min
Equipment/technology	Computer, projector with slideshow for initial instructional input
	Y and I Endings graphic organizer (Appendix A); colored word and suffix cards, glue
Start/stop signals	Students will begin moving when the teacher states the word
	Students will stop the movement activity when the teacher claps twice. They should respond by repeating the two claps, standing

(continued)

(continued)

	straight with arms by their sides and making eye contact with the teacher
Skill cues	Model for the students raising arms in a y shape – keep arms straight, reach wide
	And raising arm up with fist made for "i" shape – keeps arms straight, reach to the sky
Safety cues	Make sure students have appropriate space while doing their movements
Teaching style	Direct instruction; practice
Assessment	Formative
Format of assessment	While the students are engaged in the activity, move about the room and observe them. Use a checklist to record their understanding of the concept.
Transition activity	Have the students stand by their chairs and follow you in a few stretches. – Wrap arms around the opposite shoulder and hug yourself
	– Spread your feet out wide and stretch down to touch your toes
	Then have the students take a seat and begin the extension activity

Modifications/Accommodations: If any students are unable to stand for the movements, allow them to sit and do movements using arms only. For students unable to move their arms in the "i" or y shape, they can move their head or bend their bodies, or give students a rope like object (jump rope, string, etc.) and allow them to make the shapes with the object.

For more advanced students, you may read a paragraph or series of sentences that contain words that will have "y" or "i" endings which will need to be decoded by using context clues. For instance, baby, baby's, and babies, which introduce possessives. Have students make the corresponding motions for the appropriate ending taking into account the context clues. For example: *The baby's mommy took his candy away. The baby's fingers were very sticky from the candies.*

Lesson Plan: Hula Hoop Transition

Suggested Grade Level: 3/4

Lesson Overview

Engagement (10 min): Ask students to make an ordinal list of 5 things that they did earlier in the day, on the playground, in another last class, etc. Introduce the concept of transitions. Access their prior knowledge by discussing what the word

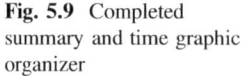

Fig. 5.9 Completed summary and time graphic organizer

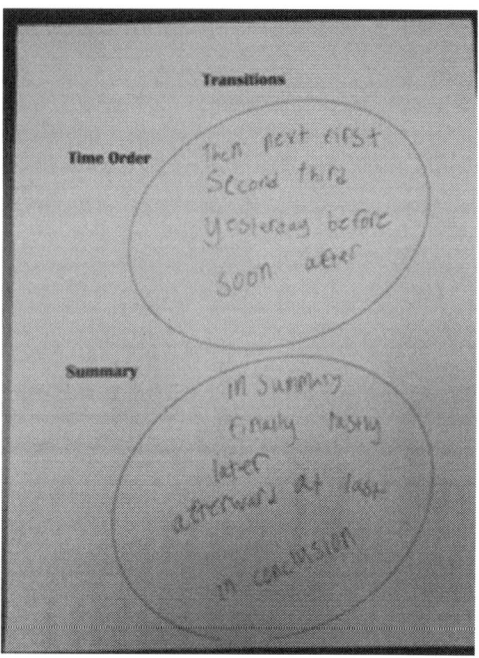

means and have students write a short paragraph from the list they made. Have some share while you record transitions on the board.

Instructional Input (10 min): Refer to students' paragraphs. Show on the board a list of transitions and discuss types and purpose. Give students the graphic organizer (see Fig. 5.9).

Cooperative Practice (15 min): Have students use the organizer to record transitions they are already familiar with, referencing the words you recorded earlier and the list displayed on the board. They may work individually, with a partner, or in groups to continue adding.

Movement Activity (20 min): Students will demonstrate their understanding of transitions by passing a hula hoop in a group activity.

Extension (5 min) Give students a paragraph that contains the types of transitions you have been focusing on and have them highlight them with different colored markers or highlighters to indicate the type of transition.

Closure (2 min): Ask students if they have any questions about the transitions they found in the paragraph and clarify any questions they have. If no questions are asked, ask for a few students to give some examples they found. Recap the lesson and dismiss.

NCTE	Students apply knowledge of language structure, language conventions (e.g., spelling and punctuation), media techniques, figurative language, and genre to create, critique, and discuss print and non-print texts
CCSS	CCSS.ELA-LITERACY.W.4.3.C
	Use a variety of transitional words and phrases to manage the sequence of events
Goals	Students will use non-locomotors movement to demonstrate their understanding of transition words
Objective	The students will pass a hula hoop without the use of their hands from one person to another in a circle and changing directions to demonstrate understanding of transition words

Description of Hula Hoop Activity

Engagement

- Ask students to make a list of 5 things they did in order earlier in the day, on the playground, in their last class, etc.
- Introduce the topic of transitions. Access their prior knowledge by discussing what the word means and that people transition all the time from one thing to another. We transition from one lesson to the next, to the playground from class, from lunch to recess, from one grade to the next. Have students turn their list into a short paragraph. Read an example of your own if needed.

Instructional Input

- Have a couple of students share their writing and record on the board any transition words they used such as "first," "next," "then," and "after". Point out that these are time order transitions and explain any other types that you may have recorded from their sharing. Explain why we need transitions and show two sentences on the board such as *I went shopping. I ate lunch.*
- Show how the two sentences can be tied to together with a transition to connect the idea of time in writing. *I went shopping and then I ate lunch.*
- Ask students if they can think of any other transitions, and record those as well
- Explain that there are transition lists that students are able to use when writing, but they need to understand the types and functions of transitions and not just memorize a list. Give students a graphic organizer with the following transition categories: Summary and Time Order (see Fig. 5.9).
- Explain what both types are and refer to what students have used in their paragraphs. Show some examples of summary transitions if none were present in the paragraphs. Depending on students' level and understanding of the topic, adjust the number of categories by adding Comparison, Concession, Addition, Contrast, Consequence, Emphasis, or Space Transitions.

Individual or Cooperative Practice

- Have students use the graphic organizer by writing transitions they are already familiar with in the different categories of transitions, referencing the words you recorded earlier. They may work with a partner or in groups to continue adding. Walk around the room and note any categories that students haven't listed any transitions for, and address this with the whole class and assist them in generating some examples.
- Show a list of both Summary and Time Order transitions mixed together on the board and have them continue using the graphic organizer to appropriately place the transitions. Walk around and check their understanding. You may also have a copy of the graphic organizer posted on the board that you add to for visual reinforcement.

Cooperative Activity: Hula Hoop Transitions

- Tell students that they are going to do an activity that allows them to physically show when a transition occurs in writing. Review safety cues. Have the students transition by assisting with moving the desks apart for the activity.
- Have students stand in a circle holding hands with one another with the hula hoop through one student's arm. Make sure there is a space that is large enough for one or two circles to be formed. Ten students per circle is optimal (Figs. 5.10 and 5.11).
- Begin reading a selection of text. The students will pass the hula hoop to each other around the circle going in one direction. They will accomplish this by

Fig. 5.10 Students move the hula hoop with the story

Fig. 5.11 Students step through the hula hoop with the story

moving their arms, stepping through the hoop, and moving their bodies through it to move the hoop from one person to the next without letting go of their neighbor's hand. When another transition is heard the process is repeated.

- Read part of a selection making sure that the students are passing the hoop. Let several students pass and then read a transition placing emphasis on it. Remind them to say the transition, stop the hoop, and send it back the other direction.
- Continue reading but only stress the next transition word without further prompting. Continue reading normally as they become more aware of the transitions. Read enough so that each student has had a chance to move through the hoop a few times.
- Use the stop signal to end the activity. You may choose to read back through the paragraph and have them snap when they hear a transition for further reinforcement and assessment.

Extension

Have the students transition by assisting with moving the desks back again. Then have students sit down and begin work on the extension activity. Give students a paragraph that contains the types of transitions you have been focusing on and have them highlight them with different colored markers or highlighters to indicate the type of transition.

Closure

Ask students if they have any questions about the transitions they found in the paragraph and clarify any questions they have. If no questions are asked, ask for a few students to give some examples they found. Recap the lesson and dismiss.

Suggested time frame	45–50 min
Equipment/technology	Computer, projector with slideshow to display words, graphic organizer (see Fig. 5.9), one hula hoop per group, copies of a paragraph that includes transitions and highlighters
Start/stop signals	Students will hold hands and begin moving the hula hoop when the teacher begins reading the text
	Students will stop the movement when the teacher says "freeze". Students can answer with "ice" making eye contact with the teacher
Skill cues	Model for the students various movements to move the hula hoop from one person to another. Remind students to
	– Keep hands locked
	– Bend and stretch your body to move through
Safety cues	All desks and other furniture must be moved out of the way to clear a space for the students to be in a circles
Teaching style	Direct instruction; practice; cooperative practice
Assessment	Formative
Format of assessment	While the students are engaged in the activity, move about the room and observe them. Use anecdotal notes to record observations
Transition activity	Have the students assist with moving the desks apart for the activity and then back again. Then have students sit down and begin work on the extension activity

Modifications/Accommodations: If any students are unable to stand, allow these students to sit in the circle holding hands and let them pass the hula hoop when it is his or her turn. For students who may not be able to pass the hula hoop, let a peer either try to pass the hula hoop over their body or walk a circle around them with the hula hoop. If students are developmentally ready, you may include more types of transitions in the lesson.

Lesson Plan: Poetry for Multiple Voices and Movements

Suggested Grade Level: 4/5

Lesson Overview

Engagement (5 min): Play a visually stimulating onomatopoeia video to get students seeing the words and hearing the sounds.

Instructional Input (10 min) Read and display the short poem "Onomatopoeia" by Eve Merriam. Use the poem to explain and point out onomatopoeia as well as alliteration. Demonstrate how words can make sounds that add to the meaning of a poem.

Guided Practice (5–7 min) Read and display "Fossils" by Ogden Nash. Have students pick out alliteration and examples of onomatopoeia. Connect how these devices add to the meaning of the poem.

Whole Class Activity (10 min) Divide class into four groups. Practice choral reading using the poem "Grasshoppers" by Paul Fleischmen.

Instructional Input (5–7 min) Model the five movements and have students practice.

Whole Class Activity (25 min) Do first choral reading with Groups One and Two Reading Voice One and Voice Two and Groups Three and Four performing the movements. Have students switch roles and do a second reading. Discuss how movements connect to the sounds and meaning of the poem.

Extension (5 min) In their journals, have students write a few sentences explaining how the movements reflected the meaning of the poem.

Closure (2 min): Review onomatopoeia and alliteration and how poets use these devices to create meaning.

NCTE	2. Students read a wide range of literature from many periods in many genres to build an understanding of the many dimensions (e.g., philosophical, ethical, aesthetic) of human experience
CCSS	6. Students apply knowledge of language structure, language conventions (e.g., spelling and punctuation), media techniques, figurative language, and genre to create, critique, and discuss print and non-print texts
	CCSS.ELA-LITERACY.RF.4.4.B
	Read grade-level prose and poetry orally with accuracy, appropriate rate, and expression on successive readings
	CCSS.ELA-LITERACY.L.5.5.A
	Interpret figurative language, including similes and metaphors, in context
Goals	Students will understand how sound effects, specifically alliteration and onomatopoeia, influence a poem's meaning. Students will work to improve their reading fluency
Objectives	Through the use of movement during a choral reading, students will analyze and discuss how sound effects impact a poem's meaning
	Through choral reading, students will demonstrate fluency by using appropriate rate, accuracy, expression, and phrasing

Description of Poetry for Multiple Voices and Movements Activity

Engage

- To engage the students, play the YouTube video Everyday Grammar: Onomatopoeia about onomatopoeia. There are several to choose from that are entertaining and demonstrate the concept well.

- Explain that writers express meaning through the images they create in the reader's mind with descriptive words and even through the sounds that the words can make.

Instructional Input

- Read and display a short poem like "Onomatopoeia" by Eve Merriam to demonstrate how words can make sounds. Use the poem to point out and highlight with different colors the examples of onomatopoeia and alliteration.

Guided Practice

- Read and display Fossils by Ogden Nash. Have students pick out alliteration and examples of onomatopoeia. If you have an interactive white board, allow students to come forward and mark the examples.
- Connect how these devices add to the meaning of the poem. You may want to provide students with hard copies so they can mark or highlight words in the poem as well.

Choral Reading Guided Practice

- Next, tell the students that they will be reading a poem designed for multiple voices but that they will be adding multiple movements as well. The movements will help them interpret the meaning but also point out how poets create meaning through images, sounds, and word choice.
- Divide the class into four groups and number them one through four. Place Groups One and Three on one side of the room and Groups Two and Four on the other side with a clear space/line down the middle. Have students transition by clearing the desks so there is space for this.
- Use a poem like "Grasshoppers" by Paul Fleischman and have Groups One and Two be Voice One and Groups Three and Four be Voice Two. Use the start signal and have them practice reading the poem to establish fluency and a consistent rate. Students can be given paper copies but also display the poem on the board and color code the selections.

Movements: Model and Practice

- Once students are familiar with the poem, discuss how the alliteration and the sounds created during the choral reading add to the meaning. Then tell the students that they will be adding movements to the reading as well.
- Display and model the movements for the students and have everyone practice along with the verbal and visual cues provided in the poem where the movements will correspond. Tell the students that everyone will have a chance to read and do the movements but that groups will have different roles for the readings. See Fig. 5.12 for descriptions of the movements.

Movement #1 Sap's Rising- Bend over and touch toes, roll slowly upward and

reach to the sky and wiggle fingers

Movement #2 Grasshoppers Hopping- hop in place

Movement #3 Vaulting- crouch and then pop up- hop a little ways up but stay in
place

Movement #4 Grass- Bounders- marching in place

Movement #5 Grass Soarers- arms out wide and move in a soaring motion

---

Fig. 5.12 Movement descriptions

Choral Reading with Movements

- For the first reading, have Group One read Voice One and Group Two read Voice Two. Groups Three and Four will perform the corresponding movements. Have the poem and movements displayed on the board so that the groups will know what to do. Use the start signal to begin the reading.
- After the reading is done then switch and have Groups Three and Four read and Groups One and Two do the movements.
- Use the stop signal and have the student's transition back to their desks. Ask students to think about how the movements and sounds created during the choral reading added to or helped them interpret meaning. Ask them to locate and even mark with highlighters specific words that help create sounds that help support the meaning and subject of the poem, discussing alliteration and onomatopoeia.

Extension

In their journals, have students write a few sentences explaining how the movements reflected the meaning of the poem. Using the same or similar format and using a different poem, have students create their own group movements to reflect the meaning of an assigned portion or for the poem as a whole. After the reading, have students discuss how the movements they created reflect the meaning. Have students write their own poems using onomatopoeia and alliteration.

Closure

Close the lesson by reviewing terms and re-emphasizing how word choice affects meaning in a poem.

Variations

The movements can be altered/modified so that students are able to read and move at the same time. Therefore, the class can be divided in half as Voice One and Voice Two and can have corresponding movements to perform as well.

Also: Using any appropriate poem, have students create dance moves or movements for each line of a poem that they feel represents that line. Groups can take one to three lines depending on length of the poem and number of groups/students. A chosen student or group may narrate while the individual groups perform their interpretive dances or movements when their line is read. Have students discuss verbally or in writing how they chose the dance moves/movements to capture their lines' meaning. Then ask questions about how the movements in each line add to overall meaning of the poem and which dance moves/movements specifically reference certain sound effects like onomatopoeia and alliteration.

Suggested time frame	50 min
Equipment/technology	Visual media for demonstration at the beginning. Interactive whiteboard if possible. Copies of poems for each student with movements indicated. Highlighters
Start/stop signals	Students will begin moving when the teacher says, "Begin"
	Flicker the lights twice to signal students to stop moving and look to the teacher
Skill cues	Model for students each of the movements required for the featured poem Movement #1 Sap Rising – Bend over and touch toes, roll slowly upward and reach to the sky, and wiggle fingers
	Movement #2 grasshoppers hopping
	– Hop (on one foot) in place
	Movement #3 vaulting bounders—crouch and then pop-up
	– Hop up but stay in place
	Movement #4 marching – marching in place with knees waist high
	Movement #5 grass soarers – arms out wide and move in a soaring motion
	If other poems are used, possible movements can include but are not limited to shuffling feet back and forth, swaying hips, shimmy, arms out and moving in circles, flapping arms like wings, forward leg kick, and elbow to knee touch
Safety cues	Make sure that students are far enough apart from one another so they do not collide when arms are out. Make sure desks and other obstacles are removed from their area so when students bend over and raise up they do not hit anything
Teaching style	Direct Instruction; practice; large group activity
Assessments	Q&A
Format of assessment	Informal observation
Transition activity	Have students arrange desks for activity and return them back

Modifications/Accommodations: Students who are unable to stand can be seated and do the soaring motion or the arm flapping. They could also bend at the waist and raise up with hands in the air with fingers wiggling. The teacher can also decide on alternate movements for students, who may have physical limitations.

For example, for movement #3, a student may press their hands to the floor for the crouch movement and extend their arms to the sky for the pop-up. The complexity of the poem can be adjusted for students who are developmentally ready for more of a challenge.

Lesson Plan: Poetry in Motion

Suggested Grade Level: 5/6
Lesson Overview
Engagement: (5–7 min): *I Won't Hatch* by Shel Silverstein dramatic reading with movements. Group discussion.
Instructional Input (5–10 min): Modeling of analysis using *I Won't Hatch*. Instructions for group activity. Post visually as well.
Guided Practice (5–7 min): Show *I Won't Hatch* on the board. Have students pick out examples of the figurative language.
Transition: Move to small groups using the copy of the poems they are given. Like poems group up.
Cooperative Learning (20 min): Students will analyze the poem as a group creating movements for the figurative language.
Group Presentations (10–15 min): Have groups present their poems and movements for the other members of the class.
Closure (2 min): Review figurative language devices common to the poems and how the movements chosen reflected the meaning.

NCTE	6. Students apply knowledge of language structure, language conventions (e.g., spelling and punctuation), media techniques, figurative language, and genre to create, critique, and discuss print and non-print texts
CCSS	CCSS.ELA-LITERACY.RL.5.4
	Determine the meaning of words and phrases as they are used in a text, including figurative language such as metaphors and similes
Goals	Students will use movements to represent various types of figurative language and sound devices in poetry to help them learn the meaning of the words as well as their impact on the poem itself
Objective	The students will demonstrate an understanding of figurative language and poetic techniques and their impact on a poem by using non-locomotors movements such as twisting, bending, and hopping in place to represent the following: simile, metaphor, onomatopoeia, hyperbole, personification, alliteration, symbol, and imagery

Description of Poetry in Motion Activity

Engagement

- As the engagement activity, the teacher will read a short poem such as *I Won't Hatch* by Shel Silverstein, while performing exaggerated movements for the figurative language in the poem.
- Tell students that figurative language can create mental pictures and even sounds in poetry and these add to the meaning of the poem.
- Choose which figurative language to review/discuss for the lesson depending on students' understanding and familiarity with the devices. Show the word, (such as simile) the definition, and an example on the board.
- Lead a class discussion explaining how the movements you performed earlier were chosen to represent the figurative language present and how those devices influenced the meaning of the poem.

Guided Practice

- Show *I Won't Hatch* on the board. Have students pick out examples of the figurative language. If you have an interactive whiteboard, allow students to come forward and mark the examples.
- Connect these to your movements earlier, reperform them, or even have students follow along if time allows. Discuss how these devices add to the meaning of the poem. You may choose to have students record the information on a graphic organizer, copy of the poem, or a skeleton note-taking guide for reference during the cooperative activity.

Cooperative Activity

- Divide the class into small groups of four students each. Use the jigsaw method so that each group has a different poem with mainly different poetic devices with some overlap. Create the groups by handing students copies of the poems and having them get into groups according to like poems.
- Explain to the students that each group will analyze the poem for examples of figurative language—simile, metaphor, onomatopoeia, hyperbole, personification, alliteration, symbol, imagery, and meaning.
- Students will mark their selected poem and then choose motions to represent each one of the figurative language or sound devices that best fits the definition of the word and reflects the meaning of the poem. See Fig. 5.13 for an example.

Simile, Line Two: "like a tightrope-walker"	Hold arms out and put one foot in front of the other walking a couple of steps
Simile, Line Five: "Or a kid skipping rope"	Moving arms up and down and hopping up and down

Fig. 5.13 Examples from *The Base Stealer* by Robert Francis

Students will also answer the three critical thinking questions. Set the timer to begin the activity.

Additionally, each group may select student roles, which will also assist the teacher in assessing and managing. Possible roles are as follows:

- Manager–student who makes sure that each student, including themselves, has a poetic device to create a movement for once they have been located in the poem, oversees practice, and checks to make sure that the group is ready to present.
- Device coder–student who marks the poem when the group is locating the poetic devices and records group input on meaning of the poem.
- Narrator–student who reads the poem during the presentation to the class, while the other group members act out the motions when they come to a poetic device in the poem.
- Speaker–student who discusses with the class the group's movement choices for the figurative language and poetic devices, and how that impacts the meaning.

For additional individual accountability in the cooperative learning activity, the teacher may require each student to individually create a movement for at least one device in the poem. When the timer goes off, end the activity or adjust accordingly.

Cooperative Activity Instructions
Have students do the following:

- Individually read the poem. Define any unfamiliar words.
- As a group locate the featured poetic devices and have the Coder mark the poem for the following poetic devices: simile, metaphor, onomatopoeia, hyperbole, personification, alliteration, symbol, and imagery.
- Divide up the poetic devices so that each person in the group has an equal number.
- Individually, create movements for your chosen poetic devices.
- Practice performing for the presentation. Have Narrator quietly read the poem while the group incorporates each member's movements. Make sure that you have room so that you do not hit or run into one another.
- As a group, answer/discuss the questions at the bottom of the poem handout. Speaker, be prepared to share answers with the whole class once the poem is read and the movements are performed.
- Present poem and movements when called on. Narrator will read the poem while the group members perform. Speaker will read the questions and give the group's answers.

Cooperative Activity Presentation
Use an online student selector tool like the one found on www.classtools.net to choose which group goes first.

Have the narrator read the poem title and then read the poem as the members of the group perform their non-locomotors movements each time one of the key concepts is read aloud.

Once each group has performed then have the group's speaker address the following critical thinking questions that all students have collaboratively answered.

- What is the poem about?
- What types of figurative language and sound devices did your group find in the poem? Please give two examples.
- Explain how the movements that were chosen help portray the meaning of the poem.

Closure

Close the lesson by reviewing figurative language and how the motions created by the different groups represented the poetic devices and added to the meaning of the poems.

Poetry Suggestions:

"The Base Stealer" by Robert Francis
"Dreams" by Langston Hughes
"April" by Marcia Masters
"Harlem" by Langston Hughes

Suggested time frame	50 min
Equipment/technology	Visual media for demonstration at the beginning. 1 copy of a poem per group, highlighters for marking
Start/stop signals	Online timer—www.online-stopwatch.com
Skill cues	Explain to students that when they create movements to represent the poetic devices they can use any of these types of movements or a combination of them. Demonstrate the following: Bend, twist, hop in place, shimmy, big clap, wave arms, etc.
Safety cues	During the preparation and presentation, make sure that the students' desks are grouped far enough apart to give them plenty of room to practice. Also, make sure there is an area at the front of the room or in the middle for them to present. Also, tell the students to hold out their arms and make sure that they are at least an arm's width apart from each other to avoid collisions with each other
Teaching style	Direct Instruction/Cooperative Learning
Assessments	Observational Checklist: While groups are working together check for understanding
Presentation rubric	The presentation of the poem and subsequent discussion questions each group addresses will show if students understand the poetic devices and their influence on the poem's meaning.
Format of assessment	Observation during the activity and informal Q&A once the activity has ended
Transition activity	At your desk make a list of the figurative language devices and representative movements used today

Modifications/Accommodations: Remind groups of students to use movements that everyone in the group can do. For example, they may need to be seated and use only their upper bodies (arms, head, torso, etc.). The number and complexity of figurative language examples can be adjusted according to students' developmental levels as well as the complexity of the poems used.

References

English Language Arts Standards. (n.d.). Retrieved September 28, 2016, from http://www.corestandards.org/ELA-Literacy/.

Francis, R. *The base stealer*. PoemHunter.com, www.poemhunter.com/poem/the-base-stealer/. Accessed on October 4, 2016.

Hughes, L. *Harlem*. Poetry Foundation, www.poetryfoundation.org/poems-and-poets/poems/detail/46548. Accessed on November 9, 2016.

Merriam, E.. *Onomatopoeia*. http://faculty.education.illinois.edu/j-levin/Davis/onomatopoeia.html . Accessed on November 9, 2016.

Nash, O. Fossils. In *Power poetry*. http://www.powerpoetry.org/famous-poems/fossils. Accessed on October 4, 2016.

NCTE/IRA Standards for the English Language Arts. (n.d.). Retrieved September 28, 2016, from http://www.ncte.org/standards/ncte-ira.

Silverstein, S. (2016). I won't hatch. In *Where the sidewalk ends* [Voice of America]. Everyday Grammar: Onomatopoeia. [Video File]. Retrieved from www.youtube.com/watch?v=-uxFwmYIHwk.

Chapter 6
Movement in the Science Classroom

Tonya D. Jeffery, Kimberly Moore and Tommye Hutson

Abstract This chapter is about some of the benefits of incorporating movement into the science curriculum. The authors offer several activities aligned to the major content areas of science, as well as the Next Generation Science Standards (NGSS) and the Common Core Standards that effectively integrate movement into science to benefit both student learning and physical activity. The science content areas included in this chapter are: life science, earth science and physical science.

Teaching science can be a challenge, especially for beginning teachers at the elementary school level (Davis & Smithey, 2009). At the elementary level, science teachers are responsible for teaching life science, physical science, and earth science through engagement in authentic scientific practices. In addition, elementary teachers often struggle with how to design and implement engaging, inquiry-based instruction with their students (Banchi & Bell, 2008). It is essential that all K-12 students have access to high-quality science education that provides them with the knowledge and skills to become scientifically literate citizens who are prepared to attend college and pursue science, technology, engineering, and math (STEM) careers in an effort to be competitive in our global workforce. The National Science Teachers Association (NSTA) recommends the adoption and implementation of the *Next Generation Science Standards* (NGSS) as an effective, research-based approach to accomplish these goals and to transform science education (NSTA Position Statement, 2013).

The *NGSS* provide an opportunity for teachers and science educators to consider changing their practices in an effort to enhance the learning of science concepts for

T.D. Jeffery (✉) · K. Moore
Texas A&M University, Corpus Christi, TX, USA
e-mail: tonya.jeffery@tamucc.edu

K. Moore
e-mail: kim.moore@tamucc.edu

T. Hutson
Western Governor's University, Salt Lake City, UT, USA
e-mail: Tommye.Hutson@wgu.edu

© Springer Nature Singapore Pte Ltd. 2018
S.C. Miller and S.F. Lindt (eds.), *Moving INTO the Classroom*,
Springer Texts in Education, DOI 10.1007/978-981-10-6424-1_6

all students (NGSS Lead States, 2013). The NGSS incorporates three-dimensions of practices into lesson activities: (a) disciplinary core ideas, (b) crosscutting concepts, and (c) science and engineering practices. The disciplinary core ideas (DCIs) are grouped into four domains: the physical sciences; the life sciences; the earth and space sciences; and engineering, technology and applications of science. According to NGSS (2013), the DCIs have the power to focus K-12 science curriculum, instruction, and assessments on the most important aspects of science. The cross-cutting concepts (CCCs) have application across all domains of science and they are a way of linking the different domains of science. They include: Patterns, similarity, and diversity; Cause and effect; Scale, proportion and quantity; Systems and system models; Energy and matter; Structure and function; Stability and change. According to NGSS (2013, Appendix G), "These concepts need to be made explicit for students because they provide an organizational schema for interrelating knowledge from various science fields into a coherent and scientifically-based view of the world." The science and engineering practices (SEPs) focuses on what scientists and engineers do to investigate the natural world and what engineers do to solve problems, design, and build systems. The SEPs explain what is meant by 'inquiry' in science and the range of cognitive, social, and physical practices that it requires (NGSS, 2013, Appendix F).

However, modifications to current practices can present some challenges for teachers as they begin to learn about these standards and try to apply them to their classroom teaching practices. In addition, incorporating the NGSS' science and engineering practices, disciplinary core ideas, and crosscutting concepts into lesson plans can be a daunting task for teachers, especially in the crunch for time to meet state and district mandates. Sometimes these challenges impact teachers' desires to implement engaging lessons that allow students to show their innovation, creativity, and imagination in science (Jeffery, McCollough, & Moore, 2015).

In an effort to prepare students to be competitive in this global workforce and successful in a STEM career, there have been calls to expand STEM education to include the arts and design, transforming STEM into science, technology, engineering, arts, and math (STEAM) in the K-20 classroom (Maeda, 2013). Students must not only have STEM knowledge but also be innovative, critical thinkers, and have strong problem solving skills (Oner, Nite, Capraro, & Capraro, 2016). STEAM, which includes the arts and arts integration has become a moving force in this transformation in an effort to reinvent our schools, communities, and nation (Eger, 2013). Hence, the arts have been integrated into the STEM disciplines, designated as STEAM, to provide students with well-rounded experiences and the social skills and knowledge necessary to be productive and capable citizens in this fast-paced society. Examples of how arts integration has been incorporated into various science classrooms will be explored later in this chapter.

As mentioned in the introductory chapter, national recommendations call for schools to offer physical activity as part of the planned academic lessons to teach language arts, math, social studies, science, and other subjects through movement. This chapter will outline some of the benefits of incorporating movement into the science curriculum and then offer suggestions for activities and lesson plans that effectively integrate movement into science to benefit both student learning and physical activity. The lesson plans follow the 5E Instructional Model of inquiry-based lessons utilizing the Engage, Explore, Explain, Elaborate, and Evaluate phases (Bybee et al., 2006). Engage is the first part of the lesson that hooks the students and/or piques their curiosity about the scientific concept emphasized in the lesson. The teacher may or may not tell students what the concept actually is during this stage. Many teachers allow students to discover the concept through explorations in the next phase. The purpose of the Explore is to allow students the opportunity to investigate the scientific concept being studied usually through hands-on, minds-on activities in cooperative groupings. The Explain portion of the lesson allows students to share their findings from the Explore activity and explain their understanding of the science concept in their own words in small groups and/or report to the whole class. The teacher should clear up any misconceptions students may have about the concept and also introduce new terminology to students. During the Elaboration phase of the lesson, students build upon their knowledge and apply their understanding of the scientific concept to brand new experiences and applications during hands-on activities. Students are also encouraged to utilize and incorporate any new terminology into explanations, discussions, reporting of any data analyses and/or conclusions formed during this phase. The Evaluation is the final phase of the 5E lesson cycle in which students complete an activity that assesses their scientific content knowledge related to the lesson's objectives. The teacher can assess student learning by utilizing a variety of assessment strategies to measure students' understanding of the concept individually, in groups, or in organized, whole-class discussions. However, ongoing assessment is an integral part of the philosophy of the 5E Instructional Model. The 5E lesson activities are designed to be implemented sequentially through learning experiences of increasing complexity (Miele & Adams, 2016).

Results from one research study have shown the feasibility of incorporating classroom-based physical activity programs into science lessons in an effort to decrease the childhood obesity epidemic. Finn and McInnis (2014) implemented the *Active Science* curriculum with forty-seven fifth and sixth graders and two teachers. In this study, various physical activity exercises and technologies (heart rate monitors and pedometers) were integrated into the science curriculum to introduce the concept of healthy lifestyles through regular physical activity and nutrition and simultaneously taught important concepts and principles in science. Science standards covered included the structure and function in living systems, personal health, nutrition, and scientific investigations. Students took part in fitness walks, agility exercises, cardiovascular exercise, Zumba dance, etc. The goal was to get the students to use the physical activity data (steps, average heart rate, calories) in the science curriculum. The findings suggest incorporating movement into traditional science curriculum helps promote physical activity skills, scientific inquiry skills, and exposure to the use of technology during the curriculum.

In addition to physical activity, previous research suggests several strategies have emerged for teaching science through movement integration (Becker, 2013; McMullen, Kulinna, & Cothran, 2014; Nichols & Stephens, 2013; Varelas et al.,

2010; Webster, Vazou, Goh, & Erwin, 2015). These strategies include interdisciplinary methods, in which the teaching and learning of science is integrated with other disciplines, such as language arts and the arts: drama, theater, dance, and music. Creative drama, is a method to teach and authentically assess science, and also follows a social constructivist model that simulates the process of teaching for conceptual understanding based on using kinesthetic awareness (Osmond, 2007). Examples include role-playing, improvisation, pantomime, and script writing (Yoon, 2006). In role play, the role is described to students then they act according to their roles. In improvisation, the context or task is given to students, then they may act in a non-verbal presentation like mime or gesture or movement (Abed, 2016). For example, a study by Hendrix, Eick, and Shannon (2012) incorporating creative drama activities was designed to help thirty-eight upper elementary students learn difficult science concepts. They found creative drama to be an effective strategy when used as an extension to the pre-existing inquiry-based science curriculum; integrating creative drama fosters high levels of student engagement as learners explore new ideas through collaboration with peers.

Research suggests integrating science and literacy to assist children in learning science concepts through reading and scientific inquiry (Ansberry & Morgan, 2010). An example of this is implementing the Readers' Theater strategy into an elementary science classroom to build reading fluency and vocabulary in science (Kinniburgh & Shaw, 2007). Readers' Theater requires teachers taking content from a science textbook or an informational trade book and transposing it into a script for students to read and act out (Flynn, 2004). Furthermore, Readers' Theater scripts bring science content to life and allow students to add their own creativity and personalities to the parts through active expressions (Kinniburgh & Shaw, 2007).

Another example of learning science vocabulary through integrative movement can be accomplished by participating in active station rotations (Pries & Hughes, 2012). In this study, groups of students were asked to apply new vocabulary words to familiar objects and provide nonlinguistic representations of the words. Nonlinguistic representations of words can either be kinesthetic, visual, or sensory experiences and allows students to have a better connection to the words (Marzano, Pickering, & Pollock, 2001). The students participated in three activities in which they explored the science concepts of energy, Newton's laws, and simple machines and were allowed to play with various objects at the stations: (1) beat drums for sound energy, (2) a Yo-yo for force and motion, and (3) playing with wind-up toys on an inclined plane for simple machines. Encouraging the students to play with the objects provided kinesthetic experiences for students to connect to the new vocabulary words being learned (Pries & Hughes, 2012).

Nichols and Stephens (2013) explored movement integration through arts-based learning which incorporates processes of the scientific method and the creative processes that artists experience when creating, interpreting, and expressing art. They found that utilizing arts integration techniques in the science classroom through their creative drama activities for K-6 students can benefit students in learning both artistic and scientific concepts. Moreover, in the science education field, a significant body of research exists related to both models and modeling and how their role facilitates learning science concepts (Abed, 2016; Dorion, 2009; Lee, 2015; Varelas et al., 2010). When studying the nature of science, models are representations of phenomena, objects, events, ideas, and systems studied in classrooms to improve science teaching and learning (Varelas et al., 2010). Models may be expressed in various forms or representations: action, writing, speech, or other symbolic forms. In Varelas et al. (2010), students engaged in reading children's literature, performed hands-on explorations, and other integrated science literacy activities. In these drama activities, children were asked to become the things they were learning, such as making dramatic enactments of molecular behavior in different states of matter and of food webs in a forest community. The researchers found that dramatizing scientific phenomena via kinesthetic body movements offers an opportunity to engage young children with each other in fun interactions and provides a more holistic and experiential approach to learning science.

Similarly, Burgin and Butler (2016) employed a 5E role-play simulation activity for 24 students to explore the relationship between ecosystems. During the Explore phase, three students simulated the role of airplanes, in which they spread their arms like wings and walked up and down imaginary runways to intentionally hit or not hit the eagles flying in the sky; the majority of students were fish and had to avoid being caught by the bald eagles, and a couple of students representing eagles had to catch at least five fish in order for their young to survive. This integrated movement activity fostered the students' science learning and created an atmosphere that was engaging for students to grasp the concept and helped students to model real world scientific issues. Yoon (2006) categorized this type of drama in science as physical simulations in which students in such activities try to understand the science concept through *role play*, and *use their bodies as actors* (physical simulations) in a theatrical sense.

Creative drama was also utilized by Abed (2016), in which eighty-six students used their bodies as a learning tool to construct, transform, and express for themselves what it meant to be a molecule in the various phases of matter. One of the most significant results of this study was that the average and low achieving students benefited from this drama activity. Abed recommends employing drama in teaching science to provide classrooms with additional differentiation strategies to meet the needs of all learners.

Becker (2013) examined an integrated arts lesson that combined the study of modern dance with a science unit on force and motion. Results suggest that incorporating creative movement in the lesson made science learning memorable for the elementary students and afforded them the opportunity to use their body to express their ideas, engage in the thinking process and solve problems kinesthetically. Furthermore, according to Becker, utilizing dance in academic disciplines helps children to develop skills such as creativity, communication, critical thinking, and collaboration, which are skills frequently missing from regular classroom instruction. Therefore, incorporating dance movements and practices into the science classroom aligns well with the discipline and goals of science education.

Lee (2015) analyzed the biomechanics associated with human movement with fifteen fifth-grade students working with stop-motion animation (SAM) software and slow-motion cameras. The purpose of the study was to demonstrate how technology can be used to support students' modeling of human body movement organized around the theme of animation and to teach students how to convert those visual data into new representations. Like Varelas et al. (2010), Lee (2015) found that the key aspects of the scientific practice of modeling can be effectively brought in at the elementary level. Hence, this is another example of the benefit of how movement integration in a science classroom enhances science content knowledge and scientific inquiry skills.

Life Science

One of the major content areas covered in elementary science is life science. Life science, in secondary and higher education, includes disciplines such as anatomy and physiology, aquatic science (or oceanography), biology, botany, environmental science, and zoology. The NGSS (2013) are built upon the notion of learning as a developmental progression and there is increased sophistication of student thinking from one grade level to the next. According to the NGSS (2013), the disciplinary core ideas (DCIs) essential to elementary school students in grades K-2 include an understanding of the following: structures and processes (using observations to describe patterns of what plants and animals need to survive); growth and development of organisms (parents and offspring); organization for matter and energy flow in organisms; information processing; interdependent relationships in ecosystems; and cycles of matter and energy transfer in ecosystems. For example, K-2 students are expected to explore the natural world by examining evidence that living organisms have basic needs, thus setting the expectation that the local environment must provide for those needs, such as a plant's need for sunlight and water to live and grow (NGSS-1-LS1-2). Furthermore, they are expected to recognize and sort living organisms by physical characteristics such as color, size, body covering and shape (usually involving leaves from trees). For grades 3–5, more in-depth content knowledge is placed on interdependent relationships in ecosystems (food web, predator/prey relationships), cycles of matter (life cycle, water cycle, rock cycle) and energy transfer in ecosystems (food chains, biotic and abiotic systems), inheritance and variation of traits; and biological evolution—unity and diversity (fossils, extinction of animals, natural selection).

When learning about life science in the early grades, understanding that all life needs energy made available in Earth systems ties all three content areas (life, physical, and Earth) together as students realize that life cannot exist otherwise. As students move from kindergarten through grade 5, life science content that elementary students are expected to understand includes interdependence, life cycles and the principles of heredity. With age and practice, students can be expected to take measurements and record those measurements (collect and record data) meaningfully and accurately. A number of higher order thinking skills (HOTS) are introduced and reinforced through effective science instruction each year, scaffolding on experiences and enriched learning opportunities if such are provided.

As elementary students progress in their understanding of life science content, they are expected to develop a deeper understanding of connections that exist between the three content areas—physical, Earth, and life science. They should expand their recognition of life science as the content expands to include such topics such as the basic needs of organisms and reliance on the local ecosystem to meet those needs, adaptations that allow organisms to survive in unique environments, inherited characteristics versus learned behaviors, genetic inheritance, and interactions within an ecosystem such as prey/predator relationships. Furthermore, at each successive grade level, the life science content is grounded in practices that are reflective of their cognitive development level. Observing changes that occur in living organisms such as planting a seed and watching it throughout its eventual development of new seeds helps young students as they develop understanding of a complete life cycle. By the time that they have completed 5th grade content, students are expected to describe energy (initially provided by the Sun) as it moves through various food chains and food webs from producers to consumers and decomposers, predict the effects of changes in ecosystems caused by living organisms (including human beings), compare the structures and functions of different species that help them to survive in their native ecosystems and describe the processes of photosynthesis and metamorphosis.

Activity Name: Metamorphosis

Suggested Grade Level: 3.

NGSS Standards: ES-LS1.B: Growth and Development of Organisms
Students who demonstrate understanding can develop models to describe that reproduction is essential to the continued existence of every kind of organism; and organisms have unique and diverse life cycles.

http://www.nextgenscience.org/sites/default/files/3.IVT%205.6.13With%20Footer.pdf.

Common Core State Standards: CCSS.ELA-Literacy.SL.3.1D.
Explain their own ideas and understanding in light of the discussion.
http://www.corestandards.org/ELA-Literacy/SL/3/.
Goals: Students will use locomotors movement to learn the four stages of the life cycle of a butterfly [egg, larvae (caterpillar), pupa (cocoon/chrysalis), and butterfly].
Objectives: The students will perform a series of movements to demonstrate an understanding of the life cycle of a butterfly.

Suggested time frame	30–40 min
Equipment/technology	Computer and projector; access to the internet Life cycle card sort activity (4–5 sets for the class) Large images of each stage of the butterfly life cycle to be placed on the walls in four corners (areas) of the classroom + labels for each stage (station 1 = egg, station 2 = larvae/caterpillar, station 3 = pupa/cocoon, station 4 = butterfly) + four large arrows to show direction of stages Plant leaf (2 large cut-outs placed on the floor for students to stand on for the egg and larvae/caterpillar stages) (stations 1 and 2) Potato sacks (4–5)—pupa/cocoon stage (station 3) Feather or paper wings (4–5)—butterfly stage (station 4)
Start/stop signals	To start activity say, "Start" To stop the activity the teacher says "Metamorphosis." have the students say "Metamorphosis," stop what they are doing, and look at the teacher for further instructions. This should be repeated until everyone is still and has eyes on the teacher for further instructions
Skill cues	Model for the students the various movements that correspond with the life stages of a butterfly at each station. Exaggerate movements These skills should focus specifically on the PE movements gained from integrating movement. For this activity, students will gain the ability to complete arm movements and stretching. Students also will learn the proper technique of a squat and other stretches **Egg**—stay low, bottom to heels, hug knees **Transition to caterpillar**—Students will complete one forward roll from the egg position to the cocoon stage, then lay on their tummies. Then students will move like a caterpillar, from their gut and the rest of their body will follow in a wavelike motion, like a worm. (Remember caterpillars do not have bones in their bodies.) **Cocoon**—stand straight, tighten muscles **Butterfly**—flap arms up and down, small leaps
Safety cues	Remind the students to be at least an arm's width away from the walls, desks, chairs, and other people when they are doing their movements especially in their groups. Tell the students to be considerate of other students, so they do not bump into them
Teaching style	Guided discovery; modeling; practice; cooperative learning
Assessments of content through the activity	Observational checklist—see Appendix B for a sample checklist; anecdotal notes
Transition activity	Have the students stand by their chairs, cross their arms across their chest (butterfly stance), breathe in and out deeply three times, and then be seated

Description of Metamorphosis

Introduction: Metamorphosis—Life Cycle Card Sort with Movements (*Engage*)

- The Metamorphosis will include the Engage and Explore activities, which are meant to be part of a full 5E lesson plan on this topic.

  a. The Life Cycle Card Sort with Movements begins by showing students the YouTube video: Life cycle of a Butterfly https://www.youtube.com/watch?v=O1S8WzwLPlMactivity

  b. Ask students probing questions related to the video. **What did you observe about the first stage of development?** (eggs) **Where can the eggs found?** (On the leaf of a plant) **What happens when the eggs hatch? (larvae stage)? What happens once the caterpillar starts to grow?** (It sheds its skin, continues to eat, it stops eating once it's big enough and transforms into a pupa/cocoon/chrysalis stage). **How long does it take for the butterfly to then develop?** (about 15 days) **What is the life cycle of a butterfly called?** (metamorphosis)

- Next show on the board the complex term 'metamorphosis' that students may or may not be familiar with. Ask students if they know what the word means or how it is pronounced. Some students may know this term, but reassure them that learning how to say, spell, and understand a complex word like this one is something they are capable of. Visually demonstrate how this particular word can be broken down into parts called roots, prefixes, or suffixes (see Chap. 4's ELAR example).

- Explain to students that in order to facilitate their learning and retention, they will be learning movements that represent the life cycle of a butterfly, called metamorphosis. Have the students pronounce the term 'metamorphosis'. Repeat if necessary.

- Have the students get into groups of four to complete the Life Cycle Card Sort. Have the life cycle stages printed on one set of cards, the definitions printed on another set, and the illustrations/images of each stage on another set. Have students match the life cycle stage, with the correct definition, and illustration. Once each group has completed the card sort, have each group report their card sorting. Students can also be asked to record these words and definitions on a worksheet or their own paper. Adjust the number of cards for grade and developmental level.

- Finally, as a whole group, have students execute the movements for each card by calling out: Egg, Larva/Caterpillar, Pupa/Cocoon, and Butterfly. Encourage exaggeration of movements.

Explore Activity: Life Cycle Movements

- Next, show the students the four corners or areas of the classroom that have an image of each stage of the life cycle of a butterfly on the wall. Students will rotate from their card sort groups to each station, starting with Station 1, then Station 2, Station 3, and Station 4 in this order to model the life cycle of a butterfly. Students will remain at each station for 30 s. Then students will return to their tables/desks.
- Then, model for students the movement they are to make at each station:

    a. **Station 1** (Egg): Students are to crouch to the floor in the position of a squat and wrap their arms around their knees on the plant leaf. Students should stay in this position for 30 s. When the teacher instructs them to get ready to move to Station 2, students will transition to a caterpillar by following the next steps. See Fig. 6.1 for a photo of students in the "egg" stage.

    b. **Station 2** (Larvae/Caterpillar): Students will complete one forward roll from the egg position to the larvae stage, then lay on their tummies. Then students will move like a caterpillar, from their gut and the rest of their body will follow in a wavelike motion, like a worm (see Fig. 6.2). (Remember caterpillars do not have bones in their bodies.)

    c. **Station 3** (Pupa/Cocoon): Students are to climb into the potato sacks and stand still, keeping their muscles engaged, to symbolize this stage in the life cycle of a butterfly.

    d. **Station 4** (Butterfly): Students are to put on the wings, flap arms up and down, and make small leaps to move like a butterfly.

- Have students rotate through the Life Cycle Stage stations two times exploring the life cycle of a butterfly.
- Model the transition activity from the above chart and have students perform the transition activity before being seated.

Cooperative Group Activity: Butterfly, Butterfly Song with Movements

- Show students the YouTube video: Butterfly, Butterfly song: https://www.youtube.com/watch?v=8rvGUevGxDk
- After viewing the video once, tell students they will sing along the next time and execute the movements for each stage of the life cycle as a whole group, using the movements from the Explore activity.

Modifications/Adaptations: For students with physical disabilities, create movements that the student can complete for each of the cycles. For example, instead of squatting, they may be able to bend at the waist and wrap their arms like a hug.

Fig. 6.1 Students are in the "egg" stage

Fig. 6.2 Students are in the "caterpillar" stage

Earth Science

Earth science is the second content area taught by elementary school science teachers. Earth science, in secondary and higher education, includes content from astronomy, geology and environmental systems. As with life science, the ability to make and record objective observations is highly valued. When students make and record observations within an Earth science context, they are often observing events and processes that are cyclical in nature. Specifically, in grades K-2 the first major observations are of local weather conditions and seasonal patterns of sunrise and sunset. Recognition of patterns and connections between observed conditions and daily activities is stressed as well as observing the appearance of other objects in the sky (clouds, moon, stars, etc.). When learning about weather in the early grades, students are expected to move from understanding the cyclical nature of the seasons and their impact on personal life to more complex cycles such as the rock, lunar and the water cycles. With age and practice, they are expected to measure, record and graph weather information over longer periods of time in order to identify patterns in weather. Similarly, they are expected to record, recognize and correctly sequence the lunar cycle. Hence, as students progress from grades 3–5, more emphasis is placed on Earth's place in the universe (lunar cycle and solar system); the history of the Earth (global patterns of rock formations, earth's forces, such as earthquakes); plate tectonics (how Earth's plates move); the roles of water in the Earth's surface processes (water cycle, availability of water, complex patterns of changes, global movements of water); weather and climate; and biogeology (how living things affect the physical characteristics of their regions) (NGSS, 2013).

Activity Name: Pop Rocks—Rock Cycle Interpretive Dance

Suggested Grade Level: 4/5.

NGSS Standards: 4-ESS2-1; 5-ESS2-1
Water, ice, wind, living organisms, and gravity breaks rocks, soils, and sediments into smaller particles and move them around.

Common Core State Standards: CCSS.ELA-Literacy.SL.4.5; SL5.5

Include multimedia components (e.g., graphics, sound) and visual displays in presentations when appropriate to enhance the development of main ideas or themes.
   http://www.corestandards.org/ELA-Literacy/SL/4/.

Goals: Students will use music and dance movements to improvise the rock cycle and its processes.
Objectives: The students will create an interpretive dance with movements to demonstrate an understanding of the rock cycle and its processes; students will gain

an understanding of how a rock can move through the different stages of the rock cycle (terminology: igneous rock, sedimentary rock, metamorphic, magma, lava, volcanic eruptions, weathering, erosion, wind, sediments, heat, and pressure).

Suggested time frame	30–40 min
Equipment/technology	Computer and projector; access to the internet
Start/stop signals	To start activity say, "Let's Rock It" To stop the activity the teacher says "Rocks!" Have the students say "…Paper, Scissors!" stop what they are doing, and look at the teacher for further instructions. This should be repeated until everyone is still and has eyes on the teacher for further instructions
Skill cues	Remind students that interpretive dance is a way for them to move their arms, legs, and body in various movements that corresponds with their understanding of the rock cycle and its processes
Safety cues	Remind the students to be at least an arm's width away from the walls, desks, chairs, and other people when they are doing their movements especially in their groups. Tell the students to be considerate of other students, so they do not bump into them
Teaching style	Guided inquiry; simulation; practice; cooperative learning
Assessments of content through the activity	Observational checklist; anecdotal notes
Transition activity	Have the students stand by their chairs, touch their toes (as if collecting rocks off the ground), slowly raise up, stand straight, breathe deeply, and then be seated

Description of Pop Rocks: The Rock Cycle Interpretive Dance

Introduction: Pop Rocks—The Rock Cycle Interpretive Dance

- This activity is the Elaborate portion of a 5E lesson (after the Engage, Explore, and Explain portions of a 5E lesson on the rock cycle). Students will apply their current understanding of the rock cycle processes to a new situation. Students will demonstrate their understanding of the rock cycle and its processes through physical movement, by creating an interpretive dance routine.
- Place students in groups of three to four.
- Provide each student group with a set of rock cycle terminology cards. (Prior to the start of this activity, the teacher should create sets of terminology cards utilizing the terms from the rock cycle word wall (see Fig. 6.3) for each student group.)
- Explain to students that each group will come up with interpretive dance movements for the terminology on the rock cycle word wall (see Fig. 6.3) to

Weathering	Erosion	Heat	Pressure	Sediments	Wind
Igneous rock	Metamorphic rock	Sedimentary rock	Volcanic eruption	Cooling	magma
lava	water	gravity			

Fig. 6.3 Rock cycle word wall

demonstrate their understanding of the rock cycle and its processes (terminology: igneous rock, sedimentary rock, metamorphic, magma, lava, volcanic eruptions, cooling, weathering, erosion, wind, water, gravity, sediments, heat, and pressure). Each group's interpretive dance routine should last no more than 1 min.

- Instruct students that each performer in the group must hold up the appropriate terminology cards for each term being performed during their interpretive dance routine.
- Allow 10–15 min for each group to discuss and practice their interpretive dance routine.
- The teacher will find and play appropriate 'pop music' for the Pop Rock Interpretive Dances.
- The teacher can set a timer for 60 s for each group's dance routine.
- While one group of dancers stand and perform their Rock Cycle Interpretive Dance routine, the rest of the class should be seated on the floor. After each performance, the audience should be encouraged to applaud for their peers.
- The teacher will assess students' understanding of the rock cycle processes by observing each groups' interpretive dance performance and by engaging in a discussion with each team and the entire class after each performance. The class discussions post-dance should last no longer than 3–4 min.

Cooperative Group Activity—Rock Cycle Conga Line

- Each student will receive a Rock Cycle Word Wall card.
- Explain to the students that they will be practicing arranging the rock cycle word wall (terminology) cards into the proper order based on the type of rock and process.
- The student will use movement to improvise their science term while in the conga line. Students should be encouraged to exaggerate movements.
- The music will start and students will join the conga line in a position based on their card.

Extension: Post the terminology cards on the wall and refer students to them during the rest of the rock cycle unit.

Modifications/Adaptations: For students with physical disabilities, the students may sit and perform the movements or they can be partnered with someone to assist them with the movement. Pair students who may need encouragement during playtime. Be sure that there is enough room around the desks and tables for students with physical disabilities to move about the room.

Physical Science

Physical science is the third content area taught in K-5 science classrooms. Physical science, in secondary and higher education, includes disciplines such as chemistry and physics. Within those fields, the ability to make and record objective observations is a critical skill. When students—regardless of age—make and record observations, they are observing matter and/or energy. In early science learning, matter is considered anything that has mass and takes up space. When learning about matter in the early grades, matter is described in terms of its physical properties. As students move from kindergarten through grade 5, physical properties that younger elementary students can be expected to recognize include relative size, mass, shape, color and texture. With age and practice, they are expected to meaningfully and accurately collect and record data. According to the NGSS (2013), in grades K-2 the emphasis in physical science is on the structure and properties of matter; chemical reactions; forces and motion (pushes and pulls, speed, direction, and motion); types of interactions (objects touch or collide and cause a change in motion); conservation of energy and energy transfer (types of energy and energy transformations); relationships between energy and forces; wave properties; electromagnetic radiation; and information technologies and instrumentation. In grades 3–5, an even greater emphasis is placed on structure and properties of matter (mass, weight, measurement); force and motion (Newton's laws, gravitational forces; electric and magnetic forces; chemical reactions; energy; and waves.

Activity Name: Motion Sports

Suggested Grade Level: K-2.

NGSS Standards: KPS2-1, K-PS2-2
Pushes and pulls can have different strengths and directions; pushing or pulling on an object can change the speed or direction of its motion and can start or stop it.

http://www.nextgenscience.org/sites/default/files/k%20combined%20DCI%
20standards%206.13.13_0.pdf

Common Core State Standards: CCSS.ELA-Literacy.SL.3.1D
Explain their own ideas and understanding in light of the discussion.
http://www.corestandards.org/ELA-Literacy/SL/3/.

Goals: Students will use kinesthetic movement to simulate forces and motion.
Objectives: The students will perform a series of movements via sports challenges
to demonstrate an understanding of how pushes and pulls can have different
strengths, change the speed or direction of its motion and can start or stop it.

Suggested time frame	30–40 min
Equipment/technology	Tug-of-war (2–4 ropes) (borrow from physical education teacher)
Start/stop signals	To start activity, ring a bell To stop the activity the teacher will ring a bell. Have the students 'freeze' in place, stop what they are doing, and look at the teacher for further instructions. This should be repeated until everyone is still and has eyes on the teacher for further instructions
Skill cues	Model for the students the various movements that correspond to the various motion sports challenges
Safety cues	Remind the students to be at least an arm's width away from the walls, desks, chairs, and other people when they are doing their movements especially in their groups. Tell the students to be considerate of other students, so they do not bump into them
Teaching style	Guided discovery; modeling; practice; cooperative learning
Assessments of content through the activity	Observational checklist; anecdotal notes
Transition activity	Have the students stand by their chairs, touch their toes (as if collecting rocks off the ground), slowly raise up, stand straight, breathe deeply, and then be seated

Description of Motion Sports

• This is an *Explore* activity after an engaging activity on force and motion.

Introduction: Motion Sports

(Four students at each station…or simultaneously as a whole class, but in groups)

• **Tug-of-War** (Station 1) (Pulling forces; change in direction of motion and can start or stop it)

 – Groups of 4 students will participate in a tug-of-war challenge; two students on each end of the rope.

- Students will record their responses to the questions (Describe the forces in this motion sport; What forces are acting on the rope? etc.)

- **Row Your Boat** (Station 2) (Pulling on an object can change the speed or direction)

  - Pairs of students will sit on the floor facing each other with legs stretched out, feet touching, grab each other's hands and pull in both directions as if rowing in a boat. See Fig. 6.4 for a photo of students in the position.
  - Encourage the students by saying **Row slowly, then faster** (speed up the rowing), **faster, slow down, slower, stop, etc.**
  - Students will record their responses to the questions on their own piece of paper (Describe the forces and motion in this motion sport).

- **Arm wrestling** (Station 3) Push and pulling forces have different strengths and directions; pushing or pulling can start or stop its motion)

  - Pairs of two students will participate in arm wrestling competitions.
  - Students will record their responses to the questions (Describe the forces and motion in this motion sport)

- **Human Chains** (Station 4) (Pushing an object can change the speed or direction of its motion)

  - Pairs of students will sit on the floor, backs-to-backs (see Fig. 6.5); students will interlock arms as a chain, pull in their legs where their knees are up; use

Fig. 6.4 Students participating in "Row Your Boat"

the force of their legs to pull themselves and each other up into an upright position where both students are standing on their feet.

- Students will record their responses to the questions (Describe the forces and motion in this motion sport; what challenges did you experience when trying to stand upright with your partner? Communication is important—communicate as scientists do when there is a problem to solve; How did you and your partner communicate?)

Cooperative Group Activity: 4-Person Human Chain Challenge

- Have groups of four (4) students create a human chain and repeat the activity from above, but the challenge this time is that all four students have to work together to complete the challenge with four people.
- Students will spend 30 s to develop a plan and reach consensus; practice; etc.
- Groups of four (4) students will sit on the floor, backs-to-backs (facing away from each other); students will interlock arms as a chain, pull in their legs where

Fig. 6.5 Students preparing for "Human Chains"

their knees are up; use the force of their legs to pull themselves and each other up into an upright position where both students are standing on their feet.

- After this challenge, students will record their responses to the questions (What challenges did you experience when trying to stand upright with your group? What forces were acting on each of you?)

Extension: Have students reflect on the experiences. What is another motion sport that can be incorporated in this lesson? What type of forces will be acted upon/experienced for this motion sport?

Modifications/Adaptations: For students with physical disabilities, the students may sit and perform the movements or they can be partnered with someone to assist them with the movement. Be sure that there is enough room around the desks and tables for students with physical disabilities to move in their space without injury.

References

Abed, O. (2016). Drama-based science teaching and its effect on students' understanding of scientific concepts and their attitudes towards science learning. *International Education Studies, 9*(10), 163–173.

Ansberry, K., & Morgan, E. (2010). *Picture-perfect science lessons, expanded 2nd edition: Using children's books to guide inquiry* (pp. 3–5). Arlington, VA: NSTA.

Banchi, H., & Bell, R. (2008). The many levels of inquiry. *Science and children, 46*(2), pp. 26–29.

Becker, K. M. (2013). Dancing through the school day: How dance catapults learning in elementary education. *The Journal of Physical Education, Recreation & Dance, 84*(3), 6–9.

Burgin, S., & Butler, B. (2016). Controversial environmental issues explored through interdisciplinary perspectives. *Science Scope, 39*(4), 41–48.

Bybee, R., Taylor, J., Gardner, A., Scotter, P., Powell, J., Westbrook, A., et al. (2006). *The BSCE 5E instructional model: Origins and effectiveness*. Colorado Springs, CO: BSCS.

Davis, E. A., & Smithey, J. (2009). Beginning teachers moving toward effective elementary science teaching. *Science Education, 93*, 745–770. doi:10.1002/sce.20311.

Dorion, K. R. (2009). Science through drama: A multiple case exploration of the characteristics of drama activities used in secondary science lessons. *International Journal of Science Education, 31*(16), 2247–2270. doi:10.1080/09500690802712699.

Eger, J. (2013). STEAM…Now! *The STEAM Journal, 1*(1), 1–7. doi:10.5642/steam.201301.08.

Finn, K., & McInnis, K. (2014). Teachers' and students' perceptions of the active science curriculum: Incorporating physical activity into middle school science classrooms. *The Physical Educator, 71*, 234–253.

Flynn, R. M. (2004). Curriculum-based Readers Theatre: Setting the Stage for Reading and Retention. *The Reading Teacher 58* (4):360–365

Hendrix, R., Eick, C., & Shannon, D. (2012). The integration of creative drama in an inquiry-based elementary program: The effect on student attitude and conceptual learning. *Journal of Science Teacher Education, 23*, 823–846.

Jeffery, T. D., McCollough, C., & Moore, K. (2015). Puff mobile derby student engineers. *Science Scope, 39*(4), 64–71.

Kinniburgh, L., & Shaw, E. (2007). Building reading fluency in elementary science through readers' theatre. *Science Activities, 44*(1), 16–23.

Lee, V. (2015). Combining high-speed cameras and stop-motion animation software to support students' modeling of human body movement. *Journal of Science Education Technology, 24,* 178–191. doi:10.1007/s10956-014-9521-9.

Maeda, J. (2013). STEM + Art = STEAM. *The STEAM Journal, 1*(1), 1–3. doi:10.5642/steam. 201301.34.

Marzano, R.J., Pickering, D.J., & Pollock, J.E. (2001). Nonlinguistic representations. In *Classroom instruction that works: Research-based strategies for increasing student achievement.* Alexandria, VA: ASCD.

McMullen, J., Kulinna, P., & Cothran, D. (2014). Physical activity opportunities during the school day: Classroom teachers' perceptions of using activity breaks in the classroom. *Journal of Teaching in Physical Education, 33,* 511–527. doi:10.1123/jtpe.2014-0062.

Miele, E. A., & Adams, J. D. (2016). Guided-choice learning in out-of-school environments. *Science Scope, 39*(6), 52–55.

National Science Teachers Association (NSTA). (2013). *Position statement: The next generation science standards.* Arlington, VA: National Science Teachers Association.

NGSS Lead States. (2013). *Next generation science standards: For states, by states.* Washington, DC: National Academies Press.

Nichols, A., & Stephens, A. (2013). The scientific method and the creative process: Implications for the K-6 classroom. *Journal for Learning through the Arts, 9*(1), 1–12.

Oner, A. T., Nite, S., Capraro, R. M., & Capraro, M. M. (2016). From STEM to STEAM: Students' beliefs about the use of their creativity, *The STEAM Journal, 2*(2). doi:10.5642/steam.20160202.06.

Osmond, C. R. (2007). Drama education and the body: I am therefore I think. In L. Bresler (Ed.), *International handbook of research in arts education* (pp. 1109–1118). Dordrecht: Springer.

Pries, C. H., & Hughes, J. (2012). Inquiring into familiar objects: An inquiry-based approach to introduce scientific vocabulary. *Science Activities, 49,* 64–69.

Varelas, M., Pappas, C. C., Tucker-Raymond, E., Kane, J., Hankes, J., Ortiz, I., et al. (2010). Drama activities as ideational resources for primary-grade children in urban science classrooms. *Journal of Research in Science Teaching, 47*(3), 302–325. doi:10.1002/tea.20336.

Webster, C. A., Russ, L., Vazou, S., Goh, T. L., & Erwin, H. (2015). Integrating movement in academic classrooms: Understanding, applying and advancing the knowledge base. *World Obesity, 16*(8), 1–10. doi:10.1111/obr.12285.

Yoon, H. (2006). The nature of science drama in science education. In *9th International Conference on Public Communication of Science and Technology (PCST-9).* Seoul, Korea.

Chapter 7
Lesson Plans for Moving in the Science Classroom

Tonya D. Jeffery and Kimberly Moore

Abstract This chapter features six full-length inquiry-based lesson plans that utilize the 5E Instructional Model and incorporate the Next Generation Science Standards (NGSS) and the Common Core State Standards (CCSS). At the elementary level, science standards are incorporated into the English Language Arts objectives for the CCSS. There are two life science lessons, two earth science lessons, and two physical science lessons. Although there are specific grade levels from K-5 attached to each lesson, the lesson plans could easily be modified and/or scaffolded to address science standards at other grade levels.

Life Science Lesson Plan: Busy Bees

Suggested Grade Level: second grade
   Lesson Overview

Engage Activity (5 min) Watch "Pollination Rock."

Transition Students will return to their table groups to begin the Cheetos Pollination Experiment.

Explore Activity (20 min) Cheetos Pollination Experiment.

Transition Students will each get a bit of hand sanitizer before beginning the explain activity.

Explain Activity (10 min) PowerPoint with graphic organizer on Flowers and Pollination.

T.D. Jeffery (✉) · K. Moore
Texas A&M University—Corpus Christi, Corpus Christi, TX, USA
e-mail: tonya.jeffery@tamucc.edu

K. Moore
e-mail: kim.moore@tamucc.edu

© Springer Nature Singapore Pte Ltd. 2018
S.C. Miller and S.F. Lindt (eds.), *Moving INTO the Classroom*,
Springer Texts in Education, DOI 10.1007/978-981-10-6424-1_7

Elaborate Activity (30 min) Students work in groups to dramatize the rap, "Yo I'm a Flower".

Evaluate Activity (5 min) Students complete a 3–2–1 exit ticket.

Next-generation science standards (NGSS)	
Disciplinary core ideas	Interdependent relationships in ecosystems • Plants depend on animals for pollination or to move their seeds around (2-LS2-2)
Cross-cutting concepts	Structure and function • The shape and stability of structures of natural and designed objects are related to their function(s) (2-LS2-2)
Science and engineering practices	Modeling in K-2 builds on prior experiences and progresses to include using and developing models (i.e., diagram, drawing, physical replica, diorama, dramatization, or storyboard) that represent concrete events or design solutions • Develop a simple model based on evidence to represent a proposed object or tool (2-LS2-2)
Performance expectation	Develop a simple model that mimics the function of an animal in dispersing seeds or pollinating plants (2-LS2-2)
CCSS	Recall information from experiences or gather information from provided sources to answer a question (CCSS.ELA-LITERACY.W.2.8)
Goals	The students will use dance movement to dramatize and model how plants depend on animals to reproduce
Objectives	Students will identify how bees help plants to reproduce through pollination

Detailed Description of Lesson

Activity Preparation:

Teacher will need to prepare a paper sandwich bag (with the top half cut) for each student.

- A cutout picture of a flower needs to be glued to each bag. (Each bag needs to be filled with a handful of Cheetos.)
- Desks need to be arranged in groups of three to four students unless the class is already sitting at table groups. Put one small hand sanitizer in the middle of each table. Put a small spray bottle of water and paper towels at each table to clean up Cheetos.
- Teacher will write the following either on chart paper or the white board:

    - Pollination is when insects, birds, bats and the wind take pollen from one flower to another. Pollination allows the plants to make new seeds and reproduce (make baby plants)!

Engage Activity: **Pollination Rock**

- The teacher tells the students that they will be learning about pollination. The teacher asks the students if they know what pollination is.
- After getting some information from the students about their background knowledge, the teacher invites them to stand up. The teacher tells them that they are going to watch a video, Pollination Rock found: https://www.youtube.com/watch?v=V5yya4elRLw. The teacher tells them at the end of the video they will be asked these two questions:

  - What living things are pollinators?
  - What non-living things are pollinators?

- The teacher tells the students that during the video, they will have a chance to dance. They will be following the teacher's lead as they take one step to the right and clap their hands. They will then take one step to the left and clap their hands. They will repeat this movement throughout the video. Please note: The teacher may want to practice this movement/routine a few times with students before starting the video.
- At the end of the video, the teacher asks the following questions:

  - What living things are pollinators? (insects, birds, humans, dogs, bats)
  - What non-living things are pollinators? (water, wind).

Transition Now that we have begun to learn about pollinators and pollination, we are going to do an activity that helps us to better understand how bees move pollen from one flower to another.

Explore Activity: **Cheetos Pollination Experiment**

- The students will work in groups of 3–4. Each student is given a brown or white lunch bag that has a flower glued on it and a handful of Cheetos inside.
- The students are told that they are now bees and the Cheetos represent nectar. The most important rule in this activity is: DON'T LICK YOUR HANDS!
- The students are instructed to remove one of the Cheetos from their bag and eat it but they must not LICK THEIR HANDS!
- The students then rotate clockwise (with arms out as wings, making a buzzing sound) to the next student's space. The students will only be rotating within their table groups. The bags remain at their original location.
- The students then remove one of the Cheetos from their new bag and eat it. This continues until the students are back at their original seat.
- The teacher then says, **Oh my! Your hands are quite messy. Please wipe your hands on the bag to your right.** The students wipe their hands on their neighbor's bag and get orange Cheetos dust on the bag.

Transition Students will need to utilize the water bottles to spray their hands or it may be necessary to take a restroom break to clean their hands, if there isn't a sink in the classroom. **We are ready to do our next activity, but we have a few**

problems. We still have some orange hands in the room. The teacher will direct the students to take turns cleaning their hands off using sanitizer or the spray water bottles.

Explain Activity:

- Students will be given this handout: http://www.agclassroom.org/ID/teacher/doc/materials/pollination_experiment.pdf. They will work independently to complete the handout, though they may consult an elbow buddy if they get stuck.
- Once students have completed their handout, volunteers are selected to share their responses. Teacher asks:

  - **What attracts the bees to the flower?** (bright colors, nectar)
  - **Do the bees mean to move the pollen from flower to flower?** (no, it sticks to them accidentally)

Elaborate Activity Yo, I'm a Flower.

- The teacher tells the students that they are going to get a chance to come up with their own creative moves to a rap. The teacher lets them listen to this rap: http://billybproductions.com/lyrics-yo-im-a-flower/.
- The words to the rap are written on a piece of chart paper. The following words are highlighted:

  - Power
  - Flower
  - Bee

Note The teacher may choose or let groups choose to add extra words to choreograph such as nectar and seeds.

- The students are to work in groups to decide on a motion for each of these three words. One group at a time then performs their rap incorporating their chosen motions (see Figs. 7.1 and 7.2). *Note* The teacher can also have the groups teach the whole class and the whole class imitates the moves that the creators have just taught them.
- Follow-up questions:

  - **Why do the flowers need the bees?** (to spread the pollen)
  - **Why do the bees need the flowers?** (to make honey from nectar)
  - **What are the benefits of pollination?** (plants to reproduce or make new seeds)

Evaluate Activity 3–2–1 Exit Ticket.

Fig. 7.1 Student performing her chosen motion for flower

Fig. 7.2 Student performing her chosen motion for power

- The final activity is an assessment. Students will individually complete the 3-2-1 Exit Ticket (written on a half sheet of paper in Appendix B):
  - 3 things they learned today
  - 2 questions they still have
  - 1 opinion about the lesson.

Suggested time frame	70 min
Equipment/technology	Computer and projector; access to the internet
Materials	• Brown or white paper lunch bags (one per student) • Cut out pictures of flower (one per student) • Cheetos (6–10 per student) • Hand sanitizer • Water spray bottle and paper towels (one per table or group) • Student Explanation of Activity handout (one per student) • Yo, I'm a Flower Rap written on chart paper (one per class) • 3-2-1 Exit Ticket (one per student) (Appendix B)
Start/stop signals	The teacher will tell the students that their signal today to stop what they are doing, get still, quiet, with eyes and attention toward the teacher is: **BEES LOVE HONEY** The teacher will say **BEES** (and make a flying motion) **LOVE** (and put her hands on her heart) The student will respond **HONEY** (hug their bodies) When students hear "bees love honey" they should model the motion for this phrase
Skill cues	• The teacher will model to the students that when they are taking one step to the right and clap, step to the left and clap, they are to take a step about the length of their bodies • When they clap their hands, they are to do so loud enough to make a noise but not so loud to hurt their ears
Safety Cues	During both the opening song and the rap performances, students need to be aware that they don't accidentally bump into each other while they are moving and dancing
Teaching Style	Cooperative learning, small group
Assessment	3–2–1 Exit ticket 3 things I learned 2 questions I still have 1 opinion about the lesson
Format of assessment	Half page sheet that the students complete individually
Modifications	• Students who are unable to get out of their seats for the engage activity can clap along with the class. If able, they can move their shoulders and head with the music • Students who struggle with writing could have a word bank on their explain activity handout with the following vocabulary: pollen, nectar, flower
Transition activities	Students will need to wash their hands between the explore and explain activities

(continued)

(continued)

Supplemental resources	• Pollinator activity book: http://www.life.illinois.edu/entomology/ pollinators/docs/Pollination%20Activity%20Book.pdf • What is pollination? – http://www.edenproject.com/learn/for-everyone/what-is-pollination-a-diagram-for-kids • Bees Pollinating http://beespollinating.weebly.com/uploads/1/4/0/ 9/14096894/whats_the_buzz_on_bees_materials_.pdf • PowerPoint on Plants, Flowers, and Pollination: https://www.tes. com/teaching-resource/plants-flowers-and-pollination-powerpoint-6257344

Earth Science Lesson Plan: Weather Wise

Suggested Grade Level: Kindergarten
Lesson Overview

Engage Activity (10 min) Weather Words and What They Mean video with movement (based on the book by Gail Gibbons).

Transition Students line up to get ready for their weather walk.

Explore Activity (20 min) Weather walk.

Transition Students come back into the classroom and find their seats. The teacher will lead the students in a stretch to the sky. Then the teacher will tell them to stand on their toes and see if their hands can touch the clouds.

Explain Activity (15 min) Weather Word Illustration.

Elaborate Activity (15 min) Weather Charades.

Evaluate Activity (10 min) Weather Forecasting.

Next-generation science standards	
Disciplinary core ideas	Weather and climate • Weather is the combination of sunlight, wind, snow, or rain, and temperature in a particular region at a particular time. People measure these conditions to describe and record the weather and to notice patterns over time (K-ESS2-1)
Cross-cutting concepts	Patterns • Patterns in the natural world can be observed, used to describe phenomena, and used as evidence (K-ESS2-1)
Science and engineering practices	Analyzing and interpreting data • Use observations (firsthand or from media) to describe patterns in the natural world in order to answer scientific questions (K-ESS2-1)

(continued)

(continued)

Next-generation science standards	
Performance expectation	Use and share observations of local weather conditions to describe patterns over time (K-ESS2-1)
CCSS	With prompting and support, ask and answer questions about unknown words in a text. We need to add these standards to each of the lesson plans (CCSS.ELA-LITERACY.RI.K.4)
Goals	Students will use movement and their five senses to make observations about today's weather and to act out key vocabulary words
Objectives	1. Students will take a weather walk 2. Students will use their observations about the weather to make predictions 3. Students will expand their weather word vocabulary

Detailed Description of Lesson

Activity Preparation

- The teacher will need to have a calendar where the class records the weather daily. It could be a pocket chart calendar, done on a whiteboard that's saved daily, or on chart paper. See Fig. 7.3, an example of a commercial calendar but it certainly can be teacher made.
- The teacher should create a designated space for the actors for the charades game and a place where the audience members sit. The teacher can use painter's tape to delineate where the "stage" is for the actors during the game.
- The class will daily record what the sky looks like (sunny, cloudy, rainy) and they will also record the temperature as very hot, hot, warm, cool, cold, and very cold.
- The teacher also may want to have a simple bar graph to display this data.

Fig. 7.3 Commercial pocket chart weather calendar

Engage Activity Weather Words and What They Mean.

- The teacher tells the class they will be watching a video of the book *Weather Words and What They Mean* by Gail Gibbons. The video can be found here: https://www.youtube.com/watch?v=UeJohy6cHl4
- Tell students that they will be reading lots and lots of weather words. Ask them what weather words they already know. The teacher will record on chart paper the weather words they already know.
- The teacher then tells the class to see if they could remember three new words by the end of the video. The teacher tells the students that as the video introduces new weather words, they are going to imitate the movements made by the teacher.
- Teacher shows the video. As each new word is introduced, the teacher will create a simple motion to express that word kinesthetically. The teacher asks the students to stand and instructs them to imitate the movements as s/he does them. See Fig. 7.4 for examples of motions.
- After the video, ask for volunteers to record new words that the students remember and add them to the list.

Transition Tell the students it is time to get their meteorologist hats on. The class has already talked about being meteorologists as they go on their daily walk to observe the sky and the weather.

Explore Activity

- The class will go on a weather walk. This can be a 10–15 min walk outside around the school campus. Students may or may not need to put on their jackets depending on the temperature.
- Once the class is outside, the teacher asks the students to make observations. The teacher reminds students to use their five senses to make observations:

  - **What do you see?** (clouds, rain, and sunshine)
  - **What do you feel?** (wind and air temperature)
  - **What do you smell?** (smell of fresh rain)
  - **What do you hear?** (leaves blowing in the wind or crunching under my feet).

Transition Students will take off their jackets (if necessary) and return to their seats. The teacher will lead the students in a stretch to the sky. Then they will stand on their toes and see if their hands can touch the clouds.

Explain Activity

- Each student will get one word to illustrate on an index card. The teacher can choose from the following words (based on the background knowledge and

Weather Word	Motion
Lightning	Make a big lightning symbol with your hand moving across your body and bending your knees.
Wind	Both hands sway from side to side.
Tornado	The teacher will make a funnel motion using the whole body. The teacher will start by making a large circle with both hands above the head. Continue to make slightly smaller circles with your hands. The circles will get smaller and smaller as you bend your knees. Finally both hands will touch the ground as the funnel cloud touches down.
Rain	Start with hands above the head with fingers spread apart. Wiggle your fingers and slowly move hands down until they rest on both sides of the body.
Fog	Put your right hand above your eyes as if you are searching for someone. Shift the weight of your body from left to right. (Movement will be similar to a side lunge to the left, then right.)

Fig. 7.4 Weather Motions

level of understanding of her students): temperature, sun, rain, snow, dew, evaporate, frost, thunderstorm, cloud, drop, shower, cumulus, cirrus, tornado, air pressure, wind, winter, summer, fog, drizzle, shower, electricity, rainbow, hail, and hurricane.

- The teacher can use a combination of allowing students to choose their own word (from generated list) or assign students words. The teacher should have some pictures/poster/books to help the students as they do this activity.

- Once the students have had time to draw their pictures and write the word, they will share their illustrations with the class. (These words can be added to a class word wall.)

Elaborate Activity Weather Charades.

- Teacher will create charade cards using the words introduced in the video (see Fig. 7.5). On each card, teacher will write the word and add a picture to represent the word. Several of the words from the book can be downloaded: http:// prekinders.wpengine.netdna-cdn.com/wp-content/uploads/2015/02/weather-word-cards.pdf.
- Students will be put in groups of two or three. Each group will be handed one card. They will have 2 min to discuss with their partners how they will act out the word.
- One group of actors will stand and dramatize their word while the rest of the class should be seated on the floor. The students will act out their weather word without using any words. The students on the floor will call out the word that they think their classmate is dramatizing.
- The teacher can set a timer for 60 s. If the class has not guessed within this time, the students can reveal the word.
- The class can keep track of how long it took them to guess each word.

Evaluate Activity

- The lesson ends with the students completing a Weather Forecast sheet. Before they begin this activity independently, the teacher directs their attention to the class calendar.
- The teacher asks the following questions:
  - **Does anyone remember what the weather was like yesterday?**
  - **How did you know that?** (We recorded that data on the calendar yesterday.)

temperature	air pressure	moisture	wind	cloud	dew
frost	Fog	drizzle	shower	rain	flood
thunderstorm	thunder	lightning	rainbow	snow	snowflake
sleet	blizzard	hail	wind	tornado	hurricane

Fig. 7.5 Weather words

– **What is the weather like today?** (The teacher will then record on a class calendar.)

• **Today you are going to be making a weather forecast about tomorrow's weather. Why do you think it's important to forecast the weather?** (Prepare activities, know what to wear, umbrella?)

• Students then independently complete the evaluation activity Appendix B.

Suggested time frame	70 min
Equipment/technology	Computer and projector; access to the internet
Materials	• Index cards (2 per student) • Weather Calendar • Weather Forecasting handout (1 per student) in Appendix B
Start/stop signals	The teacher will say, "It's raining, it's pouring." The students will respond, "The old man is snoring." The class with the teacher will then make a snoring sound progressively getting quieter until they are quiet and looking at the teacher
Skill cues	Students are reminded that they are meteorologists when they take their walk. This is not recess where they can run freely. They are to remain quiet outside so that they can make observations
Safety cues	Students can easily get excited during charades. The actor needs to be reminded to remain on stage (area designated with tape or some other way). The audience members/charade guessers need to stay in the audience section which the teacher will clearly explain prior to the beginning of the activity
Teaching style	Guided discovery, Whole group
Assessment	Weather forecasting
Format of assessment	Handout where students predict tomorrow's weather
Modifications	Students in kindergarten have varying writing abilities. For students who still struggle with letter formation, giving them dotted words for the evaluation activity that they can trace will be helpful. More proficient students should be encouraged to write a complete sentence when they are forecasting the weather
Transition activities	Students will need to line up before and after their walk. Depending on the weather, they may need to put on their jackets. The teacher will lead the students in a stretch to the sky. The teacher will tell them to stand on their toes and see if their hands can touch the clouds
Supplemental resources	• http://betterlesson.com/next_gen_science/browse/2059/ngss-k-ess2-1-use-and-share-observations-of-local-weather-conditions-to-describe-patterns-over-time • Oh Say Can You Say, What's the Weather Today? By Tish Rabe • http://www.elementary-educator.com/lesson_plan_day_1_weather_unit.pdf

Physical Science Lesson Plan: Let There Be Light

Suggested Grade Level: first grade
Lesson Overview

Engage Activity (10 min) Bear's Shadow read aloud.

Transition Students will move from the carpet where they heard their read aloud to table groups for science investigations.

Explore Activity (20 min) Light investigations.

Transition Groups will have their materials managers return the flashlights and objects to their teacher. The rest of the group will make sure that their desk/table is cleared.

Explain Activity (15 min) Light Foldable.

Elaborate Activity (10 min) Walk to the Light.

Evaluate Activity (5 min) Hand Signals.

Next-generation science standards	
Disciplinary core ideas	Electromagnetic Radiation • Some materials allow light to pass through them, others allow only some light through and others block all the light and create a dark shadow on any surface beyond them, where the light cannot reach. Mirrors can be used to redirect a light beam. (1-PS4-3)
Cross-cutting concepts	Cause and effect • Simple tests can be designed to gather evidence to support or refute student ideas about causes. (1-PS4-1), (1-PS4-2), (1-PS4-3)
Science and engineering practices	Planning and carrying out investigations • Plan and conduct investigations collaboratively to produce data to serve as the basis for evidence to answer a question (1-PS4-1), (1-PS4-3)
Performance expectation	Plan and conduct an investigation to determine the effect of placing objects made with different materials in the path of a beam of light (1-PS4-3)
CCSS	Ask and answer questions about key details in a text read aloud or information presented orally or through other media (CCSS. ELA-LITERACY.SL.1.2)
Objective	Students will conduct an experiment and draw conclusions about what objects allow light to pass through them
Goals	i. Student will make predictions about how light will move through different objects
	ii. Students will use the vocabulary terms transparent, translucent, and opaque to describe how light moves through objects

Detailed Description of Lesson

Activity Preparation:

- The teacher will write the following three words and definitions either on chart paper or a whiteboard:

    - Transparent—lets all light through
    - Translucent—lets some light through
    - Opaque—lets no light through

- The teacher will need to collect four objects for each group (at least one transparent, one opaque, and one translucent). Suggestions include magnifying lens, water bottle, rock, and book.
- The teacher will need to prepare squares of aluminum foil, wax paper, and plastic wrap for foldable activity.
- The teacher will need to print and cut out cards for the last two activities.
- The teacher will need to make signs on construction paper, cardstock, or poster board labeled: OPAQUE, TRANSPARENT, TRANSLUCENT

Engage Activity Bear's Shadow.

1. The teacher will be reading the book Bear's *Shadow* by Frank Asch. The teacher may choose to read the picture book or use this YouTube video: https://www.youtube.com/watch?v=DDnCGqwOdv0
2. The teacher tells the student that Bear has a problem in this story. Their job is to figure out what Bear's problem is and how he solves it.
3. After the story is read, the teacher asks the following questions:

    a. **What was Bear's problem?** (he couldn't get rid of his shadow)
    b. **What did Bear try to do to get rid of his shadow?** (shut the door, nail it down)
    c. **What finally made Bear's shadow go away?** (when the sun went down)
    d. **What was the source of light in the story?** (the sun)
    e. **What deal did Bear make with his shadow?** (that the shadow could go fishing and they would each catch a fish)

4. The teacher will introduce students to three new vocabulary words: transparent, translucent, and opaque. The teacher says each word and asks for a volunteer to read the definition. The class claps and repeats each word (one clap for each syllable).
5. The teacher then asks the class if they know that shadows are light bouncing off of opaque objects.

Transition Now that we got to hear about Bear's experience with light, we are going to do our own Light Investigations.

Explore Activity Light Investigations.

   i. The teachers tell the students that they are going to do an investigation.
  ii. At their table groups, they will find a flashlight and four objects: magnifying lens, water bottle, rock, and book.
 iii. The students will work in table groups to conduct their investigation:

    a. First, they will write the names of their four objects on their student lab sheet (see Appendix B).
    b. They will then predict what will happen if they shine the flashlight on their objects.
    c. One student holds the flashlight while the other student stands on the opposite end of the object as they test their objects one at a time (see Figs. 7.6, 7.7 and 7.8).
    d. They then record the results. They decide whether each object is transparent, translucent, or opaque.

Transition Each group has a materials manager that will return the materials from their investigation and bring back to the group the materials they need to create their foldable.

Explain Activity Light Foldable (see Fig. 7.9).

Fig. 7.6 Students test a translucent object

Fig. 7.7 Students test an opaque object

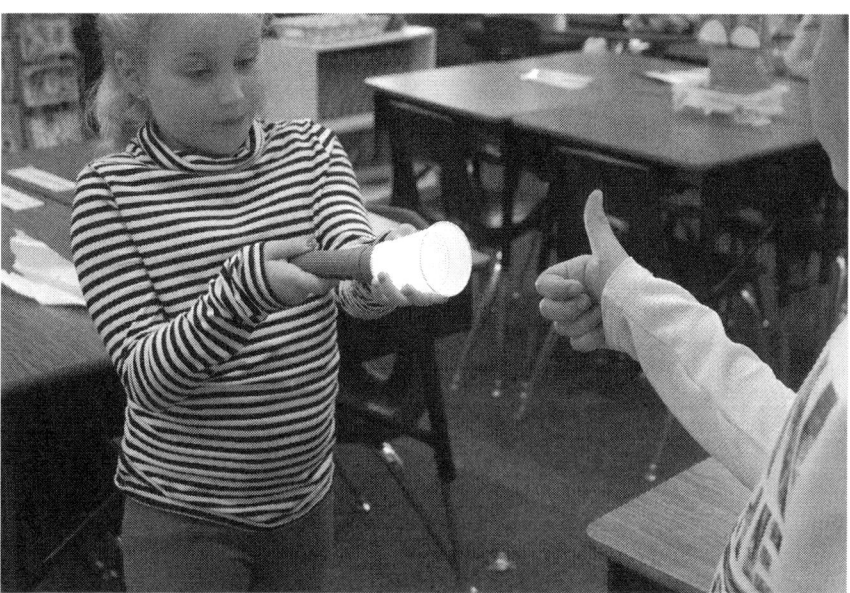

Fig. 7.8 Students test a transparent object

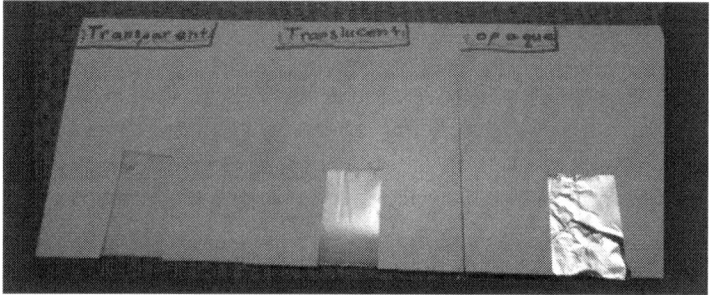

Fig. 7.9 Light foldable

- The students will be given a piece of white copy paper. They are to make one vertical fold in their paper. This activity will be done as a whole group. The teacher will be modeling and monitoring to make sure students follow directions.
- They will then make two cuts in their paper to create three flaps. The students will label the flaps: Transparent, Translucent, and Opaque. *Note* Teachers may choose to do steps one and two for their students to save time.
- They will then glue a small square of plastic wrap on the transparent flap (make sure to only put glue around the edges), a small square of wax paper on the translucent flap, and a small square of aluminum foil on the opaque flap.
- The students will then lift their flaps and write the definitions for each word underneath the flap.

Elaborate Activity Walk to the Light Game.

- The teacher will have placed three easily visible posters, each with a different: word transparent, translucent, or opaque, around the room (one on each end and one in the middle).
- The teacher will show pictures of objects one at a time. The class will walk to the sign that correctly matches the object: transparent, translucent, and opaque.
- The teacher will go through 6–8 pictures.

Evaluate Activity Hand Signal Quiz.

- The teacher tells the students that they have one last challenge where they will use hand signals to demonstrate what they have learned about light.

  - If an object is opaque, the students will put up their right hand beside their body, making a stop gesture since light will NOT go through.
  - If an object is transparent, the students use their right arm to make a big figure eight motion because ALL light will go through. The teacher will model this movement. The students should lunge to the left and lunge to the right as they

make their figure eight. If they want to make the movement even bigger, the students can bend their knees as they move their arm and upper body.
 - If an object is translucent, the students will move their arm from right to left but not bend their knees and only make a small movement to show that only SOME light goes through.

• The teacher will show the students 6–8 object cards and have the students respond with their hand signals.

Suggested time frame	60 min
Equipment/technology	Computer and projector; access to the internet
Materials	• Foldable (one per student) • Scissors (one per student) • Glue (one per student) • Squares of wax paper, saran wrap, aluminum foil (one per student) • Signs (one per class): transparent, translucent, opaque • Transparent objects (one per student): magnifying lens, plastic cup, or water bottle (one per group) • Translucent objects (one per group): thin curtain or fabric, sunglasses • Opaque objects (one per group): book, rock • Student lab recording sheets (one per student) • Pictures of translucent, transparent, opaque objects (one per class) – Pictures can be found here: http://fourthgradenpes.weebly.com/uploads/2/4/0/0/24006226/transparent_translucent_opaque_sort.pdf
Start/stop signals	Teacher says: "Sunrise" (and puts hands above her head) Students say: "Sunset" (and put hands to their sides)
Skill cues	Remind students that they are to use small walking steps when they play the *Walk to the Light* game. They need to be facing toward the sign and walk with their hands by their sides
Safety cues	Tell students that they need to be responsible with their flashlights. They need to be sure to flash the light only on objects, not in their eye
Teaching style	Guided discovery, whole group activities
Assessment	Group assessment
Format of assessment	Oral questioning
Modifications	Some students will struggle with being able to write quickly. The teacher may opt to already have the names of the objects written on their student lab recording sheet. The teacher could also choose to have definition pre-printed that the students glue into their foldable
Transition activities	Each group has a materials manager that will return the materials from their investigation and bring back to the group the materials they need to create their foldable
Supplemental resources	1. National Science Teachers Association (NSTA) first grade: light and sound http://ngss.nsta.org/DisplayStandard.aspx?view=topic&id=4 2. Read-aloud: *I See Myself* by Vicki Cobb

Life Science Lesson Plan: Circles of Life (Adapted from AIMS Activity)

Suggested Grade Level: fifth grade
Lesson Overview

Engage Activity (5 min) Flocabulary Food Chains.

Transition Students will go outside for the next activity. They will need to get coats (depending on weather) and line up.

Explore Activity (20 min) Catch Me if You Can.

Transition Students will need to move from outside to inside, putting up their coats and returning to their seats.

Explain Activity (15 min) Catch Me if You Can Debrief.

Elaborate Activity (10 min) Four Corners Food Chain.

Evaluate Activity (10 min) Food Chain Writing Activity.

Next-generation science standards	
Disciplinary core ideas	Interdependent relationships in ecosystems • The food of almost any kind of animal can be traced back to plants. Organisms are related in food webs in which some animals eat plants for food and other animals eat the animals that eat plants. Some organisms, such as fungi and bacteria, breakdown dead organisms (both plants or plants parts and animals) and therefore operate as "decomposers." Decomposition eventually restores (recycles) some materials back to the soil. Organisms can survive only in environments in which their particular needs are met. A healthy ecosystem is one in which multiple species of different types are each able to meet their needs in a relatively stable web of life. Newly introduced species can damage the balance of an ecosystem (5-LS2-1)
Cross-cutting concepts	Systems and system models • A system can be described in terms of its components and their interactions (5-LS2-1)
Science and engineering practices	Developing and using models • Develop a model to describe phenomena (5-LS2-1)
Performance expectation	Develop a model to describe the movement of matter among plants, animals, decomposers, and the environment (5-LS2-1)
CCSS	Pose and respond to specific questions by making comments that contribute to the discussion and elaborate on the remarks of others (CCSS.ELA-LITERACY.SL.5.1.C)
Goals	Students will use movement to simulate the interdependent relationships within an ecosystem
Objectives	(a) Students will identify the role that each living thing plays in the food web (b) Students will explain how energy is transferred within an ecosystem

Detailed Description of Lesson

Activity Preparation

- Teacher will need to cut ribbon or yarn long enough to fit around the students' wrists.
- The teacher will need to designate an outdoor area. If there aren't clear boundary marks, the teacher may want to use cones so that the students know where they may run.
- The teacher needs to spread pattern blocks or some other small objects in the playing area outside.
- The teacher will put the four signs up in the four corners of the classroom for the Elaborate activity.
- Teacher will have key vocabulary words on a word wall: producer, primary consumer, secondary consumer, tertiary consumer, herbivore, omnivore, predator, and prey.

Engage Activity Flocabulary Food Chain

- Teacher tells students that they will be continuing their studies of living things in an ecosystem. As they watch the video, they are to notice examples of producers, primary consumers, secondary consumers, and decomposers.
- The teacher instructs students to get up on their feet. Then, the teacher tells them that it's time to move. They may move in their place, however, they choose (as long as they don't touch a neighbor).
- When they hear the word eat, they are to make an eating motion.
- When they hear the word energy, they are to make a muscle.
- When they hear the words food chain, they make circles with their fingers as in Fig. 7.10.
- The class moves to the video: https://www.youtube.com/watch?v=ylNqv0E_Ge8 Flocabulary Food Chains.
- The teacher then asks or explains:

  – **What are examples of producers?** (grass, plankton)

Fig. 7.10 Finger circles

- **What are examples of primary consumers, animals that are herbivores or plant eaters?** (grasshopper, shrimp)
- **What are the predators they show in the video?** (snake, hawk, humans, bear, fish)

  A predator that eats a primary consumer is called a secondary consumer.
  A predator that eats a secondary consumer is called a tertiary consumer.
  What are two examples of decomposers? (bacteria, fungi)

Transition Students will go outside for the next activity. They will need to get coats (depending on weather) and line up.

Explore Activity Catch Me if You Can
Procedure for Game:

- Inform the students they are going to play a game of tag that will simulate a natural food chain.
- Divide the students into three even groups. Each group will be assigned a different color of yarn. Have the students help each other tie the yarn around their wrists in a bow that can be easily removed at the end of the game.
- Explain that the animals the students are simulating are represented by the colors of yarn. Students with brown yarn are grasshoppers, those with yellow yarn are lizards, and those with red yarn are hawks.
- Discuss the predator/prey relationships in this food chain:

  - Hawks hunt only lizards.
  - Lizards hunt only grasshoppers.
  - Grasshoppers eat only grass. (Represented by the pattern blocks.)

- Give each student a plastic bag to be used as a stomach and explain how the game will work (see Fig. 7.11).

  - Those students who are grasshoppers must gather pattern blocks from the ground and put it into their plastic bags.
  - The students playing lizards will try to tag the grasshoppers. If they are successful, the grasshopper is "eaten" and the contents of their bag are emptied into the lizard's bag.
  - The students playing hawks will try to tag the lizards, and get the contents of their bags.
  - Lizards and hawks may NOT pick up pattern blocks from the ground.

- For the animal to survive, they must not be tagged during the game and their stomach (plastic bag) must be filled by the game's end:

  - Grasshoppers—snack size bag
  - Lizards—sandwich bag
  - Hawks—quart size bag

Fig. 7.11 Student with filled plastic bag representing the stomach

Game Play:

- In round one, there are an equal number of grasshoppers, lizards, and hawks.
- In round two, there are more grasshoppers, but equal numbers of lizards and hawks.
- In the final round, there are more grasshoppers than lizards and more lizards than hawks.

Transition Now that the students have played several rounds, it is time to go inside and have a discussion about what happened in the game.

Explain Activity Catch Me If You Can Debrief.
The teacher leads the class in a whole group discussion:

- **Why did each round end?**
- **Which round was the shortest? The longest? Why?** (Shortest round was when there was equal number of primary, secondary, and tertiary consumers. Longest was round three. Energy is lost at each level so there need to be many more primary consumers than tertiary consumers.)
- **How do you think the game would be different if there was a larger or smaller area where you could run?** (Larger area—The rounds would probably last longer since it would be easier for the prey to escape their predators.)
- **How does the size of the ecosystem affect predator/prey relationships?** (the smaller the ecosystem in terms of square miles, the quicker the animals will be eaten/die)

- **How is this game like a real ecosystem?** (the predator/prey relationships are the same) **How is it different?** (Real ecosystems are much more complex. We didn't even have decomposers.)
- **Where does grass get energy?** (sun)
- **Where does the grasshopper get energy? The lizards? The hawks?**

Elaborate Activity Four Corners Food Chain.

- The teacher has put signs labeled: Producer, Primary Consumer, Secondary Consumers, and Decomposers in each of the corners of the classroom.
- The teacher selects one volunteer to count to 10 with their eyes closed. Students move around the room. By the time the volunteer is at 10, all students need to choose one corner.
- The counter then calls out one member of the food chain. If the counter calls out decomposer, then all the students who were decomposers sit down.
- The remaining students must give one example of the member of the food chain identified in their corner.
- The game continues until there is only one student left (or the teacher declares those standing winners).

Evaluate Activity Food Chain Writing Activity.

The students will be instructed to illustrate and label their own food web. This is an evaluation, however, we should encourage the students to be creative and create food webs other than the ones we have demonstrated throughout the lessons. See Appendix B.

Suggested time frame	60 min
Equipment/Technology	Computer and projector; access to the internet
Materials	• Pattern blocks (50–100) • 3 colored ribbon (green, yellow, and red enough for one per student) • Snack bags, sandwich bags, quart bags (one per student) • Cardstock signs: producer, primary consumer, secondary consumers, decomposers • Copies of evaluate writing/drawing activity (one per student). See Appendix B
Start/stop signals	Teacher says: "One, Two, Three" Students reply: "All Eyes on Me"
Skill cues	The teacher reminds the students to make sure they are looking up as they play the *Catch Me if You Can* game so that they don't accidentally run into another student
Safety cues	Students will be playing a simple tag game. It is important the teacher models that we tag our classmates lightly on their arms or back. The teacher will also remind the students before the four corner food chain game that whenever we are moving in the classroom, we use walking feet not running feet

(continued)

(continued)

Teaching style	Whole group activities
Assessment	Food chain writing and drawing
Format of assessment	Paper and pencil task
Modifications	For students who struggle with mobility, in the supplemental resources there is an online interactive food chain game
Supplemental resources	(a) Food chain online interactive game: https://www. sheppardsoftware.com/content/animals/kidscorner/foodchain/ foodchain.htm (b) Chains of life: http://eteamscc.com/2016/chains-of-life/ (c) Food chain song: https://www.youtube.com/watch?v= ttpNGJcpJ68
Transition activities	Students will go outside for the next activity. They will need to get coats (depending on weather) and line up

Earth Science Lesson Plan: Lorax Lives

Suggested Grade Level: fourth grade
Lesson Overview

Engage Activity (30 min) *The Lorax* Reader's Theater.

Transition Students will need to take out laptops or iPads if the class has enough for at least one device to every two students. If not, students will go to a computer lab or desktop computers in their classrooms.

Explore Activity (30 min) Environmental Research.

Transition Students will need to put up their computers and return to their original seats.

Explain Activity (15 min) Sharing Research.

Elaborate Activity (30 min) Making Environmental Posters.

Evaluate Activity (10 min) Environmental Poster Presentations.

Next-generation science standards	
Disciplinary core ideas	Natural resources • Energy and fuels that humans use are derived from natural sources, and their use affects the environment in multiple ways. Some resources are renewable over time, and others are not (4-ESS3-1)
Cross-cutting concepts	Cause and effect • Cause and effect relationships are routinely identified and used to explain change (4-ESS3-1)

(continued)

(continued)

Next-generation science standards	
Science and engineering practices	Obtaining, evaluating, and communicating information • Obtain and combine information from books and other reliable media to explain phenomena (4-ESS3-1)
Performance expectation	Obtain and combine information to describe that energy and fuels are derived from natural resources and their uses affect the environment
CCSS	Make connections between the text of a story or drama and a visual or oral presentation of the text, identifying where each version reflects specific descriptions and directions in the text (CCSS. ELA-LITERACY.RL.4.7)
Goals	Students will use movement to dramatize how human activities impact the environment
Objectives	1. Students will do independent research to learn about ways that humans impact a variety of environments around the world 2. Students will identify things that humans can due to positively impact their environment

Detailed Description of Lesson

Activity Preparation

- The teacher needs to gather materials for the poster activity.
- The teacher may need to rearrange the classroom to allow space for the students to move during the Reader's Theater.

Engage Activity: The Lorax Reader's Theater

- The class will read *The Lorax* using the following Reader's Theater script: https://www.sps186.org/downloads/basic/433305/lorax%20readers%20theater. pdf. This script has 15 parts (13 narrators plus the Lorax and the Once-ler).
- Teacher will assign parts to students. If the class has more than 15 students then the play can be read twice through with the remaining students being audience members.
- Students will read-aloud the script. As they are reading, they are encouraged to use their bodies to dramatize the story (see Fig. 7.12).
- The teacher can ask probing questions if the students are struggling with generating movement: **How do you think the Once-ler stands? Walks? What kind of look on his face?**

  - **How can you show the movement of the Truffla trees swaying in the wind?**
  - **How would the Brown Barba-loots move when they are frisking around?**

Fig. 7.12 Students dramatizing the "Once-ler" chopping at the "Truffula Tree"

- At the conclusion of the Reader's Theater, the teacher will then ask the following questions:
  - **What was the land of the Lorax like before the Once-ler arrived? Did it seem like someplace you'd like to live? What parts of your own environment would you be sad to see go?**

- **Why does the Lorax speak for the trees?**
- **How does the Once-ler's Thneed business hurt the land of the Lorax? What happens to the Swomee-swans, the Brown Bar-ba-loots, and the Humming-fish? How could things have been different if the Once-ler listened to the Lorax?**
- **What do you think the boy hearing the story will do with the Truffula seed that the Once-ler tosses to him? What would you do if you were the boy?**
- **Do you think the Lorax and his friends will come back if new Truffula Trees grow? Explain your answer. Where do you think they have been?**

Transition Students will need to take out laptops or iPads if the class has enough for at least one device to every two students. If not, students will go to a computer lab or utilize desktop computers in their classrooms.

Explore Activity Environmental Research.

- Students will explore three websites to obtain information about how humans impact their environment. Students can work individually or in pairs.

  i. Rainforest

     a. Students will explore the following website: http://www.ri.net/schools/West_Warwick/manateeproject/Rainforest2/interesting.htm
     b. They will answer the following questions to guide their research:

        i. How can mining for gold in the rainforest affect its ecosystem?
        ii. How do poachers affect the food webs of animals in the rainforest?

        What does the article say could happen by removing just one plant or animal from the rainforest? Why do you think that is? (Hint: Think food webs!)

- Coral Reef

  - Play game on laptop or iPad: http://www.ausarabexplore.info/interactives/coral/coral.html
  - Create a T-chart that includes 'Practices that are good for the reef' on the left side and "Practices that are not good for the reef" on the right side.

- Toxtown

  - Ask students to explore Toxtown:: http://www.toxtown.nlm.nih.gov/flash/city/flash.php
  - Have them go to one of the six locations: city, farm, port, town, border, southwest
  - Have students click on three different parts (for example beaches, boats, rivers) and record the environmental impact.

Transition Students have been working at computers. They need to put up their computers and return to their assigned seats.

Explain Activity Sharing Research.

- The teacher will call on partners to share their research from the Explore activity. The teacher will focus the discussion through questioning:
  - **What natural resources are in this environment?**
  - **What is the impact of removing these resources?**
  - **What are the causes of pollution?**
  - **What can be done to help lessen humans' negative impact on the environment?**

Elaborate Activity Making Environmental Posters.

- For the next activity, students are responsible for creating a poster that describes the sources of pollution and what they can do to positively impact their environment.
- Students will work in groups of 3–4 to make their posters. The teacher will provide markers and poster board.
- The students will then practice presenting their posters. As part of their presentation, they are to act out their solutions to positively impacting the environment. (For example: planting trees, picking up trash, riding their bikes to school rather than driving in a car).

Evaluate Activity Environmental Poster Presentations.

- Groups of students will present their posters to the whole class.
- After showing their poster, students will act out their solutions for how they can positively impact their environment.

Suggested time frame	Two 60-min class times: • Engage, Explore, Explain on Day One • Elaborate and Evaluate on Day Two
Equipment/technology	Computer and projector; access to the internet
	iPads, laptops, or desktop computers (one for every two students)
Materials	• Poster board • Markers • Copies of Reader's Theater of *The Lorax*
Start/stop signals	Teacher says: "POLLUTION" Students respond: "STINKS" (and they hold their nose and make a sad face)

(continued)

(continued)

Skill cues	Students are encouraged to use dramatic arm motions when they are acting in the reader's Theater. Before reading, the teacher can have the students practice standing on their toes and reaching as high as they can. The students will then practice getting as small as they can when they are trees coming down
Safety cues	As students practice their dramatization, they need to be aware of not disturbing other students and other objects in the classroom
Teaching Style	Guided discovery
Assessment	Group poster assignment
Format of assessment	Poster
Modifications	Students with more limited mobility can be encouraged to move the parts of their body with mobility or can try and move an object like a scarf, pool noodle, or ribbon
Supplemental resources	Lorax full-length play: https://sites.google.com/site/goinggreenstudy/home/teachers/text-and-media/the-lorax-the-lorax-play
	The Great Kapok Tree by Lynne Cherry https://www.youtube.com/watch?v=gw0arFtHeVw http://www.earthsciweek.org/classroom-activities/ngss
	http://www.seussville.com//games/lorax/
Transition activities	Students will need to take out laptops or iPads if the class has enough for at least one device to every two students. If not, students will go to a computer lab or desktop computers in their classrooms

Physical Science Lesson Plan: Puff Mobile (Adapted from an AIMS Activity)

Suggested Grade Level: third grade
Lesson Overview

Engage Activity (5 min) Zoom Puff Mobile Video.

Transition The materials manager will collect materials needed for the project.

Explore Activity (30 min) Designing and Testing the Puff Mobile.

Transition The class will all contribute to cleaning up their trash and return to their seats.

Explain Activity (15 min) Explaining the Results.

Elaborate Activity (15 min) Testing the Puff Mobile—Take Two.

Evaluate Activity (10 min) Puff Mobile Writing and Self-evaluation.

Next-generation science standards	
Disciplinary core ideas	Forces and motion • Each force acts on one particular object and has both strength and a direction. An object at rest typically has multiple forces acting on it, but they add to give zero net force on the object. Forces that do not sum to zero can cause changes in the object's speed or direction of motion (3-PS2-1)
Cross-cutting concepts	Cause and Effect • Cause and effect relationships are routinely identified (3-PS2-1)
Science and engineering Practices	Plan and conduct an investigation collaboratively to produce data to serve as the basis for evidence, using fair tests in which variables are controlled and the number of trials considered (3-PS2-1)
Performance expectation	Planning and carrying out investigations • Plan and conduct an investigation to provide evidence of the effects of balanced and unbalanced forces on the motion of an object (3-PS2-1)
CCSS	Explain their own ideas and understanding in light of the discussion (CCSS.ELA-LITERACY.SL.3.1.D)
Goals	Students will use movement (the force of their breath) to move a small vehicle
Objectives	• Students will identify what forces impact the movement of their Puff Mobile • Students will identify the cause/effect relationships between the design of their Puff Mobile and its ability to move • Students will identify the cause/effect relationships between the force that they use to breathe on the Puff Mobile and its ability to move

Detailed Description of Lesson

Activity Preparation

- The teacher will prepare Puff Mobile making kits: 10 straws, 4 mint lifesavers or small wooden wheels, 1 piece of paper, a roll of tape, and a pair of scissors for each group.
- The teacher will make one raceway per group. The teacher will use a meter stick to mark in 10 cm increments on a piece of butcher paper. This will make the testing activity run much more smoothly. The teacher should mark up to 200 cm. It works best to use the perimeter of the classroom or a hallway for racetracks.
- The teacher will borrow cones from the physical education teacher to mark the starting line for each raceway.

Engage Activity: Zoom Puff Mobile Video

- The students are told that they will be exploring forces that make things move. They will be building a Puff Mobile which is a vehicle that is made out of: 10 straws, 4 wheels, and 1 piece of paper. They will receive a pair of scissors and a roll of tape as well.
- To warm up their creative engineering and design minds, they will watch the first minutes of this video Puff Mobile—Zoom Sci—Zoom Into Engineering: http://www.youtube.com/watch?v=-Ovun2Yx4Qg
- Teacher will ask:

  - **What is an engineer?**
  - **What problem did the engineers in the video encounter?** (air blew back at them rather than moving the vehicle forward)
  - **What kind of things do you need to consider when making your vehicle?** (how to make the wheels even and able to roll, shape, weight)

Transition The materials manager will collect materials needed for the project.

Explore Activity Designing and Testing the Puff Mobile.

- Students will be told that they will be experimenting today, as engineers do. Their challenge is to design a car that, by blowing, will move the farthest. This is a cooperative group effort. Teams will be judged on how well they work together as a team.
- Students will be shown the materials they will have to work with and be given the student worksheet.
- They will be divided into groups of 3–4 students. The groups will have 5 min to discuss their plan. Then team members will have 15 min to construct, name, and sketch their original design (blueprint) on paper.
- The students will then be given their materials. They will have 15 min to construct their Puff Mobile. Students will have 5 min to estimate and record the distance that they predict their vehicle will travel and decide who will be the Puffer. Students can take turns puffing. They can also choose to have two students at once on their bellies puffing together.
- Students will have 5 min to time their trials. Instruct them to measure the distance traveled and record it next to the estimate. Students will be given warnings at 1 min and 30 s.
- Teachers may ask questions such as, **How can you improve your design for greater distance?** but cannot give any kind of direct advice.

Transition The class will all contribute to cleaning up their trash and return to their seats. **Now it is time to communicate your results to the rest of the class**.

Explain Activity Testing and Class Discussion/Explaining the Results.

- Each Puff Mobile will be tested. See Fig. 7.13 for a photo of the "test." After each test, the group will share with the class how they constructed the vehicle. Other class members will be invited to share what they noticed when the vehicle was tested and give suggestions for improvement.
- If it worked well, groups can be asked as to what they did to enhance the distance of their vehicle. Teacher will ask probing question to guide conversations:

    - **What were the forces that impacted the movement of the vehicle?** (friction, gravity, force of breath being blown on the vehicle)
    - **What reduced the friction?** (if the lifesavers were placed in such a way that they could roll easily)
    - **What increased the friction?** (too much tape)

Fig. 7.13 Students test their puff mobile

– **What else impacted how far the vehicle went?** (if the group took breaks between breaths, how deep of a breath and how close the student's' mouth was to the vehicle)

Elaborate Activity Testing the Puff Mobile—Take Two.

- Students will be told that they have a chance to modify and improve the design of their Puff Mobile a second time. Their goal is to improve their own previous group distance, during 5 sec of blowing. Students will discuss their sketches/blueprint for modifying their design again. Teachers will also award each group team points for working together.
- Have the students consider: What worked well in their first attempt? What did they learn from observing other groups? Did they think of any new ideas that they could try since their first attempt?
- The procedures from attempt one will be repeated: 5 min to discuss, 15 min to redesign.
- Testing will occur at the same time. Students will record their new distance.

Evaluate Activity Puff Mobile Writing and Self-evaluation.

- Students will use the writing prompts to reflect on their experience:

  – How did you change your Puff Mobile on your second trial?
  – What would you change if you had another trial?
  – What are you wondering now?

- As a whole group, allow students to share some of what they've written if time allows.

Suggested time frame	75 min
Equipment/technology	Computer and projector; access to the internet
Materials	• Plastic Straws (10 per group) • Wheels either lifesavers or small wooden craft wheels(4 per group) • Scotch tape (1 roll per group) • Sheet of paper, 8½″ × 11″ (1 per group) • Meter Stick or tape measure (1 per group) • Scissors (1 per group) • Puff mobile sheet (one per student)—see Appendix B • Stopwatch (1 per group) • Orange cones at the starting line (1 per group) • Butcher paper (2 meters per group)
Start/stop signals	Students will echo (repeat) a clapping pattern that the teacher initiates: two slow claps followed by three quicker claps

(continued)

(continued)

Skill cues	Teacher will demonstrate proper stance for "puffing." Get on knees or your belly and lean forward. The vehicles are most likely to move if the students get on their bellies and blow directly at the vehicle at the angle they wish it to move
Safety cues	Students need to be careful when holding scissors, moving with scissors and where they leave their materials. Students need to also be reminded to take breathing breaks (similar to blowing up a balloon) if they feel themselves beginning to get winded or light headed as they are puffing
Teaching style	Guided discovery
Assessment	Self-reflection and evaluation
Format of assessment	Journal writing
Modifications	Students with physical limitations may have difficulty getting on the floor on their bellies. They may still participate if the teacher can set the runway up on desks or a long table
Transition activities	The class will all contribute to cleaning up their trash and return to their seats

References

AIMS Education Foundation. (2004). Puffmobiles. *Popping with power* (pp. 114–119). Fresno, CA: AIMS Education Foundation.

AIMS Education Foundation. (2012). Catch me if you can. *Concerning critters: Adaptations* (pp. 196–200). Fresno, CA: AIMS Education Foundation.

Asch, F. (1985). *Bear shadow*. New York City, NY: Simon & Schuster.

Berger, L. Weather forecast sheet. Retrieved from http://betterlesson.com/lesson/resource/3224058/weather-forecast-sheet-3-pdf?from=email_bl_dd_lessonfile_1_name.

Brennan, B. (2011). Yo, I'm a flower rap. Retrieved from http://billybproductions.com/lyrics-yo-im-a-flower/.

Bydlowski, D., & Ribits, F. (2011). Pollination rock. Retrieved from https://www.youtube.com/watch?v=V5yya4elRLw.

Carlton, J. (2013). Transparent, translucent, or opaque sort. Retrieved from http://fourthgradenpes.weebly.com/uploads/2/4/0/0/24006226/transparent_translucent_opaque_sort.pdf.

English Language Arts Standards. (n.d.). Retrieved December 1st, 2016, from http://www.corestandards.org/ELA-Literacy/.

Gibbons, G. (1990). *Weather words and what they mean*. New York City, NY: Holiday House.

Moore, K. (2014). Puff mobile engineering. Retrieved from http://eteamscc.com/2014/puff-mobile-engineering/.

Moore, K. (2016). Chains of life. Retrieved from http://eteamscc.com/2016/chains-of-life/.

NGSS Lead States. (2013). *Next-generation science standards: For states, by states*. Washington, DC: National Academies Press.

National Agriculture Literacy Curriculum. (2013). Pollination experiment. Retrieved from http://www.agclassroom.org/ID/teacher/doc/materials/pollination_experiment.pdf.

Zoom. (2008). Puff mobile-zoom sci-zoom into engineering. Retrieved from https://www.youtube.com/watch?v=-Ovun2Yx4Qg&t=79s.

Chapter 8
Movement in the Social Studies Classroom

Angel Cartwright and Christopher Freeman

Abstract This chapter is about some of the benefits of incorporating movement into the Social Studies curriculum. The authors offer several movement activities organized around a traditional content-based approach to the discrete Social Studies, while the activities have also been aligned to the new C3 framework for ease of implementation. The Social Studies content areas included in this chapter are: history; geography; economics; government; citizenship; culture; science, technology, and society; global connections; and self and society.

Integration of movement into the Social Studies classroom can be mutually beneficial for both Physical Education and Social Studies, and should be considered a potential solution to the lack of time and resources given to both in the current standardized-test driven educational landscape. This chapter of the textbook considers positive effects of movement integration in the Social Studies content classroom, while also providing examples of how movement can be integrated into various aspects of the Social Studies curriculum.

There is an increased interest in content integration within the United States educational system (Lynott, 2008; Webster, Russ, Vazou, Goh, & Erwin, 2015). For educators desiring to see the academic benefits of a holistic approach to their academic content, mixing and blending of content fields has become a popular educational practice (Benes, Finn, Sullivan & Yan, 2016; Lynott, 2008; Orlowski, Lorson, Lyon & Minoughan, 2013; Webster et al., 2015). This cross disciplinary practice stems from societal and political influences creating an environment where content integration is necessary and beneficial (Chen, Cone, & Cone, 2011). One reason for the increased focus on integrating curriculum is the influence of high-stakes testing, which has narrowed the focus of many schools to standardized

A. Cartwright (✉) · C. Freeman
Midwestern State University, Wichita Falls, TX, USA
e-mail: angela.cartwright@mwsu.edu

C. Freeman
e-mail: Freeman.christopher72@yahoo.com

© Springer Nature Singapore Pte Ltd. 2018
S.C. Miller and S.F. Lindt (eds.), *Moving INTO the Classroom*,
Springer Texts in Education, DOI 10.1007/978-981-10-6424-1_8

test preparation, leaving little time and attention for the devalued non-tested subject areas, which include Physical Education, Social Studies, and Art (Berliner, 2011). Though there is no doubt that literacy and mathematics are crucial to students' academic development, a narrow focus on these content areas has caused a significant decrease in attention to content areas that are not deemed high priority; Physical Education alone has seen its allotted time decrease by as much as 35% since the implementation of policies such as "No Child Left Behind" [NCLB] (Berliner, 2011). This reallocation of priorities, and thus of time, discussed in Chap. 1, creates an educational environment that leaves preschool through grade twelve (P12) practitioners in search of other avenues of instruction. One promising avenue is the integration of movement into the content classroom. Movement integration into the Social Studies classroom, in particular, is a topic which deserves greater exploration, as both content areas have been negatively impacted by policies privileging other content areas. As time will be necessarily limited for both Physical Education and Social Studies, it is imperative that P12 practitioners capitalize on strategies that can increase students' engagement and achievement within the content classroom environment.

Physical Education has traditionally taken a back seat role to core content (Kirk & Kirk, 2016), and as a result of policies like NCLB, Social Studies is joining it; therefore, the resulting educational gaps must be addressed (Berliner, 2011). An important acknowledgement of this issue came in the form of the Obama administration's "60 min of play" policy (Kirk & Kirk, 2016). Kirk and Kirk (2016) demonstrate that 60 min of educational-based movement activities can improve students' knowledge in a content area while expanding upon the national movement requirements. Although the "60 min of play" policy emphasizes children's need for physical movement, the policy does not mandate sufficient time allotments for physical activity in schools compared to that of previous years (Adams-Blair & Oliver, 2011; Berliner, 2011). Though not a comprehensive solution, Obama's "60 min of play" policy acknowledge that the epidemic of childhood obesity is exacerbated by the mainly sedentary environment of the P12 classroom; the policy drew attention to the impact decreased Physical Education can have on students (Adams-Blair & Oliver, 2011; Berliner, 2011). The effects of the standardized-test driven relocation of instructional time extend beyond students' physical fitness. Berliner's (2011) study raises concerns that devaluing subjects such as Physical Education and Social Studies leads to a society with a generally underdeveloped citizenry. He argues that the decline in instructional time in areas such as Physical Education and Social Studies is correlated with a shift in societal values (Benes et al., 2016; Berliner, 2011). Thus, P12 practitioners should find ways in which they can ameliorate the deficits created by test-driven policies.

Integrating content correctly and without loss to either subject matter can be a daunting task for many P12 practitioners. As with technology integration, most P12 practitioners simply do not know where to start the movement integration process (Goh et al., 2013). This leads to many questions about the nature of integration and the validity of integration; however, in true content integration, the integrity of both subjects is maintained. One relevant method for achieving content integration is the content linkage approach (Lynott, 2008), which views the use of Physical Education goals linked with other subjects goals as a viable option in the movement integration theory.

Approaching Social Studies with physical movement integration holds the possibility of creating a more engaging classroom in which students enjoy increased levels of success while capitalizing on the limited time allotted for both subjects. When time is limited, every moment counts, and student behavior and task redirections can consume precious time. Integrating physical movement into the Social Studies classroom is beneficial in this respect, as students' ability to escape the confines of their desk and actively move during class reduces the chances that redirection will be necessary by the classroom teacher (Skoning, 2008). Increased achievement through enhanced engagement is in line with current educational trends, many of which are focusing on the idea of limited management through maximum engagement (Webster et al., 2015). Movement integration creates a whole new level of hands-on learning where traditional, and even some technology-based approaches, fall short.

As with any successful educational initiative, the primary goal of movement integration into the core content classroom is student success. Integrating movement into the Social Studies classroom benefits students physically by helping to bridge the gap left by decreased instructional time in Physical Education and can decrease the need for behavioral redirections. However, these benefits alone are unlikely to motivate most P12 Social Studies practitioners to consider movement integration for regular use in their classrooms. Because time in the P12 classroom is always short, practitioners cannot commit to strategies that do not lead to increased academic achievement for their students. Therefore, increased achievement in the core content areas should be the key goal of movement integration.

Movement integration enhances student understanding of Social Studies concepts by providing a concrete context in which to learn the sometimes abstract concepts that make up Social Studies content. In addition to providing environments in which students can actively practice applying their content knowledge in ways that would be difficult in more traditional methods, key concepts that are ingrained with multiple sensory experiences build a solid foundation for students to recall the content (Chen et al., 2011). These types of learning experiences are particularly important for concepts such as citizenship, which by nature is difficult to learn outside of interpersonal interactions. Thus, movement integration based in cooperative learning strengthens students' understanding of concepts like citizenship, while creating space in which they can develop characteristics such as self-motivation, self-discipline, and social skills (Chen et al., 2011).

Movement integration into the social studies classroom meets multiple needs of the P12 practitioner and can be a beneficial, positive mode of instruction (Chen et al., 2011). Benefits to students include attention to physical health (Adams-Blair & Oliver, 2011) and a positive outlet for tensions that can accumulate throughout the day (Skoning, 2008). These benefits, combined with the opportunity to learn and apply Social Studies concepts and skills, make a strong argument for movement integration into the P12 Social Studies classroom. Social Studies content in the United States is currently undergoing a shift as the National Council for the Social Studies moves away from the ten thematic strands to the College, Career, and Civic Life (C3) Framework (National Council for the Social Studies [NCSS], 2013). The change represents a paradigm shift from content-based Social Studies instruction to skills-based Social Studies instruction. This chapter is organized according to the traditional thematic strands, as most state standards still reflect a content-based organization; the section titles reflect the commonly used content wording, as follows: (1) NCSS strand 2, Time, Continuity, and Change, is discussed as History; (2) NCSS strand 3, People, Places, and Environments, is discussed as Geography; (3) NCSS strand 7, Production, Distribution, and Consumption, is discussed as Economics; (4) NCSS strand 6, Power, Authority, and Governance, is discussed as Government; (5) NCSS strand 10, Civic Ideals and Practices, is discussed as Citizenship; (6) NCSS strand 1, Culture, is discussed as Culture; (7) NCSS strand 8, Science, Technology, and Society, is discussed as Science, Technology, and Society; (8) NCSS strand 9, Global Connections, is discussed as Global Connections; and two strands, (9) NCSS strands 4 and 5, Individual Development and Identity and Individuals, Groups, and Institutions, respectively, are discussed as Self and Society. Though the chapter is organized around a traditional content-based approach to the discrete Social Studies, the chapter activities are aligned to the new C3 framework for ease of implementation.

History

Though only one of the disciplines that makes up Social Studies, the concept of history, dominates elementary Social Studies instruction and materials (Brophy, Alleman, & Halvorsen, 2012). Learning history helps elementary-aged students understand societies, the role of the arts and sciences in the pursuit of bettering societies, and the role of political action in the shaping of societies (Stockard & Wogan, 2010). In the larger context of Social Studies, students learn how contextual factors have driven historic events. Student learning is built on an increased ability to apply historiographical concepts, including causation, change and continuity, historical evidence, and contextual motivation (Brophy et al., 2012). The concept of chronology is fundamental to developing these and other historical thinking skills central to the Social Studies; indeed, chronology is the first skill identified in the History dimension of the National Council for the Social Studies (NCSS) College, Career, and Civic Life (C3) Framework (2013). The movement activity below is designed to meet these curricular goals while increasing students' physical movement. As opposed to labeling the chronological order of the Social Studies content events on an activity sheet or a smartboard, students apply the vocabulary as they reenact the Ancient Olympic Ceremonies. Multiple reenactments allows for reinforcement of key content as students are increasingly able to retell the story and apply chronology vocabulary in subsequent reenactments.

Activity Name: Chronology of the Ancient Olympic Ceremonies

NCSS C3 Alignment: Grades K-2

D2.His.1.K-2.
By the end of grade 2: Create a chronological sequence of multiple events.

Goals The students will learn the concept of chronology and apply chronological vocabulary to reenact and retell the historical roots of the Olympic Games.

Objectives The student will be able to: place events in chronological order while applying chronology vocabulary.

Suggested time frame	20 min, though each additional reenactment/retelling will increase the time frame
Equipment/technology	mirrored bowl—bowl wrapped in foil; paper towel tube torch; yellow scarf for sun; three sheets for priestesses and runner; projector
Start/stop signals	Count down from ten for students to get in their costumes and places. Say, "action!" to indicate beginning of the reenactment. Repeat each time for rotating through the groups. Say, "End scene!" to indicate the ending of the reenactment
Skill cues	Model for students reaching, running in place, marching, hands above head, passing the torch gracefully
Safety cues	Clear an area in the class for student performance so there are no obstacles to collide into. Students should stand at arm's-length for self-space. Remind students to keep hands and props to themselves
Teaching style	Direct instruction; reenactment
Assessments of content through the activity	Observational checklist—note when student correctly applies chronological awareness as described by the grade-level goals
Transition activity	Return materials to box, return to desks for extension activity (see Sect. "Geography")

Description of Chronology of the Ancient Olympic Ceremonies Activity

Introduction: Olympic Games

- Ask students what they know about the torch and what it symbolizes.

  - Make sure that students answers/teacher input includes information such as

    Lighting of the torch symbolizes the official opening of the Olympic Games. The torch travels from Greece to the host country because the Olympics began in ancient Greece.

- Give students a brief overview of the purpose and importance of the torch by referring students to the handout: http://www.olympic.org/documents/reports/en/en_report_655.pdf.

  - Direct student attention to the historic aspect on page 4.

Activity: Chronology of the Lighting the Torch for the Olympic Games Movement

- Explain to students that they will gain a greater understanding of the order of events that take place during the lighting of the Olympic torch (refer to the above link to the student handout).
- Divide students into groups of five and provide props.
- Ask students to read the story of the chronology of the torch lighting to identify individual roles in the lighting (sun, holder of the bowl, priestess who lights the torch, priestess who receives the torch, runner who receives the torch).
- Ask student groups to prepare a reenactment to retell the story of torch lighting, using chronology vocabulary (first, after, before, next, last).
- Ask student groups to present their reenactments to the class to check for understanding.
- Reinforce that we do the lighting ceremony in a similar way in the present because it was done this way in the past.

Extension If time permits, ask student groups to write short stories using chronology vocabulary.

Modifications/Adaptations Students with limited motor function can be assigned appropriate roles such as assigning a limited mobility student the role of "holder of the bowl."

Geography

Brophy et al. (2012) describe the complex field of Geography as "the study of people, places, and environments from a spatial and ecological perspective" (p. 125). In the larger context of Social Studies, students learn the ways in which physical environments impact, and are impacted by, human societies. As students proceed through the lower elementary grades to the upper elementary grades, they move from learning where things are located to why civilizations and landmarks are located in certain places (Stockard & Wogan, 2010). Because of the abstract nature of political geography and the scale of physical geography, Geography content can be difficult for students to comprehend (Brophy et al., 2012). For these reasons, Geography instruction should be as concrete and active as possible. The movement activity below is designed to concretize the concept and purpose of directions. As opposed to using pencils to interpret activity sheet maps, students will move around the school while they interpret a school map.

Activity Name: Olympic Torch Journey

NCSS C3 Alignment: Grades K-2

D2.Geo.1.K-2.
By the end of grade 2: Construct maps, graphs, and other representations of familiar places.

Goals The student will learn how to create and use maps of the school.

Objectives The students will be able to create and use maps to locate culturally significant locations in their school.

Suggested time frame	30 min
Equipment/technology	Projector and internet access; school maps; paper towel roll torches; large bowl for torches to "light" at final destination
Start/stop signals	Put finger on lips in "shh" gesture and open door to begin; close door behind students upon their return and have them store their torches in the appropriate place to end
Skill cues	Practice using fingers to trace routes on maps; practice slowly and quietly walking (fingers on lips in "shh" gesture)
Safety cues	Remind students to be aware of their surroundings when they are walking and looking at their maps; remind students to keep hands and torches to themselves

(continued)

(continued)

Teaching style	Cooperative learning, experiential
Assessments of content through the activity	Observational checklist: as student groups arrive, review map routes and ask for group supervisor input on group success in following the route. See Appendix D for a sample checklist
Transition activity	Return paper towel tube torches and return to seats, have students sit at their desks to brainstorm a list of culturally significant places in their town/city

Description of the Olympic Torch Journey

Introduction: The Olympic Torch Journey

- Show the video of Olympic Torch Relay to introduce topic: http://www. olympic.org/olympic-torch-relay.

  - A short clip of any leg of any Olympic Torch Relay is sufficient

- Give students a brief overview of the Olympic Torch Relay: http://www. olympic.org/documents/reports/en/en_report_655.pdf.

  - Focus on the routes and how they, and the locations highlighted, are chosen found on pages 6–8.

Activity: The Olympic Torch Journey

- Ask students to identify the school's cultural highlights (i.e., the auditorium, they gymnasium, the main office), the places the Olympic Torch would pass by if it came through their school.
- Ask students to mark the identified locations on the maps of the school.
- In groups, have students plot routes (see Fig. 8.1) that would take the Olympic Torch by a teacher-specified number of the identified locations that end at the same place.
- Provide groups of students (as many different groups as can be properly supervised) with a "torch" and have them follow their routes.
- When students arrive at the final destination, each group can add their "fire" to the large bowl, lighting the Olympic Torch.

Extension As groups arrive at the end of their routes, have group members make informational signs describing the cultural significance of each stop on the route.

Modifications/Adaptations Student grouping, supervision, and routes will be determined by student needs. Students with limited motor function can be assigned appropriate roles, such as checkpoint monitor at designated sites on the route.

Fig. 8.1 Students plotting routes on the map

Economics

Economics is the study of decision-making processes related to producing, distributing, and consuming goods and services (Brophy et al., 2012). In the larger context of Social Studies, students learn how individuals and societies have met their unlimited wants and needs with limited resources in a variety of places and times. As students proceed from the lower elementary grades to the upper elementary grades, they learn how "scarcity, specialization, interdependence, market[s], and public polic[ies]" (Stockard & Wogan, 2010, p. 169) impact the decision-making process. One of the primary concerns of elementary Economics instruction is the basic concept of producing, providing, and consuming goods and services (NCSS, 2013). The movement activity below is designed to use students' movements to demonstrate the concept of specialization. By selecting athletics, students are given the opportunity to be more active than they would if another occupation was selected.

Activity Name: Athletics as Specialized Labor

NCSS C3 Alignment: Grades 3–5

D2.Eco.4.3-5
By the end of grade 5: Explain why individuals and businesses specialize and trade.

Goals The students will learn that Olympic athletes produce a specialized service for their countries.

1: Draw a picture of Olympians training for their specialized jobs.

Objective The students will draw picture of an Olympian engaged in specialized training for his/her event and identify at least one service Olympians provide for their communities.

Suggested time frame	30 min
Equipment/technology	Projector and internet access; http://www.olympic.org/photos, paper and crayons
Start/stop signals	Say "action" for students to begin tableau; say "cut" for students to come out of tableau
Skill cues	Model tableau for students; lead students in practicing tableau with a game of Simon says
Safety cues	Ensure ample space for student movements in tableau; remind students to keep hands to themselves
Teaching style	Direct instruction, Tableau
Assessments of content through the activity	Student drawing—drawing should depict Olympians training for specific sports and include a service provided to the community
Transition activity	Return materials and create drawings

Description of Athletics as Specialized Labor

Introduction: Tableau

- Ask students if they know what a tableau is; follow up by asking if they have seen or participated in the mannequin challenge.

  - Student responses might include that they have seen or participated in the challenge, which involves freezing in place, holding a position.

- Show brief video of mannequin challenge compilations: https://www.youtube.com/watch?v=v7h5lYu7HEE.
- Explain to students that tableau is similar in that they hold the relevant pose based on a photograph, painting, story, etc.

Activity: Athletics as Specialized Labor

- Project a life-sized photo of an Olympic event that can be easily done in tableau (for example, a running race).
- Ask class: **What do you see? What stands out to you? Could you do this?**

- Ask several student volunteers to tableau (become the subject of the photo). Ask a student volunteer: **Are you having difficulty getting into this pose? Do you think you could do this in real life?**

  - Student responses to this round of tableau are likely to indicate that they can achieve the pose.

- Project a life-sized photo of one that cannot be easily done in tableau (for example, a backflip on the gymnastics beam).
- Ask class: **What do you see? What stands out to you? Could you do this?**
- Ask several student volunteers to tableau (become the subject of the photo). Ask a student volunteer: **Are you having difficulty getting into this pose? Do you think you could do this in real life?**

  - Student responses to this round of tableau are likely to indicate that they cannot achieve the pose.

- Lead class in a discussion on the specialized training required to be an Olympic athlete, pointing out that each event requires specialized training, even the ones that look easy, like running.
- Lead the class in a discussion on why people chose to do become Olympians, including personal and national pride.
- Lead the class in a discussion on how Olympic athletes' training and performances function as a service to their national communities, including national pride and notoriety.

Extension As time allows, ask students to identify types of specialized labor in their community.

Modifications/Adaptations Partner students (i.e., Think-Pair-Share) for discussion and drawing.

Government

Brophy et al. (2012) suggest that, for the purposes of elementary instruction, Government be understood as "the basic idea that governments provide facilities and services that people need but are too big in scope, expense, and so on for individuals or families to provide for themselves" (p. 166). In the larger context of Social Studies, students learn the ways in which the needs of people have been met by governments in various societies through time. When studying Government, students learn about political processes, behaviors, and decision-making, as well as governmental tasks, processes, and services (Stockard & Wogan, 2010). Though elementary students may struggle with governmental processes, they generally understand the purpose of government, as well as the ideals that form the foundation of the democratic system (Brophy et al., 2012). Fittingly, one of the first concepts that lower elementary students learn is the purpose of rules (NCSS, 2013). The movement activity below uses a sporting activity to demonstrate the purpose of rules in human relationships and activities.

Activity Name: Following the Rules in Olympic Events

NCSS C3 Alignment: Grades K-2

D2.Civ.3.K-2.
By the end of grade 2: Explain the need for and purpose of rules in various settings inside and outside of school.

Goals The student will learn the purpose of rules in Olympic competition.

Objectives The student will draw a picture of what might happen if shot putters did not follow the rules.

Suggested time frame	30 min, depending on number of students
Equipment/technology	Projector and internet access; http://www.olympic.org, hula hoop; balloons/balls; masking tape
Start/stop signals	"Ready, set, throw!" for each student to take turn as shot putter; two claps to get students' attention at anytime during the activity
Skill cues	Model shot putting with balloon/ball; have students practice throwing motions without balls Cues for shot put: • Hold shot in dominant hand, tucked under the chin (keep wrist and elbow tight) • Point opposite foot (of throwing hand) at target • Have the back foot toward the center of the circle • Squat and rotate body back • Explode toward target (explosion begins at hips, non-throwing hand is used as a guide and tracks the motion for the "putting" arm) • Release above head (up and out)
Safety cues	Make sure students and other items are clear of the throw zone; remind students to keep hands and balls to themselves After you throw, go get your ball and take it back to your line. Throw only into empty spaces, not at others
Teaching style	Direct instruction, Simulation
Assessments of content through the activity	Student drawing—drawing should depict disorderly, unsafe, and/or unfair sporting event
Transition activity	Return to seats and create drawing; share drawings

Description of Following the Rules in an Olympic Event

Preparation

- Gather required materials: hula hoop, inflated balloons (soft/plush balls could be used, as well), masking tape.
- Set shot put stations (see Fig. 8.2) up around the room in safe locations. Groups should be 3–4 students per station.

Introduction: Shot Put as an Olympic Event

- Show photos of and describe Olympic shot put (http://www.olympic.org/photos).
- Ask students **What do you see? and What do you think is happening here?**

Activity: Benefits of Rules in Shot Put

- After a brief discussion about the photo and the shot put event, organize students into station groups.
- Circulate among stations while students try to participate in the general idea of shot put, with each student getting a chance to attempt the shot put once at his/her station.

  - Note: Because students have seen only a still photo and have only a general idea of what the shot put event is, their attempts are likely to be inaccurate, with poor form and poor results. They are likely to ask how to do the shot put; for the purposes of providing two distinct experiences to compare later, simply encourage them to do it the way they think it should be done this first time.

- Show video of Olympic shot put (http://www.olympic.org/athletics-shot-put-women).

  - As students watch the video, point out good technique and the rules, such as standing in the circle and aiming for inside the wedge.
  - Refer to the skill cues in the table above.

- Direct student attention to the hula hoop and masking tape wedge already set up, explain the rules of Shot Put to students.
- Have students redo their shot put attempt with more knowledge of rules.
- Lead discussion on why we have rules in the Olympics and in class, focusing on the benefits of safety, organization, and efficiency.
- To assess student content acquisition, have students draw pictures of sporting events with rules compared to sporting events without rules.

Extension Engage in class discussion about the difference between equality and equity regarding rules, utilizing the Paralympics as an example.

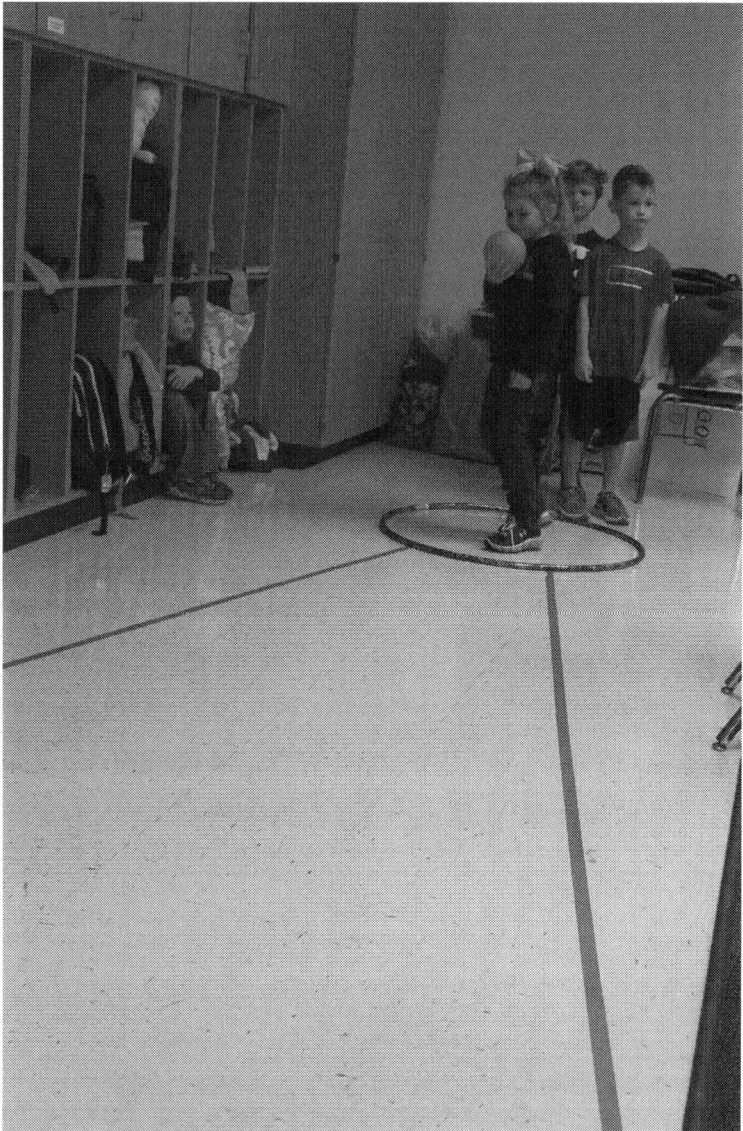

Fig. 8.2 Setup for shot put station

Modifications/Adaptations Students with limited motor function can participate with modifications such as varied ball size/weight, underhand throwing, or manipulatives to allow for alternate ways to move the ball.

Citizenship

Citizenship is related to the study Government; in the larger context of Social Studies, students learn about the rights and responsibilities of individuals in different societies. Students learn about the ideals of democracy in the lower elementary grades, and they learn how these ideals are put into practice in communities (Brophy et al., 2012). The concept of community is central to citizenship and civics education, as is the concept of working together for the common good (NCSS, 2013). In the movement activity below, an extension of the History activity above, students engage in a reenactment of the ancient Olympic ceremonies in order to investigate the purpose of the Olympics, both in the past and in the present.

Activity Name: Purpose of the Olympic Opening Ceremonies

NCSS C3 Alignment: Grades 3–5

D2.Civ.6.3-5.
By the end of grade 5: Describe the ways in which people benefit from and are challenged by working together, including through government, workplaces, voluntary organizations, and families.

Goals The students will learn how the Olympic Games serve the global common good by uniting communities in a celebration of human achievement.

Given a video and discussion on the Olympic Opening Ceremonies, the student will be able to identify how the Olympics serves the common good.

Objectives The students will be able to identify how the Olympics serves the common good.

Suggested time frame	20 min
Equipment/technology	Projector with internet connectivity
Start/stop signals	Count down from ten for students to get in their places. Say, "Action!" for dance to begin; say, "Cut!" at end of dance
Skill cues	Warm up as a class by modeling interpretive movements, such as rising slow from a crouched position to standing with arms raised to represent growth
Safety cues	Clear an area in the class for student performance so there are no obstacles to collide into. Arm's-length so no one hits another

(continued)

(continued)

Teaching style	Cooperative learning
Assessments of content through the activity	Paragraph on how the olympics have/continue to serve the common good by celebrating human achievement and interdependence
Transition activity	Return to desks to write paragraph

Description of Purpose of the Olympic Opening Ceremonies

Introduction: The Olympic Opening Ceremonies

- Show students a brief video of Olympic Opening Ceremonies Highlights

  - https://www.youtube.com/watch?v=jjt-c282q3A
  - Direct student attention to the focus on interdependence and human achievement, as well as the increased presence of dance, both traditional and interpretive, in recent Ceremonies.

Activity: Celebrating Human Interdependence and Achievement Through Dance

- Brainstorm a class list of examples of human achievement that required people to work together.

  - Examples can include going to space, building the pyramids, etc.

- Organize students into small groups and have each group select an example from the class list and compose a narrative describing the cooperative effort and the achievement.

  - An example from the building the pyramids might look something like the following:

    The bricks that make the pyramids are made of mud and straw. Some workers collect the materials and then others shape and bake them. More workers move the large bricks to the site of the pyramid. Workers move the bricks up ramps as the pyramid gets taller.

- Circulate among groups as they develop an interpretive dance/sequence of movements that reflects the narrative.

  - Require students to include specific locomotors (i.e., jump, hop, leap) or non-locomotors (i.e., twist, bend, stretch) movements at some point during the dance.

- Ask groups to take turns sharing their interpretations.
- When all groups have shared, have students return to their desks to write their assessment paragraph.

Extension Students can explore instances in which conflict impacted the Olympic Games.

Modifications/Adaptations Groups including students with limited motor function can design their interpretive movements to be accessible to all group members. Students can be provided with a scribe or complete an oral assessment.

Culture

Though it is one of the strands in Social Studies, Culture is itself not a social science. However, many of the themes within the social science disciplines of Anthropology and Sociology are found within the Culture strand (Brophy et al., 2012). Anthropology is the study of culture, with an emphasis on cultural universals as well as dissimilarities; Sociology is the study of society, which is both a reflection and creator of culture (Stockard & Wogan, 2010). In the lower elementary grades, students learn that there are similarities and differences in cultures, and that these cultural differences are represented in various art forms; in the upper elementary grades, this process of artistic representation is investigated, particularly the ways in which art can be utilized as a historical source (NCSS, 2013). In the movement activity below, students create tableaus in order to begin their analyses of the cultural elements illustrated in various Olympic posters.

Activity Name: Olympic Poster Tableau

NCSS C3 Alignment: Grades 3–5

D2.His.11.3-5.
By the end of grade 5: Infer the intended audience and purpose of a historical source from information within the source itself.

Goals The student will learn how Olympic-themed art reflects the times and cultures in which it is created.

Objectives The student will explain how the Olympic posters reflect the times and cultures in which they were created.

Suggested time frame	20 min
Equipment/technology	Computer with internet access—http://colorlib.com/wp/ history-of-olympics-poster-design/; projector
Start/stop signals	Say "action" for students to begin tableau; say "cut" for students to come out of tableau
Skill cues	Model tableau for students
Safety cues	Ensure ample space for student movements in tableau
Teaching style	Tableau
Assessments of content through the activity	Student groups create and interpret tableaus to practice creating and interpreting contemporary art
Transition activity	Return to desks to design posters

Description of Olympic Posters Tableau

Introduction: Olympic Posters

- Display an Olympic posters from the 1936 and 1964 Games.

  - Good examples can be found at https://colorlib.com/wp/history-of-olympics-poster-design/

- Ask students **What do you see? What stands out to you? What are some similarities? What are some differences?**

  - Student responses might include things like drawing/painting versus photographs, a focus on winning versus a focus on competing, people all look alike versus people look different (see below).

- **What do you think the host country in 1936, Germany, expect winners to look like? Why do you think Germany chose this visual in 1936? What does this visual tell us about Germany, and the world, in 1936?**

  - Student responses might include winning, pride, etc.
  - Student responses might include that the winners would look German, that the poster design reflects the rise of Nazism, racism, and/or fascism.

- Repeat with Olympic poster from the 1964 Tokyo.

  - Student responses might include competition, effort, etc.
  - Student responses might include that the winner could come from a variety of places and look a variety of ways, that the poster design reflects an increased appreciation for diversity and the developing world.

Activity: Design Tableau Olympic Posters

- Organize students into small groups and provide each group with an information sheet for an Olympic year and notable world events from the time period.
- Circulate among groups as they design a tableau of an Olympic poster for their Games (see Fig. 8.3).

  - Tableaus should include poses that incorporate sitting, standing, arm/leg/hand/feet/head positioning as appropriate. Student groups could also write a brief artist statement about their tableau to be shared with the other groups. Props could be created and utilized in tableaus if time permits.
  - If students have not previously done a tableau, refer to the introduction in the above economics activity.

- Ask students to share their tableaus with the other groups, and ask other groups to interpret the historical context of the tableaus.

Extension Project posters from the Games being discussed and ask students to compare and contrast the posters and tableaus.

Modifications/Adaptations Tableaus can be designed to be accessible to students with limited motor function.

Fig. 8.3 Students shaking hands to highlight good relationships

Science, Technology, and Society

The Science, Technology, and Society (STS) strand focuses on the ways in which scientific and technological advances, often precipitated by individuals, have impacted societies through time (NCSS, 2013). In addition to fostering critical reflection on the ways in which our current societies have been shaped by scientific and technological advances, the STS strand is also used to encourage students to think critically and problem solve about current issues and events; contextualizing both progress and problems associated with technological and scientific advances reinforces the civic duty of citizens to be informed about the forces that shape the societies in which they live (Hickman, Patrick, & Bybee, 1987). Because of its close relationship to other content areas, particularly Science, STS standards are frequently implemented in inter-curricular lessons. Additionally, STS's focus on change over time and the impact of change on all aspects of society and culture, including economics, government, and transportation, leads to its frequent implementation alongside other Social Studies strands. This type of intra-content integration is illustrated by the movement activity below, which is an extension of the Geography movement activity above.

Activity Name: Running the Olympic Torch Through Time

NCSS C3 Alignment: Grades 6–8

D2.Geo.7.6-8.
By the end of grade 8: Explain how changes in transportation and communication technology influence the spatial connections among human settlements and affect the diffusion of ideas and cultural practices.

Goals The student will learn how technology has and may continue to change the Olympic Torch Relay.

Objectives The student will describe how technology has helped change the lighting and journey of the Olympic torch.

Suggested time frame	30 min
Equipment/technology	Projector and internet access; school maps; paper towel roll torch; large bowl for torches to "light" at final destination; pictures representing barriers; drawing supplies
Start/stop signals	Put finger on lips in "shh" gesture and open door to begin; hold up hand palm forward in stop gesture at each barrier
Skill cues	Practice slowly and quietly walking (fingers on lips in "shh" gesture)

(continued)

(continued)

Safety cues	Remind students to be aware of their surroundings when they are walking and looking at their map
Teaching style	Experiential
Assessments of content through the activity	Barrier drawings
Transition activity	Show favorite drawing to classmates upon return to the classroom

Description of Running the Olympic Torch Through Time

Introduction: Running the Olympic Torch

- Show video of Olympic Torch Relays to introduce topic: http://www.olympic. org/olympic-torch-relay.
- Give students a brief overview of the Olympic Torch Relay: http://www. olympic.org/documents/reports/en/en_report_655.pdf.
- Draw attention to changes in transportation technology shown in video and handout.

  - Direct student attention particularly to the ways in which the Torch has traveled through snow, water, air, and space.

Activity: Overcoming Obstacles in Running the Olympic Torch

- Organize students into small groups and provide groups with a "torch" and a map to another location on school grounds.

  - Identify the classroom (starting place) as Athens, and identify the ending place as the host city for the Olympic Games.

    The host city could be the school's home city, or it could be the actual host city from a recent/upcoming Olympic Games.

  - Predetermined routes should be marked on the maps with each map following a different order while going by specified locations.
  - At each of the specified locations, place information sheets describing an obstacle or barrier that Olympic Torch bearers will encounter, such as a large body of water, mountains, desert, wind, rain, etc.

- Review the basics of interpreting and using a map.
- Instruct student groups to follow their maps through the school, walking quickly and quietly as they proceed from Athens to the host city.
- Inform student groups that they will encounter obstacles/barriers on their way At each obstacle/barrier, student groups will stop to draw a picture (see Fig. 8.4) of how their group would overcome the obstacle to deliver our torch to the Olympic Games' host city.

Fig. 8.4 Students drawing obstacles/barriers encountered

- When all groups arrive at the host city, return to the classroom.
- Ask student groups to share their plans for overcoming the barriers/obstacles on the Torch's journey.

Extension Students can research the ways in which the Olympic Games have helped drive technological and scientific advances in areas such as medicine, transportation, communication, etc.

Modifications/Adaptations Oral presentation helps students with developing small motor skills to demonstrate knowledge of technological developments that help with transportation tasks. Students can navigate smaller spaces if they have limited mobility and try to determine ways to navigate barriers when movement is difficult.

Global Connections

In part, due to the changes in societies brought about by technological and scientific advances (see Sect. "Science, Technology, and Society"), humankind must now face issues that are larger than the scope of the individual nation-state. Societies change at a rapid pace, and the impacts of these changes are known to and felt by societies around the world (NCSS, 2013). The Global Connections strand of Social

Studies plays an important role encouraging students to see more than the local and national context of their society. Globalization requires an understanding of our interdependence, as well as a critical evaluation of the costs and benefits of glob-alization (Risinger, 2014). Balancing the opposing goals of national interest and global priorities (Stockard & Wogan, 2010) will require citizens trained to engage in informed dialogue in pursuit of cooperation and compromise (Risinger, 2014), and the Global Connections strand provides context for developing these citizen-ship skills.

Activity Name: Impact of War on Olympic Games

NCSS C3 Alignment: Grades 3–5

D2.Geo.12.3-5.
Explain how natural and human-made catastrophic events in one place affect people living in other places.

Goals The student will learn how a natural disaster impacted the 1908 Olympic Games.

Objectives The student will research how countries worked collaboratively to help London put on the 1908 Olympic Games.

Suggested time frame	20 min
Equipment/technology	Projector and internet access—http://www.gettyimages.fi/detail/news-photo/scene-showing-bosco-trescasi-italy-buried-under-lava-after-news-photo/3333840#april-1906-scene-showing-bosco-trescasi-italy-buried-under-lava-after-picture-id3333840; blindfolds; toilet paper
Start/stop signals	Blow a whistle to begin the relay, blow whistle to end the relay
Skill cues	Model relay challenges • giving directions in blindfold challenge • wrapping in mummy challenge
Safety cues	Clear unnecessary furniture for manageable blindfold path Gentle blindfolding Hands at sides
Teaching style	Experiential
Assessments of content through the activity	Student discussion
Transition activity	Return classroom furniture Human chain relay to collect and dispose of toilet paper

Description of 1908 London Games: Coming Together After Adversity

Introduction: Relays

- Share with students that the 1908 Olympic Games were the first to feature a relay. In the relay, running, which had previously been an individual sport, became a team sport.

Activity: 1908 Relay

- Organize students into groups of four and have them model the two phases of the relay.
  - One pair of students in the group does the blindfold challenge (see Fig. 8.5), in which one student wears a blindfold and moves from the start to the finish line based on the verbal directions of his/her partner.
  - One pair of students does the mummy challenge (see Fig. 8.6), in which one student wraps another in toilet paper to resemble a mummy, after which the "mummy" student must navigate from the start to the finish line.
- Have student groups complete the relay challenges, then discuss the ways in which they had to help their teammates.
- Project a photo of the destruction of the 1906 eruption of Mount Vesuvius http://www.gettyimages.fi/detail/news-photo/scene-showing-bosco-trescasi-italy-

Fig. 8.5 Blindfold challenge

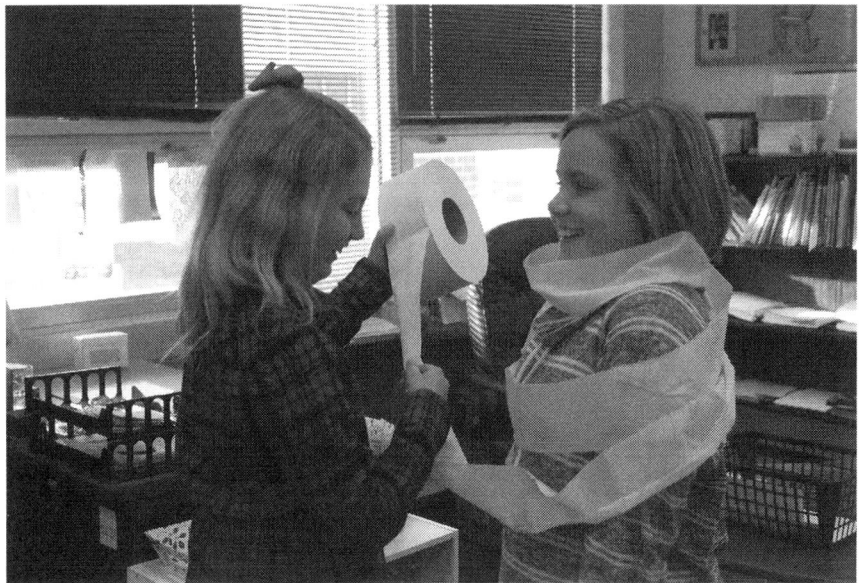

Fig. 8.6 Mummy challenge

buried-under-lava-after-news-photo/3333840#april-1906-scene-showing-bosco-trescasi-italy-buried-under-lava-after-picture-id3333840.
- Explain that the photo shows the devastation of a volcanic eruption that required that they Olympic Games be relocated to London.
- Explain that many nations came together to help put on the Olympics and ask student groups to research how the global community came together to put on the 1908 Olympic Games.

Extension Student groups can research ways in which the Olympics have been impacted by human-made catastrophes, such as wars.

Modifications/Adaptations Students with limited motor function can fulfill appropriate roles in the relay, such as the direction-give in the blindfold challenge or the wrapper in the mummy challenge. Teachers can also create relay movements that are appropriate for a specific student's limitation.

Self and Society

The Individual Development and Identity and Individuals, Groups, and Institutions Strands investigate the ways in which individuals and groups shape and are shaped by the societies in which they live. Though two separate strands, they both frequently appear under the auspices of psychology, sociology, and anthropology in P12 educational settings, (NCSS, 2013) and their central questions are intertwined. The central quest of psychology is intimately related to the societal context in which it develops; "identity is a complex intersection of individual experience and group socialization which has a profound impact on our perception of ourselves and the world around us" (Lynskey, 2013a). Because the socialization of the classroom, the first extrafamilial experience for many children, creates a context in which an intense, personal journey is made in and shaped by public interaction (Lynskey, 2013b), P12 educators have an invested interest in positive individual and group identity development.

Group identity development, the sociological aspect of the two strands, is increasingly important in today's global society (see Sect. "Global Connections"). Though some children enter their P12 education with an awareness of racial, ethnic, socioeconomic, and gender differences (Brophy et al., 2012), some children will not. Just as the P12 classroom is the first extrafamilial socialization for many children, the classroom can also be their first exposure to difference. The ways in which P12 educators facilitate these encounters and the understandings that develop as a result are an important aspect of developing students' multicultural competencies, as first experiences in these epistemological borderlands can have lasting effects, whether positive or negative (Lynskey, 2014). For these individual, social, and civic reasons, the Individual Development and Identity and Individuals, Groups, and Institutions Strands play a key role in Social Studies education, appearing as contextual factors and social goals (Brophy et al., 2012) in many content-specific units.

Activity Name: What Ever Happened to …?

NCSS C3 Alignment: Grades K-2

D2.His.4.K-2.
Compare perspectives of people in the past to those of people in the present.

Goals The student will learn how Olympic events change to reflect cultural changes.

Objectives The student will hypothesize reasons for the discontinuation of Olympic events.

Suggested time frame	30 min, depending on number of students
Equipment/technology	Projector and internet access—https://www.olympic.org/tug-of-war, rope
Start/stop signals	Blow a whistle when it's time to start/stop olympic tug of war

(continued)

(continued)

Skill cues	Model classroom olympic tug of war • lining up along rope • holding rope with both hands
Safety cues	Clear unnecessary furniture, or find a secondary location, for ample space Remind students that the rope is meant to be held, not wrapped around hands/arms/wrists
Teaching style	Experiential
Assessments of content through the activity	Group hypotheses
Transition activity	Organize student groups to return classroom furniture to appropriate places before beginning discussion

Description of What Ever Happened to …?

Introduction: Discontinued Olympic Sports

- Project a photo of Olympic Tug of War: https://www.olympic.org/tug-of-war.
- Share with students that Olympic events have changed over time, and that tug of war used to be an Olympic event.

Activity: Tug of War

- Organize students into two groups and have them take their places at each end of the tug of war rope.

  - A tug of war rope is a length of rope with a ribbon tied around the middle. An equal number of people gather at either end of the rope; at the signal they each pull until the ribbon crosses over the middle. The team that pulls the ribbon to their side wins the game.

- When student groups are in position, blow the whistle and have them begin the tug of war event.
- Stop tug of war event when there is a winner or 30 s elapses, whichever occurs first.
- When students return to their seats, begin class discussion on possible explanations for why the event was discontinued.
- Break students into small groups and assign each group a discontinued Olympic event.
- Student groups will hypothesize possible explanations for the discontinuation of their event, focusing on changes in culture that might have been influential.

  - Information on discontinued sports and events can be found at http://www.topendsports.com/events/discontinued/list.htm.

Extension Student groups can hypothesize on future Olympic events based on contemporary cultural trends.

Modifications/Adaptations Students with limited motor function can fulfill appropriate roles, such as watching the rope to determine the winner.

References

Adams-Blair, H., & Oliver, G. (2011). Daily classroom movement: Physical activity integration into the classroom. *The International Journal of Health, Wellness and Society, 1*(3), 147–154.

Benes, S., Finn, K., Sullivan, E., & Yan, Z. (2016). Teachers' perceptions of using movement in the classroom. *The Physical Educator, 73*(1), 110–135.

Berliner, D. (2011). Rational responses to high stakes testing: The case of curriculum narrowing and the harm that follows. *Cambridge Journal of Education, 41*(3), 287–302.

Chen, W., Cone, T., & Cone, S. (2011). Students' voices and learning experiences in an integrated unit. *Physical Education and Sport Pedagogy, 16*(1), 49–65.

Brophy, J., Alleman, J., & Halvorsen, A. (2012). *Powerful social studies for elementary students*. Belmont, CA: Cengage Learning.

Goh, T., Hannon, J., Newton, M., Webster, C., Podlog, L., & Pillow, W. (2013). "I'll Squeeze It In": Transforming preservice classroom teachers' perceptions toward movement integration in schools. *Action in Teacher Education, 35,* 286–300.

Hickman, F. M., Patrick, J. J., & Bybee, R. W. (1987). *Science/technology/society: A framework for curricular reform in secondary school science and social studies*. Boulder: SSEC Publications.

Kirk, S., & Kirk, E. (2016). Sixty minutes of physical activity per day included within preschool academic lessons improves early literacy. *Journal of School Health, 86*(3), 155–163.

Lynott, F. J. (2008). Integrating other subject matter without jeopardizing physical education goals: The content linkage approach. *Strategies, 22*(1), 10–17.

Lynskey, A. C. (2013a). *Christian literature and social justice: A literary analysis*. Electronic thesis or dissertation. Retrieved from https://etd.ohiolink.edu/.

Lynskey, A. C. (2013b). Occupy classrooms: Teaching from a spiritual paradigm. In C. Dillard & C. Okpalaoka (Eds.) *Engaging culture, race, and spirituality in education: New visions*. New York: Peter Lang.

Lynskey, A. C. (2014). Dominance, denial, and dialogue. In *2014 COPLAC Annual Conference*.

National Council for the Social Studies (NCSS). (2013). *The college, career, and civic Life (C3) Framework for social studies state standards: Guidance for enhancing the rigor of K-12 civics, economics, geography, and history*. Silver Spring, MD: NCSS.

Orlowski, M., Lorson, K., Lyon, A., & Minoughan, S. (2013). A tool for integrating movement into the classroom. *Journal of Physical Education, Recreation, and Dance, 84*(9), 47–51.

Risinger, C. F. (2014). Teaching about (and with) digital global citizenship. *Social Education, 78*(5), 241–242.

Skoning, S. N. (2008). Movement in dance in the inclusive classroom. *Teaching Exceptional Children Plus, 4*(6), 170–174.

Stockard, J. W., & Wogan, M. M. (2010). *Activities for elementary school social studies*. Long Grove, IL: Waveland Press.

Webster, C., Russ, L., Vazou, S., Goh, T., & Erwin, H. (2015). Integrating movement in academic classrooms: Understanding, applying and advancing the knowledge base. *Obesity Reviews, 16*(8), 691–701.

Chapter 9
Lesson Plans for Moving in the Social Studies

Angel Cartwright and Christopher Freeman

Abstract This chapter features four full-length lesson plans that incorporate the National Council for the Social Studies (NCSS) Standards. Two of the lessons are for lower-elementary; one lesson focuses on how scarcity necessitates decision-making, and the other leads students to create a chronological sequence. The other two lessons are for upper-elementary; one lesson focuses on helping students to distinguish between fact and opinion to establish credibility, and the other lesson will help students learn how to create charts for data.

Lesson Plan: Class Dash

Grade: k-2, recommended grade 2.

Lesson Overview

Preparation Set up stations in the classroom with small treats (small pieces of candy, small toys, tokens for the class store, stickers for the sticker chart, erasers, etc.). There should be around five stations, more than students can power walk to in 10 s.

Engagement (10 min): Class Dash Activity.

Transition: Students return to seats to organize treats.

Instructional Input (5 min): Class discussion over scarcity.

A. Cartwright (✉) · C. Freeman
Midwestern State University, Wichita Falls, TX, USA
e-mail: angela.cartwright@mwsu.edu

C. Freeman
e-mail: Freeman.christopher72@yahoo.com

© Springer Nature Singapore Pte Ltd. 2018
S.C. Miller and S.F. Lindt (eds.), *Moving INTO the Classroom*,
Springer Texts in Education, DOI 10.1007/978-981-10-6424-1_9

Transition: Direct student attention to the board.

Cooperative Activity (10 min): Team Class Dash.

Transition: Move to desks for discussion and exit ticket.

Extension: Have students rank treats in order of price to reinforce the monetary aspect of scarcity.

Closure: As you collect exit tickets, ask students what scarcity is; after several answers, reinforce that scarcity means not having enough of something.

NCSS C3	D2.Eco.1.K-2. Explain how scarcity necessitates decision-making
Goals	The student will identify how cooperation with others impacted scarcity, and thus decision-making
Objectives	The student will learn the impact of scarcity on decision-making

Description of Class Dash Activity

Engagement Power walk (see skills cues below) around classroom showing students what treats (small pieces of candy, small toys, tokens for the class store, stickers for the sticker chart, erasers, etc.) are at which preset locations within the classroom. Make sure students know which items are at which stations.

Explain to students that they will be allowed to get go through the stations getting one treat from each station they visit. Organize students into groups of four or five, and give each group 10 s to power walk around the classroom visiting stations; if the stations are close together, reduce the time so that students cannot get to every station.

Transition As students finish, have them return to their seats and organize their treats from favorite to least favorite.

Instructional Input Ask student volunteers how they decided which treats to go for and which to pass. Explain to students that when we do not have enough of something to get everything we want, it is called scarcity, and it requires us to make choices about what we will get. In this case, time was what was scarce. Ask students to name some other things that can be scarce and require us to make choices. Student responses could include things like money, toys, screen time, etc.

Transition Direct student attention to the question written on the board, "What would you do differently the second time? Why?" Tell students that they will be given another chance to go through the stations, but this time as a team. Ask students to think about the question during their second time so they are ready to answer the question when they are done.

Cooperative Learning Reorganize four to five students into a new small group and give them 30 s to plan their team approach to the class dash. It is important not to create teams until just before they do the class dash, as some teams would have substantially more time than others to plan if groups were all assigned at the same time.

Transition As each team finishes the class dash, have them return to their seats to do a team debrief on how well their strategy worked. Repeat process until all students have been part of a team. When all teams have gone, ask students how it was different and why. Student responses might include: they worked together, they did not have to get to each station on their own, they were able to get more treats, etc.

Extension If time allows, have students organize their treats from what they think is most expensive to least expensive. When they are done, explain that sometimes we do not have money for all the things we want, which means we have a scarcity of money. A scarcity of money requires us to make decisions about what we buy, just like the scarcity of time required us to make decisions on what stations we visited during the Class Dash.

Closure Redirect student attention to the question on the board and have them record their answers on their exit tickets.

Suggested time frame	50 min
Equipment/technology	Stations with small treats (small pieces of candy, small toys, tokens for the class store, stickers for the sticker chart, erasers, etc.)
Start/stop signals	3–2–1 countdown to "Go" each time a group does the class dash
Skill cues	Model power walking • heel to toe • pump arms
Safety cues	Clear unnecessary furniture, or find a secondary location, for ample space Remind students to keep hands, arms, and feet to themselves during the dash
Teaching style	Simulation
Assessment	Summative
Format of assessment	Exit ticket

Modifications/Accommodations Furniture should be moved and stations located so that students with locomotors aids have space to maneuver.

Lesson Plan: Head, Shoulders, Knees, and Toes

Grade: k-2.

Lesson Overview

Engagement (5 min): Simon Says.

Instructional Input (5 min): Head, Shoulders, Knees, and Toes.

Transition Simon Says students back to desks.

Cooperative Learning (10 min): Table group sorting cards.

Extension Class list of chronology words.

Closure (2 min): Review concept of chronology.

NCSS C3	D2.His.1.K-2. Create a chronological sequence of multiple events
Goals	The student will put visual cards into chronological order
Objectives	The student will create a chronological sequence

Description of Head, Shoulders, Knees, and Toes Activity

Engagement Play Simon Says with students in order to familiarize students with touching their head, shoulders, knees, toes, eyes, ears, mouth, and nose.

Simon Says A leader gives commands to the group. If the leader prefaces the command with "Simon Says" the group should do it; if the leader does not, the group should not.

Transition Tell students that since they are so good at locating their heads, shoulders, knees, toes, eyes, ears, mouths, and noses, you are going to sing a song with a dance about them.

Instructional Input

- Sing the "Head, Shoulders, Knees, and Toes" song, modeling the motions for each of the listed body parts. After modeling the song and dance, ask students to join. Repeat until all students are easily following the sequence.
- At the end of the last song, Simon Says students to put their hands on their heads (see Fig. 9.1) and listen. Ask students which body part they would touch next in the song; ask students which body part would be last in the song. Ask students if they know what we call it when things are in the order in which they happen.

Fig. 9.1 Students place hands on their hands during Simon Says

After a few answers, clarify that we call it chronological order. Have students repeat the word after you, breaking it down by syllable. To help students with the pronunciation, have them clap on each syllable. When students are able to pronounce the word, ask them what it means again. Repeat and clarify as necessary.

Transition Simon Says students to go to table groups. Introduce the sequence cards (paper squares with visuals of each of the listed body parts) by holding each up and asking students to identify the picture. Explain that groups will be placing the mixed up cards in chronological order, reminding them that it means the order in which they appear in the song.

Cooperative Learning Circulate among student groups while they sequence mixed up cards into chronological order.

Extension If time allows, have students make a class list of chronology words. Remind students about using words like next and last when we talked about the song, and then ask them to list all of the chronology words they can think of. Student responses might include first, second, third, etc., as well as next, before, after, finally, etc.

Closure Ask students what chronological order means, clarifying as necessary.

Suggested time frame	50 min
Equipment/technology	Picture cards for each group with: 2 heads, 2 shoulders, 4 knees, 4 toes, 1 eye, 1 ear, 1 mouth, 1 nose
Start/stop signals	"Simon Says" go to your table, begin, collect sorting cards
Skill cues	Model touching head, shoulders, knees, toes, eyes, ears, mouth, and nose
Safety cues	Clear unnecessary furniture Remind students to keep hands, arms, and feet to themselves
Teaching style	Direct instruction
Assessment	Summative
Format of assessment	Observational checklist of table groups' sorting
Transition activity	"Simon Says" students into next phase of plan

Modifications/Accommodations Students with limited motor function can point to the body parts on a picture.

Lesson Plan: Credibility Red Light, Green Light

Grade: 3–5.

Lesson Overview

Engagement (8 min): Students vote on a song to which they can dance.

Transition Ask students to return to their seats to discuss the songs.

Instructional Input (5 min): Explanation of difference between fact and opinion using sentences on the board.

Transition Tell students they are going to play a version of Red Light, Green Light.

Cooperative Learning (15 min): Two supervised groups read through a passage and play Opinion Red Light, Fact Green Light

Extension Students underline facts in green and opinions in red in a new passage.

Closure Ask students to which source was more credible and why.

NCSS C3	D3.2.3-5. Use distinctions among fact and opinion to determine the credibility of multiple sources
Goals	The student will identify facts and opinions when establishing credibility
Objectives	The student will distinguish between fact and opinion to establish credibility

Description of Opinion Red Light, Fact Green Light

Engagement Direct students to a list of three song titles written on the board. The song titles are your choice, but they need to be songs you can play for a class dance. Ask students if they like to dance and to which song they would like to dance. Have students vote for a song to which the class will dance. When tally is completed, play segment of the song to allow students to dance.

Transition Have student clap for themselves as they return to their seats.

Instructional Input Write two statements on the board: "Song X is the best song." and "We danced to song X."
Ask students which one is true. There will likely be some disagreement with the first statement; ask students to share their choice for the best song. Explain that the first statement is an opinion, which means people can have disagreements without anyone being correct or mistaken. Explain that the second statement is a fact, which means that it can be proven to be correct. Explain that facts are more credible than opinions, so sources that have more facts are considered more credible than sources with fewer facts.

Transition Tell students that they will be playing Opinion Red Light, Fact Green Light to determine which of two sources is more credible. In this version, when the sentence they hear is an opinion, they do not move forward, like Red Light. When the sentence they hear is a fact, they do move forward, like Green Light. Whichever source gets them farthest across the classroom has the most facts and is the most credible. See Fig. 9.2 for a picture of students participating in the activity.

Cooperative Learning Organize students into two large groups have them read and discuss a passage with a teacher/paraprofessional. One group should get a largely factual sequence of sentences, while the other should get a largely opinion-based sequence of sentences. Discussion should focus on the facts and opinions in each source. When the group discussion is over, have student groups line up at the back of the classroom. Each group does a round of Credibility Red Light/Green Light. When both groups are done, ask students to discuss which group's source was more credible and why. Student observations might include that the group who got farthest had the more credible source because their source had the most facts.

Extension If time allows, give individual students new passages, along with red and green markers/crayons/pencils. Have students go through the passage, underlining facts in green and opinions in red.

Fig. 9.2 Students participating in opinion red light, fact green light

Closure Ask students what makes something credible.

Suggested time frame	50 min
Equipment/technology	Speakers and a few songs of teacher's choice that can be used for class dance voting Two short sequences of sentences, one largely factual and the other largely opinion
Start/stop signals	"Red light" to stop an activity when it is time to transition to another
Skill cues	Model freezing for red light/opinion and taking a step forward for green light/fact
Safety cues	Clear unnecessary furniture, or find a secondary location, for ample space Remind students to keep hands, arms, and feet to themselves
Teaching style	Direct instruction
assessment	Summative
Format of assessment	Exit ticket
Transition activity	Groups remain standing in place during credibility discussion to reinforce difference between sources, then return to seats for exit ticket

Modifications/Accommodations Students with limited motor function can move a token on their desks.

Lesson Plan: Olympic Data

Grade: 3–5.

Lesson Overview

Engagement (8 min): Ask students to make class lists of their favorite sports and favorite Olympic sports.

Transition Show photos of your "favorite" Olympic events: shot put, discus, curling, and hockey.

Instructional Input (10 min): Model classroom Olympic events.

Transition Students identify which sport was your best performance.

Collaborative Learning (20 min): Student groups do events and collect data.

Extension Students hypothesize why some events were more successful than others and brainstorm adjustments to the event that might improve performance.

Closure Have students share their data tables and hypotheses from extension, if applicable.

NCSS C3	D4.2.3-5. Construct explanations using reasoning, correct sequence, examples, and details with relevant information and data
Goals	Given an olympic event simulation, the student will be able to organize olympic simulation data into a chart
Objectives	The student will learn how to create charts for data

Description of Class Olympics Activity

Engagement Ask students to name their favorite sports; keep a list on the board. Follow up by asking about their favorite Olympic sports, also keeping a list on the board. Tell students you have favorite Olympic events, too. Show photos/videos of your favorite Olympic events (shot put, discus, curling, hockey) at http://www.olympic.org/sports.

Instructional Input Model the classroom Olympic events.

- Shot put—trying to throw a balloon from inside a hula hoop as far into an adjacent masking tape wedge as you can
- Discus—trying to throw a paper plate from inside a hula hoop as far into an adjacent masking tape wedge as you can

- Curling—trying to get a Junior Mint as far down a table as possible without it falling off the opposite end by clearing its path with the toothbrush
- Hockey—trying to get a Junior Mint into a shoebox at the far end of the table with a bent straw.

Transition Have students vote on your best performance, then ask which they would like to try.

Cooperative Learning Adjust students into four roughly equal groups by sport. Pair the shot put group with the curling group and pair the discus group with the hockey group. Provide a data collection sheet to each student. Data collection sheets will be grids with spaces for students to write names and measurements, similar to the template below.

Event		
Name	1st Attempt	2nd Attempt

Model measurement and data collection process for students:

For the Shot put and Discuss: Use a string to measure from the center of the hula hoop to where the discus/shot put landed, then use a yardstick to measure inches/feet.

Curling and Hockey: Tally successful shots (made goals in Hockey and Junior Mints within one inch of the table edge in Curling) versus unsuccessful shots.

After modeling the measurement and data collection process for each event, have groups begin the events. Circulate and monitor as students compete in the classroom Olympics events. When each group has completed their Olympic events and collected their data, have students return to their seats to organize their data into charts by performance using the template below.

Event	
Rank	Distance/accuracy
1	
2	

Extension If time allows, have students hypothesize why some events were more successful than others. Then have them hypothesize ways they could change the events (change materials, change process, etc.) that might make the event more successful.

Closure Have students share their data charts, along with their hypotheses about changing the events, if applicable.

Suggested time frame	50 min
Equipment/technology	Projector and internet access—http://www.olympic.org/photos, balloons/foam balls, hula hoops, masking tape, paper plates, tooth brushes, Junior Mints, bendable straws, shoe boxes, data sheets, pencils, string, yard sticks
Start/stop signals	Blow a whistle when it is time to start/switch/stop olympic events
Skill cues	Model classroom olympic events (see instructional input)
Safety cues	Clear unnecessary furniture, or find a secondary location, for ample space
Teaching style	Simulation
Assessment	Summative
Format of assessment	Student charts
Transition activity	Returning olympic events materials, returning to seats to create charts

Modifications/Accommodations Partners for students with limited mobility and dyscalculia.

Chapter 10
Movement in the Mathematics Classroom

Dittika Gupta and Sarah Cobb

Abstract This chapter is about some of the benefits of incorporating movement into the Mathematics curriculum. The authors offer several activities aligned to the five significant Mathematics areas or strands represented in Common Core Standards that effectively integrate movement into Mathematics to benefit both student learning and physical activity. The Mathematics content areas included in this chapter are: numbers and operations, measurement, data analysis, algebra, and geometry.

Picture a math classroom. What comes to your mind? Are the students sitting at their desks silently working practice problems or are they moving purposefully around the room engaged in a learning activity? The traditional image of a mathematics classroom depicts students working independently on worksheets. Even though children, especially young children, learn most effectively by doing and moving, the stereotypical mathematics classroom is rigidly structured, still, and solitary (DeFrancesco & Casas, 2004). This image is changing, however. Recently, a great deal of effort has been focused on bringing movement into the mathematics classroom (American Alliance for Health, Physical Education, Recreation and Dance, 2013; Centers for Disease Control and Prevention, 2013).

As discussed in Chap. 1, integrating movement into the classroom can lead to the development of the whole child: physically, emotionally, cognitively, and socially (Adams-Blair & Oliver, 2011, Erwin, Fedewa, & Ahn, 2013; Hall, 2007; Hannaford, 1995; Norris, Shelton, Dunsmuir, Duke-Williams, & Stamatakis, 2015; Skoning, 2010; Theodorakou & Zervas, 2003). Many researchers call for physical activity in a mathematics classroom as a way to increase educational achievement (Beaudoin & Johnston, 2011; Coe, Pivarnik, Womack, Reeves, & Malina, 2006; DeFrancesco & Casas, 2004), on-task behavior (Mahar, Murphy, Rowe, Golden,

D. Gupta (✉) · S. Cobb
Midwestern State University, Wichita Falls, TX, USA
e-mail: dittika.gupta@mwsu.edu

S. Cobb
e-mail: sarah.cobb@mwsu.edu

© Springer Nature Singapore Pte Ltd. 2018
S.C. Miller and S.F. Lindt (eds.), *Moving INTO the Classroom*,
Springer Texts in Education, DOI 10.1007/978-981-10-6424-1_10

Shields, & Raedeke, 2006), attentiveness (Azrin, Ehle, & Beaumont, 2006), attitude (Beaudoin & Johnston, 2011), and concentration (Caterino & Polak, 1999) as well as physical activity levels (Erwin, Able, Beighle, & Beets, 2011). Furthermore, use of movement in mathematics classrooms may help students to develop procedural flexibility: that is, not only knowing multiple procedures but also being able to apply them adaptively to different situations (Baroody & Dowker, 2003; Rittle-Johnson & Schneider, 2014; Rittle-Johnson & Star, 2007; Star & Seifert, 2006; Verschaffel, Luwel, Torbeyns, & Van Dooren, 2009).

Though physical activity is only one of the many factors that affect learning, research provides strong support for integrating purposeful movement into mathematics classrooms. Various studies suggest the positive impact of integrating movement into the classroom through the use of physical actions, such as hopping, jumping, tossing, and other locomotors skills to learn skip counting and other number operations (Wade, 2016); building, sorting, manipulating, modeling, tracing, measuring, and constructing to develop spatial sense and understanding of geometry (Howse & Howse, 2014; National Council of Teachers of Mathematics [NCTM], 2000); use of gestures as a means to provide visual attributes to graphs for the students (Noble, 2003); or integrated physical rotations, such as students rotating their own bodies to develop understanding of angles and size of turn along with direction sense (Clements & Burns, 2000). Nemirovsky and Rasmussen (2005) examined ways in which integrating movement led to an increased understanding of mathematical notation and increased fluency in manipulating equations that further highlight the need to incorporate movement into learning of mathematical concepts.

Additionally, research suggests that the outcomes of integrating movement in the classroom include increased on-task behavior as well as increased comprehension (Block, Parris, & Whiteley, 2008; Lynch, 2007; Stalvey & Brasell, 2006) and increased motivation (Vazou, Gavrilou, Mamalaki, Papanastasiou, & Sioumala, 2012). Considering prior research on movement in mathematics, this chapter focuses on lessons and activities that integrate movement purposefully into the mathematics classroom and engage students in learning different mathematical concepts in a meaningful way. The activities are designed to incorporate math into every stage of a mathematics lesson. Some activities are designed for use at the beginning of the lesson. They aim to get students excited and ready to learn mathematics, or to activate students' prior knowledge. Some activities can be used to introduce new concepts through discovery or kinesthetically involved instruction. Movement activities can also be used to reinforce concepts, giving students physical intuition for abstract ideas. Ideas are also provided in the following chapter for using movement to break up the monotony of drill and practice. Some activities can also be used towards the end of the lesson to help students make connections to their learning and make it relevant and meaningful.

The activities and lessons in this chapter are divided into five mathematics content strands: Numbers and Operations, Measurement, Data Analysis, Algebra, and Geometry. Each strand starts with a brief introduction and is then followed with activities for integrating physical activity in the mathematics classroom. Each strand has two activities, one for lower and one for upper elementary classrooms. Additionally, activity sheets and extensions are provided to make the activities accessible and easy to use.

Numbers and Operations

The elementary mathematics curriculum significantly emphasizes number and operations concepts in order to build a strong conceptual foundation for later mathematical development. Three major themes are related to this strand: (1) understanding numbers, representing numbers, relationships among numbers and number systems; (2) understanding meanings of operations; and (3) computing fluently and making reasonable estimates (NCTM, 2000). The concept of numbers and operations is especially critical in early years because during this period, students strengthen their informal knowledge of numbers and move toward more sophisticated understanding of numbers, their sizes, relationships, and operations. In particular, knowledge of two concepts is essential: basic arithmetic facts and the ability to compute with understanding using a variety of methods (NCTM, 2000). Teaching techniques that foster these skills through differentiation are vital, and the integration of movement into the classroom may provide additional opportunities for practice and understanding.

Acquiring understanding of numbers and number systems through movement can help provide a concrete foundation on which a thorough understanding of abstract number concepts can be built. Utilizing engaging activities such as hopping, jumping, tossing, and other locomotors skills may help students to learn various math concepts connected to numbers and operations. For example, students may whisper a number as they perform each step of a movement, such as throwing a ball. This activity reinforces both the steps in the physical movement and the process of skip counting (Wade, 2016). Repeating this as students' practice, the activity leads naturally to skip counting. In this way, activities primarily focused on physical education objectives can also reinforce mathematical content in the numbers and operations strand. Specific programs, such as 'Encouraging Activity to Stimulate Young (EASY) Minds', a school-based intervention for integrating physical activity into mathematics lessons, offer activities to increase students' on-task behavior and decrease sedentary time learning (Riley, Lubans, Holmes, & Morgan, 2014). For example, one activity integrates movement through a variation of the "Macarena", and another activity teaches footwork patterns in ladders to review multiplication facts.

There are many ways to engage students in learning, but integrating movement can provide significant support in learning numbers and operations. The two activities in this strand suggest ways to integrate movement to facilitate a greater understanding of the order of operations and representation of fractions by introducing and reinforcing these critical concepts.

Activity 1: Operation Stations

Suggested Grade Level: 5

Standards
CCSS.Math.Content.5.OA.A.1
Use parentheses, brackets, or braces in numerical expressions, and evaluate expressions with these symbols.

Goals Students will practice evaluating numerical expressions.

Objectives Students will simplify numerical expressions using order of operations. Students will choose the correct number operation by moving to the right location to simplify the numerical expressions.

Suggested time frame	15–20 min
Equipment/technology	One card per student with an arithmetic expression written at the top; signs (see Fig. 10.1) for parentheses, multiplication, division, addition, and subtraction locations; pencils
Start/stop signals	Begin the activity by ringing a bell and then saying "Move!" To get students' attention or end the activity, ring the bell two times
Skill cues	"Share the General Space"—remind students to be aware of their classmates in parts of the classroom that become crowded "Move left to right"—students move from left-to-right in the classroom depicting the same order in which numerical expressions are evaluated
Safety cues	Remind students to be careful of desks and chairs as well as other students when moving around the classroom. Remind students not to run in the classroom
Teaching style	Guided discovery, independent practice (if done alone) or partner work (if done in pairs)
Assessments of content through the activity	Observe and actively monitor students as they move around the room to simplify the expressions. In particular, correct students who move from a later stage back to an earlier stage. Provide assistance when necessary. Make note of students who struggle and why
Transition activity	In order to transition, have the students return to their desks and explain the order of operations to their partner for any one of the expressions they simplified

Description of Operation Stations Activity The activity reinforces the order of operations by guiding students to physically move to locations (stations) that depict the correct number operation to simplify the expressions. They will move to stations around the room for each operation, simplifying numerical expressions as they go. Students may work individually, in pairs, or in small groups, depending on the needs of the class.

Preparation:

- Make five signs: Parentheses, Multiplication, Division, Addition, and Subtraction.
- Use the signs to mark areas of the classroom as shown below in Fig. 10.1. Labels may be attached to the wall or floor. Parentheses should be at one end of the classroom; addition and subtraction should on opposite walls at the other end; multiplication and division should be on opposite walls halfway between. Make sure there is adequate space near each sign for a large group of students.
- Prepare a card for each student with an expression involving addition, subtraction, multiplication, and division, with some operations grouped in parentheses. An example would be the expression $6 \div 3 \times (2 + 1) - 1$. If you wish to repeat the activity, you will need more than one card per student (see Fig. 10.2 for more examples).

Introduction:

- Begin by reminding students of the order of operations for simplifying numerical expressions: first simplify expressions in parentheses, then perform multiplication and division operations, and finally perform addition and subtraction. Remind students of the acronym PEMDAS and the mnemonic, "Please Excuse My Dear Aunt Sally". Tell students that they will practice these steps as they move around the classroom. Point out the stations around the classroom and explain that each station represents a different step in the process.

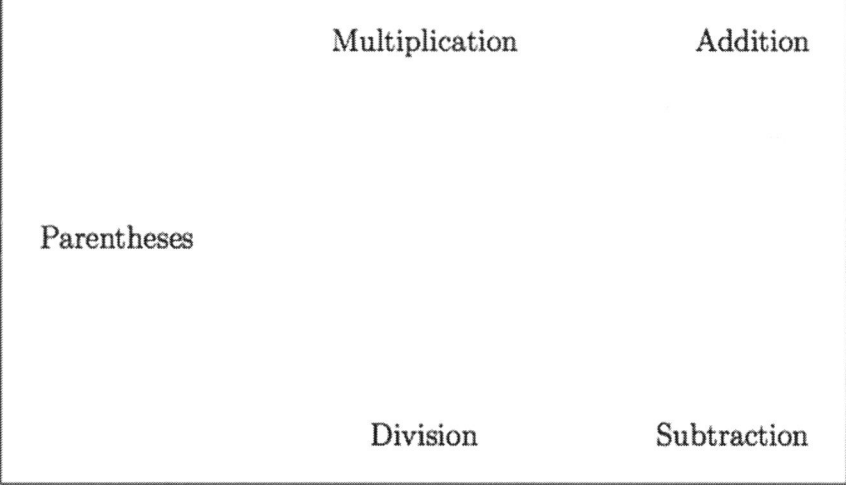

Fig. 10.1   A diagram depicting the setup for the operation stations activity

Fig. 10.2 Numerical
expression examples for
student cards

Expression	Value
$(7 + 3) \div (8 - 3) \times 3$	15
$(3 - 1) \times 4 + 2 \times 2$	12
$7 - 8 \div (3 + 1) \times 2$	3
$9 - 2 \times (3 - 1) \times 3$	1
$(4 + 4) \div (2 \times 2) + 1$	3
$8 \div 2 + 3 \times (2 + 1)$	13
$6 \div (1 + 1) - (1 + 2)$	0
$(4 + 6) \div 2 + 2 \times 3$	11
$9 - 6 \div 2 - (3 + 1)$	2

Activity:

- Give each student a card with an expression involving addition, subtraction, multiplication, and division, with some operations grouped in parentheses. An example would be the equation $6 \div 3 \times (2 + 1) - 1$. See Fig. 10.2 for further examples. The activity may be done either individually, in pairs, or in small groups. If students are working together, each student within the pair or group should be given the same expression.
- Ask students to look at their cards and decide which operation should be performed first. Students walk to the sign for that operation. Once at the sign, students simplify the expression to determine their next movement. Students write the simplified expression on their card below the original expression. So, for the example $6 \div 3 \times (2 + 1) - 1$:

- The student will first walk to the parentheses area and write $6 \div 3 \times 3 - 1$.
- The student should then walk to the division area and write $2 \times 3 - 1$.
- The student should then walk to the multiplication area and write $6 - 1$.
- Finally, the student should walk to the subtraction area and write 5.

- During the activity, students will start at the parentheses area and move towards the next numerical operation (to multiplication and division, then to addition and subtraction) depending upon the next numerical operation to be performed.
- Once all students have simplified their expressions to single numbers, instruct students to line up along one wall. Collect cards from each student and give them a new one. Once all students have a new card, begin the activity again.
- Once students have returned to their seats, review simplifying expressions again by explaining that the operations occur in three stages: first expressions in parentheses, then multiplication and division, then addition and subtraction. This corresponds to moving across the classroom in one direction (left-to-right in Fig. 10.1).

Modifications/Adaptations Students who have difficulty moving around the classroom could be given a poster representing Fig. 10.1 to be used at their desk, and they can move the card or another object around the poster to represent the order of operations. Also, the student could stretch or point in the direction of the station corresponding to the next operation. Struggling students could also be given notecards with the mnemonic "PEMDAS" to support the order of operations.

Extensions The activity can be extended by letting each student create his or her own expression and then move across the room to simplify it. Another extension could be to have a peer check the answer by moving around and solving the problem.

Activity 2: Getting to Know Our Fractions

Suggested Grade Level: 3

Standards

CCSS.Math.Content.3.NF.A.1

Understand a fraction $1/b$ as the quantity formed by 1 part when a whole is partitioned into b equal parts; understand a fraction a/b as the quantity formed by a parts of size $1/b$.

Goals Students will develop an understanding of fractions as parts of a whole by modeling various fractions.

Objectives The students will arrange themselves in groups to illustrate different common fractions. Students will develop an understanding of the part–whole concept of fractions by modeling different fractions in their groups.

Suggested time frame	20–25 min
Equipment/technology	Timer; paper bags each containing five cards with fractions written on them. Groups of six should have fractions 1/6, 1/3, 1/2, 2/3, and 5/6. Groups of 8 should have 1/8, 1/4, 1/2, 5/8, and ¾
Start/stop signals	To start the activity, blow a whistle, and start the timer The activity ends when the timer sounds
Skill cues	"Be mindful of others"—students should be aware of the movement of everyone in their groups "Be creative and work together"—students should discuss different ways of modeling the fraction and work together to illustrate the fraction
Safety cues	Remind students to be aware of their classmates as they move around. Tell them to keep hands and feet to themselves as they work to model the fractions
Teaching style	Demonstration, cooperative learning, whole-class discussion
Assessments of content through the activity	Check that groups have modeled each fraction correctly. Ask questions such as, "What have you done?"; "How is this 1/3?", or "Can you show me the fraction another way?"
Transition activity	Once students return to their seats, have students wearing a particular color of clothing stand and ask the class about the fraction representation

Description of Getting to Know Our Fractions Activity This activity takes place in two phases. First, the class as a whole will model one-half; then, the students will split into smaller groups to model other fractions.

Preparation:

- Prepare fraction cards in paper bags (see Fig. 10.3). Each group of six or eight students will need a bag with appropriate fractions for the size of the group.

Introduction:

- Remind students that fractions are used to describe an equal number of same-size pieces. Ask them, **What does the fraction one-half mean?** Answers may include such ideas as one of two equal-sized groups or one out of every two things in a collection. Engage them in a brief discussion.

Activity:

- Phase 1: Whole-Class Activity

  - If the number of students is odd, choose one student to be the group leader. If the number of students is even, let students work together without a leader.
  - Tell the students, **Half of you sit down. The other half should stay standing**. Allow students (with the direction of the leader, if there is one) to determine which students will be in each half. They may do this by pairing up and having one student of each pair stand and one sit, or by dividing into

Number of students in a group	Fraction Cards
6	$\frac{1}{6}$, $\frac{1}{3}$, $\frac{1}{2}$, $\frac{2}{3}$, and $\frac{5}{6}$.
8	$\frac{1}{8}$, $\frac{1}{4}$, $\frac{1}{2}$, $\frac{5}{8}$, and $\frac{3}{4}$

Fig. 10.3 Fraction cards for the phase 2 group activity

two groups, counting, and moving members from one group to another. If students are struggling, guide them by asking questions like, **Do you need more students standing up or more students sitting down?**

- Once students have divided in half, count the two groups aloud to show that they are the same size. Then instruct each standing student to stand next to a seated student to show that one-half can be thought of as one student of each pair. See Fig. 10.4 for an example of students participating in the activity.
- Repeat the activity twice more, choosing activities from the list below or creating your own.

  Half of the students walk to one side of the room, half walk to the other side. Half of the students face the front of the classroom and half of the students face the back of the classroom.
  Half of the students raise hands while half of the students do not raise hands (see Fig. 10.5).

  Each time, allow students to choose which students will be in each half, guiding them if necessary. If you are using a group leader, choose a new leader each time. Encourage them to mix the halves each time so that a different set of students forms each half.

- Phase 2: Group Activity

  - After modeling one-half, then divide the class into groups of 6 or 8. Not all groups need to be the same size. Give each group a bag of appropriate

Fig. 10.4 The whole-class modeling one-half

Fig. 10.5 Students modeling one-half another way

fractions. If there are an odd number of students, assign one student to be a leader of one of the groups. Set a timer for 15 min.

– Instruct each group to draw a fraction card from the bag and model that fraction in one of the ways that the class modeled one-half. For example, if a group of six draws the fraction two-thirds, they might have four students point to the front of the classroom and two students point to the back of the classroom. Move between the groups, checking that they have modeled the fractions correctly. Once they have modeled one fraction, instruct them to draw the next one and model that using a different movement.

– When the timer ends after 15 min, students return to their seats.

Modifications/Adaptations Visual representations of the fractions may be included on the cards. If the class contains students with limited physical movement, the whole class can model fractions in ways that all students can participate (for example, pointing or raising hands). Once divided into groups, students can create representations that all group members can do.

Extensions Ask students to draw figures to illustrate the different fractions that they modeled in their groups. Provide paper to the students. Students could also construct a fraction not modeled in class and illustrate it. If group leaders were needed for some parts of the activity, use the activity to introduce or discuss the idea of remainders.

Measurement

Measurement consists of describing an object or situation numerically, which is one of the most common and widely applicable concepts in mathematics. According to the *Principles and Standards for School Mathematics* (NCTM, 2000), "Measurement is the assignment of a numerical value to an attribute of an object, such as the length of a pencil. At more-sophisticated levels, measurement involves assigning a number to a characteristic of a situation, as is done by the consumer price index (p. 44)." From miles per gallon to amount of ingredients in a recipe, measurement is readily applicable to many real-world situations. Linear measurement also serves as the foundation for spatial understanding of perimeter, area, and volume.

Students in early grades compare quantities based on their perceptual judgements; therefore, teaching should incorporate activities to help amend these perceptual judgements and provide the basis for developing conceptual understanding of measurement (Outhred & McPhail, 2000; Outhred, Mitchelmore, McPhail, & Gould, 2003). Though elementary grades focus heavily on measurement concepts, considerable research offers that many secondary students do not have a thorough knowledge of the concepts (Carpenter, Lindquist, Brown, Kouba, Silver, & Swafford, 1988; Hart, 1989; Schwartz, 1995). Bragg and Outhred (2000a, b) suggest that students 6–10-years old should follow rules and procedures when using a ruler to measure length, rather than learning about length measurement through conceptual understand alone. Conceptual understanding of measurement concepts needs to be developed through practical experiences particularly because students who do not have sound understanding of linear measurements are unlikely to succeed in measuring area and volume.

Integrating movement into activities can provide students with the natural connection needed to develop the concepts of measurement. Traditional instruction in measurement has focused on "the procedures of measuring rather than the concepts underlying them" (Stephan & Clements, 2003, p. 3). Integrating movement introduces a hands-on approach that can help extend children's thinking and conceptualization of measurement by having them actively interact with their environment to develop conceptual understanding of measurement concepts. Teaching measurement concepts through real-world connections sparks students' interest and contextualizes the importance of mathematics outside of the classroom (Jones, 2011). Integrating movement with real-world connections can further increase intrinsic motivation (Vazou et al., 2012), which can be instrumental in increasing interest in class and thus developing understanding of measurement concepts. The activities in this strand suggest ways of integrating movement into learning of measurement concepts and increasing engagement and intrinsic motivation.

Activity 1: Measuring with Every Body

Suggested Grade Level: 1–2.

Standards
CCSS.Math.Content.1.MD.A.2
Express the length of an object as a whole number of length units, by laying multiple copies of a shorter object (the length unit) end to end; understand that the length measurement of an object is the number of same-size length units that span it with no gaps or overlaps.

CCSS.Math.Content.2.MD.A.2
Measure the length of an object twice, using length units of different lengths for the two measurements; describe how the two measurements relate to the size of the unit chosen.

Goals Students will practice measuring length using nonstandard units. After this lesson, students will also comprehend the need for standard units of measurement.

Objectives Using their bodies as nonstandard units of measurements, the students will express length as a number of length units. Students will practice measurement concepts such as laying nonstandard units end to end with no gaps or overlap, while also understanding that length measurement of an object is the number of same-size length units. Students will also recognize the need for a standard unit of measurement by comparing measurement answers from different groups.

Suggested time frame	30–40 min
Equipment/technology	Masking tape, pencils, paper, activity sheet
Start/stop signals	Students start the activity when the instructions are over and teacher says "measure" Students pause or stop the activity when the teacher says "rulers down"
Skill cues	"Freeze your body"—remind *counters* to keep their hands still while *units* are moving to ensure an accurate measurement Remind *units* to pay attention to precise placement
Safety cues	Tell students to work together as a team and respect the other team's space (if two groups are on one line). Remind students to be careful when walking so they do not step on the students whose hands or arms are on the floor. Make sure students have adequate space to move
Teaching style	Cooperative learning, discovery, and whole-class discussions
Assessments of content through the activity	Observe students to make sure they are measuring with no gaps or overlap. Ask questions to assess them about the units of measure for each measurement. Collect activity sheet
Transition activity	Once students have returned to their seats, discuss the inverse relationship between size of units of measure and size of measurements and the need for standard units of measurement

Description of Measuring with Every Body Activity In this activity, students will measure the length of masking tape lines using parts of their bodies as units of measure. They will practice measuring with nonstandard units by laying parts of their bodies end to end with no gaps or overlap. They will also develop an understanding of the need for standard units of measure as they discover that their measurements do not always match.

Preparation:

- In advance of the lesson, the teacher should place masking tape on the floor in straight lines. There should one line for every two students. If there is not enough space, one line for every four students will suffice. The lines need not all be the same length, but all should be between ten and twenty feet long. There should be approximately six feet between lines, so that students have room to move.

Introduction:

- Remind students that the length of a line is the number of units that can be laid along the line with no gaps or overlaps. Ask students, **What are some non-standard units of length that you have seen used?** They may mention paper clips, coins, popsicle sticks, or pencils. Say, **Today, you will measure lines in student-heights, forearms, foot-lengths, and fingers.**

Activity:

- Instruct students to find a partner and assign each pair of students to one line. Tell the students that one partner will be the *unit* and one the *counter*. If there are not enough lines for each pair, two pairs may share a line. In this case, each pair will work on one side of the line.
- The student that is the *unit* lies down on the line with feet even with the end of the line. (If two pairs are sharing the line, the *units* should lie down on opposite sides of the line rather than directly on it.) Tell the students to keep their arms at their sides but stretch their bodies as much as they can to become taller. Once students are lying down and have stretched out, instruct the *counter* to use his or her hand to mark the top of the *unit's* head next to or on the line and count it as 'one' (see Fig. 10.6). Once the *counter* has marked the position, the *unit* student will get up and move so that the *unit's* feet are even with the *counter's* hand. Students continue until they reach the end of the line. Students write down the measurement (i.e. two and a half student-heights) in the first column of the activity sheet. Emphasize that measurement is always written in units and that in this case, the unit of measurement should be student-heights.
- The students then switch roles and measure the line again, writing this measurement in the second column of the activity sheet (see Appendix C).
- Ask the class, **How many of you got the same answer both times?** Most of the class will probably answer that they received the same number of student-heights, but a few may not. Ask the class why the measurements are

Fig. 10.6 Students measuring the length of a line in student-heights

different. They might talk about how students are not the same height or how a person is not a standard unit of measure.

- Next the students measure the line in forearms. *Units* lay arms with their elbows even with the beginning of the line and fingers held together and pointing along the line. Emphasize that they should make a long straight line from elbow to fingertips. Once students have their arms in position, *counters* use their hands to mark where *unit's* fingers are and count it as one. Tell students to continue until they have found out how long their line is in forearms, then write their answer in the first column of the activity sheet. Remind them again that a measurement should always have a unit of measure and that in this case the unit of measure should be forearms. Once the line is measured, they switch roles and measure the line again.
- Ask the class again how many of the pairs got the same answer both times and discuss the reasons that measurements may be different (i.e., students' bodies are not all the same size).
- Measure the line again, this time in foot-lengths. Students can do this by walking along the line, heel to toe, while their partner counts. Each student should measure the line using their own feet and record the answer. Remind them again that a measurement should always have a unit of measure and that in this case the unit of measure should be foot-lengths (not feet).
- Measure the line one more time, this time using finger-lengths as the unit of measure. The *unit* student lays an index finger next to the line, the *counter* marks the end, and the *unit* moves the finger along. Remind students to keep their fingers as straight as possible and to be careful not to step on each other's

fingers. Again, each student should have a turn to be the *unit* and should record that measurement in the activity sheet. The unit of measure should be finger-lengths.

- Once the lines have been measured, tell students to return to their seats. Ask students which unit of measure gave the smallest number for the length and which one gave the biggest number. Discuss the reasons that bigger units of measure will give smaller numbers and smaller units of measure will give bigger numbers. Introduce the concept of standard units of measurements by explaining the need to have the same answer. For example, two students measuring one distance using forearms may find measurements of 10 forearms and 11 forearms, leading to confusion about how long the line is.

Modifications/Adaptations Students with physical impairments limiting body movements may measure lines in units of books, folders, or pencils, moving along the line as they lay down the objects. They can be the *counter* while their partner is the *unit*; the students with physical impairments can use a stick to mark points in their role as a *counter*.

Extensions Provide each student with a ruler and have them measure the line. Students may place the ruler from the beginning rather than starting from zero. Introduce the correct use of rulers and concept of inches and centimeters to the students. Point out that all of the rulers are the same length and standard units such as inches or centimeters have the same spacing, so the measurement of a line in standard units will always be the same.

Activity 2: Stretch It 'Till You Break it!

Suggested Grade Level: 2

Standards
CCSS.Math.Content.2.MD.A.3
Estimate lengths using units of inches, feet, centimeters, and meters

CCSS.Math.Content.2.MD.A.4
Measure to determine how much longer one object is than another, expressing the length difference in terms of a standard length unit.

Goals Students practice measuring in different units and compare length. Students will also relate measurements in different units by converting length measurements.

Objectives Using Tootsie Rolls, students will be able to measure to the nearest inch or centimeter. Students will be able to calculate the difference in length and convert from one unit to another unit of measurement.

Suggested time frame	20–25 min
Equipment/technology	Tootsie Rolls, paper plates or paper towels, activity sheet, pencils
Start/stop signals	Start the activity by playing music (while students are moving or measuring). Teacher can say commands such as "jump", "skip", "jumping jacks", run in place", "hop", or "stretch" while the music is playing Stop the music to get students attention
Skill cues	Remind students to hold the wrapped Tootsie Roll in their hands while engaging in physical activity • Jump: land on two feet, squash your knees • Skip in place: step, hop; reach high • Stretch: reach, feel the muscles elongating • Hop in place: start and land on same foot, squash your knees • Jumping jacks: feet wide, feet together • Run in place: pump your arms, bring your knees up
Safety cues	Remind students not to push or bump into each other. Make sure there is enough space to complete the movement before they start jumping, skipping, or stretching
Teaching style	Guided discovery, cooperative learning
Assessments of content through the activity	Teacher actively observes and monitors students during measurement. An observational checklist could be used to help assess students' understanding. The activity sheet is collected to gauge students' understanding through their work
Transition activity	Once all the physical activity is completed, students transition back to their seats to stretch the Tootsie Roll and measure it

Description of Stretch It 'Till You Break It! Activity

Preparation:

- In advance of the lesson, the teacher should have at least one Tootsie Roll per student. Space needs to be created for students to do movements such as skip in place, hop in place, jump, run in place, and stretch in place. Paper towels and preferably paper plates should be ready.

Introduction:

- Ask students their favorite candy. They may mention Skittles, M&Ms, Hershey bars, Reeses, Snickers, Milky Way, Dum Dums, or any others. Tell them that your favorite candy is Tootsie Rolls and today they will use Tootsie Rolls to practice measurements and conversion of units. Give each student Activity Sheet 2: Measuring the Tootsie Roll (see Appendix C) and a ruler.

Activity:

- Provide each student with a Tootsie Roll (or other type of stretchy candy) and a ruler. Instruct them not to eat it.
- Students unwrap the Tootsie Roll and place it on the wrapper.

- Instruct students to measure the length of the Tootsie Roll and write the measurement on Activity Sheet 2: Measuring the Tootsie Roll.
- Emphasize the units of measurement. Students can measure in centimeters. If the class has not learned centimeters, they can measure in inches. Remind them to include the unit when writing down any measurement.
- Ask students to stretch the Tootsie Roll without breaking it. They will likely be unable to stretch it much, if at all, and some may even break it. Give new Tootsie Rolls to students who break theirs.
- Have the students wrap the Tootsie Roll back in the wrapper, hold it in their hand, and stand. At this point, depending on space, the students do various movements (i.e., jump, skip in place, stretch, hop in place, jumping jacks, run in place) for 5 min (see Fig. 10.7). Play music while students are doing the movements. These movements can be done in any order and repeated any number of times, but at least three of them should be done for variety.

  - Students can jump for 1 min, skip for 1 min, stretch for 1 min, and do jumping jacks for 1 min, hop or run in place for 1 min, and end by jumping again for 1 min. *Make sure that the students are holding the wrapped Tootsie Roll in their hands during each of the movements.*
  - Set a timer or alert the students at the end of each minute.

Fig. 10.7 Students moving while holding the Tootsie Roll in their hand

- Once the movements are done, the Tootsie Rolls will be warm and stretchy. Tell the students to unwrap the Tootsie Roll and try again to stretch it. As students are stretching it, provide paper towels for them in case the candy becomes very sticky.
- Students should stretch the Tootsie Roll as far as possible without breaking it. Instruct them to measure the stretched tootsie roll using their rulers in the same unit of measurement they used for the unstretched Tootsie Roll (see Fig. 10.8). Students note the new measurement on the activity sheet. Remind them again to include units.
- Once all measurements are done, students can eat the Tootsie Roll or throw it away. Have some extra Tootsie Rolls for students who throw theirs away.
- Students then work with a partner to finish the remaining parts of the activity sheet:

  - Students fill in the measurement of the original and stretched Tootsie Roll.
  - Students convert their measurements into different units. For example, if the students measured in centimeters, then they could convert to millimeters or meters. If students measure in inches, they could convert to feet or yards (see Fig. 10.9).

Modifications/Adaptations Any student who has physical impairments limiting lower body movement should hold the Tootsie Roll in his or her hand and move hands to mimic the movements.

Extensions Students can convert between the customary and standard units such as inches and centimeters.

Fig. 10.8 Student measures a stretched Tootsie Roll

Millimeters (mm)	Centimeters (cm)	Meters (m)
1	0.1	.001
10	1	.01
1000	100	1

Inches (in)	Feet (ft)	Yard (yd)
1	.083	.028
12	1	.33
36	3	1

Fig. 10.9 Conversions table

Data Analysis

The ability to understand data is crucial for students to become aware of the world beyond themselves. As they mature, students face an increasing range of decisions: what cereal to have for breakfast, what kind of car to buy, or how to vote (Jones, 2011). Statistical literacy is necessary to enable students to make informed decisions. In light of the ever-increasing quantity of data available, statistical literacy is a key skill for effective citizenship (Shaughnessy, 2007; Van de Walle, Karp, & Bay-Williams, 2013). *Principles and Standards for School Mathematics* (NCTM, 2000) identifies five themes associated with data analysis: (1) formulating questions that can be addressed with data, collecting, organizing, and displaying relevant data to answer the questions; (2) selecting and using appropriate statistical methods to analyze data; (3) developing and evaluating inferences and predictions based on data; and (4) understanding and applying basic concepts of probability.

In the elementary grades, students' study of data analysis should help them develop the ability to use numerical summaries and graphical representations to understand data (NCTM, 2000). With simple questions and data, even kindergarten students are capable of participating in every stage of a statistical investigation (Hourigan & Leavy, 2016). Kindergarten students should be able to formulate their own questions, collect data using surveys, present the data in graphical form, and interpret the graphs (Cook, 2008). The activities in this chapter use movement to introduce students to key ideas of data analysis: making bar graphs to represent a data set and using mean, median, and mode to describe a given data set.

Activity 1: Bar Graph

Suggested Grade Levels: 1st–2nd

Standards
CCSS.Math.Content.1.MD.C.4
Organize, represent, and interpret data with up to three categories; ask and answer questions about the total number of data points, how many in each category, and how many more or less are in one category than in another.

CCSS.Math.Content.2.MD.D.10
Draw a picture graph and a bar graph (with single-unit scale) to represent a data set with up to four categories. Solve simple put-together, take-apart, and compare problems using information presented in a bar graph.

Goals The students will be introduced to bar graphs by moving and arranging themselves into different categories.

Objectives The students will create bar graphs by arranging themselves on a line.

Suggested time frame	25–30 min
Equipment/technology	Signs with months of the year, the four seasons, and possible numbers of brothers and sisters (0, 1, 2, 3, and 4 or more), masking tape
Start/stop signals	Start the activity by saying, "Let's graph!" During the activity, students should stop moving and look at the teacher when the teacher says, "Let's count!"
Skill cues	"Stand in straight lines" and "face forward". Remind students to respect and cooperate with others in deciding where each student stands
Safety cues	Make sure the area where the bar chart is built is large enough for students to move around safely. The teacher may find the need to conduct the activity in the hallway where there is more room to line up into rows. Remind students to be careful of others as they move around
Teaching style	Direct instruction, guided practice
Assessments of content through the activity	Monitor students during counting as a group. Note which students are unsure of when to stop. Assess students' understanding of bar graphs by asking questions such as: "What is a bar graph?", "How many people have a birthday in the month of August?", and "How do you know that?"
Transition activity	Once students have returned to their seats, transition by drawing a representation of the last bar graph created during the activity

Description of Bar Graph Activity The activity will introduce students to the concept of bar graphs. Students will be able to interpret and answer questions about bar graphs.

Preparation:

- Make signs before class: one for each of the twelve months, one for each of the four seasons, and one with each of the numbers 0–3 on them as well as one saying "4 or more".
- Before class, use masking tape to make a straight line and lay out twelve signs with months of the year on the line in a way that allows enough space for several students to line up in front of each sign before the class begins (see Fig. 10.10).

Introduction:

- Explain to students that it is often useful to divide objects into different categories. Give some examples, such as students in different grades, students of different ages, hair color, or height to discuss categories. If the class has already talked about classifying objects, remind them of the kinds of classifications they have done. Tell them that a bar graph is a useful way to give visual information about how objects are placed into categories.

Fig. 10.10 Setup for bar graph activity

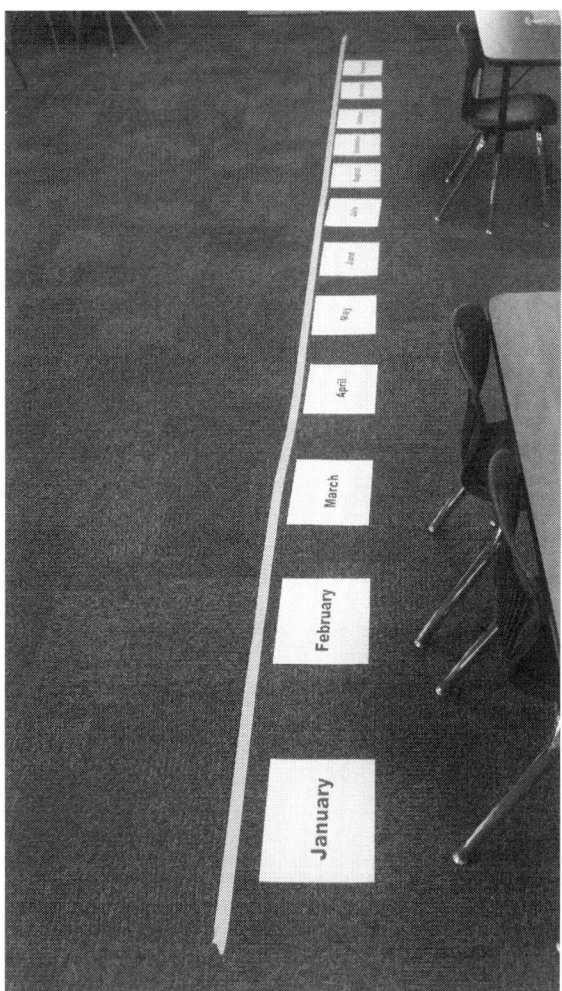

Activity:

- Explain to students that when given a signal "Let's graph", they will move to the appropriate place and line up. Remind students how to stand in a line (see Fig. 10.11).
- Tell students to find the month they were born in and line up in front of that month sign.
- Once students have formed lines, ask questions such as, **How many students were born in August?** Explain that students can find the answer by counting the students in the line in front of the "August" sign. Ask the class to count with you. Repeat the process for two other months.

Fig. 10.11 Students lined up
in front of the month of their
birth, forming a bar graph

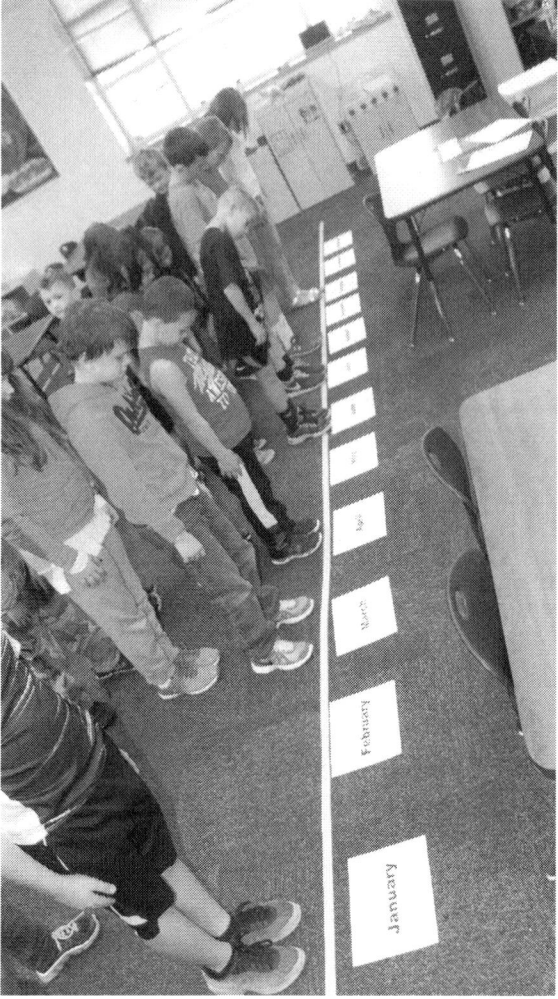

- The last student in each line picks up the sign at the back of that line and brings
  it to the teacher. Four other students are given the signs with the names of
  seasons. They lay them down where the month signs were before.
- Next, students choose their favorite season and line up in front of the corresponding sign.
- Once the students have formed lines ask, **How many students chose spring for
  their favorite season?** Ask the class to count with you. Repeat the process for
  the other seasons.
- Have the last student in each line pick up the sign for the season and five
  students lay down the numbers 0–3 and the "4 or more" sign. Tell students that
  they will now line up according to the number of sisters and brothers they have.

Clarify whether cousins, half-brothers and half-sisters, and stepbrothers and stepsisters are included in the counting.

- Once students have formed lines, ask questions such as, **How many students have one brother or sister?** Ask the class to count with you. Repeat the process for other numbers.
- Pick up all the signs and tell the students to return to their seats.
- Once all students have returned to their seats, explain that a bar graph is a way of representing the number of things in different categories. Draw the bar graphs corresponding to the data the students used in the activity.

Modifications/Adaptations Students with limited mobility may need assistance moving into the correct line, or give the student with limited mobility their sign and he or she can be the line leader.

Extensions Ask students to think of more kinds of data that can be represented with a bar graph. Examples could include things like favorite color, favorite pet, or favorite candy. Guide students through making the bar graphs. For a different extension, take a photograph of the students in bar graph configuration. Once students have returned to their seats, project the photograph and draw rectangles over each line of students to make a more abstract bar graph to help students connect the physical with the pictorial representation.

Activity 2: Mean, Median, Mode

Suggested Grade Level: 6

Standards
CCSS.Math. Content. 6.SP.B.5.C
Giving quantitative measures of center (median and/or mean) and variability (interquartile range and/or mean absolute deviation), as well as describing any overall pattern and any striking deviations from the overall pattern with reference to the context in which the data were gathered.

Goals Students will be introduced to the mean, median, and mode of a data set.

Objectives Students will define and compute the mean, median, and mode of a data set.

Suggested time frame	15–20 min
Equipment/technology	Unit cubes or other small identical objects. The total number should be six times the number of students participating in the activity
Start/stop signals	To start the activity, ring a bell To end the activity, ring the bell twice
Skill cues	

	"Stand still"—students should be careful to stand still in a straight line when computing the median. Remind them to speak softly and move carefully when forming groups and when trading cubes
Safety cues	Remind students to be aware of each other as they move around the room. Remind them to walk and not run
Teaching style	Direct instruction, cooperative learning
Assessments of content through the activity	After each definition, ask the class what the value is for their data set
Transition activity	Once students have returned to their seats, explain how to compute the mean, median, and mode of a data set

Description of Mean, Median, Mode Activity Students will be given different numbers of unit cubes. They will find the mean, median, and mode of the set of data given by the number of cubes each student has.

Preparation:

• Have a list of numbers ready to show to introduce the lesson. Have unit cubes ready to use. The total number of cubes will be six times the number of students participating in the activity.

Introduction:

• Show students a list of numbers. Tell students that a list of numbers has a lot of information in it and that some may find difficulty in summarizing the list. Tell them they will learn three ways to describe features of a set of numbers.

Activity:

• Give each student some cubes. The total number of cubes should be six times the number of students, but some students should have more than six cubes and others fewer than six. For example, in a class of 21 students distribute a total of 126 cubes. Each student will be given a group of cubes, though some will have the same amount of cubes as others in the class. The cubes should be distributed such as: 1, 2, 3, 3, 4, 4, 5, 5, 5, 5, 6, 6, 7, 7, 8, 8, 9, 9, 9, 10, and 10 cubes.
• Have each student go up to the board and write the number of cubes they are holding. This is the data set. In the example above, there would be 21 numbers written on the board. Explain that this activity will introduce the ideas of *mode*, *median*, and *mean*, which are ways to describe a data set.
• Tell students to form groups in which all students have the same number of cubes. Those students with five cubes should be in a group, while students with ten cubes should be in a group, etc. Ask students to look for the group with the most students. Tell them that the number that appears most often in a data set is called the *mode*. Ask students which group has the most people and explain that the number of cubes that each student in the biggest group has is the mode. In

the example, the largest group is the group of four students holding five cubes, so five is the *mode*. If there is a tie for largest group, explain that a data set may have more than one mode.

- Tell students to line up in order from least to greatest number of cubes they are holding. Students will still be standing with the groups they used to find the mode, but the line should be single file (students stand side by side). Once students have made a line, the student at each end sits down. Then the next student at each end, and the next, and so forth. When one or two students are left standing, explain that the *median* is the middle number of a data set arranged from smallest to largest.

  - If the total number of students is odd, one student will be left standing. Explain that the last student left standing has the median number of cubes.
  - If the total number of students is even, there will be two students left standing. Explain that the median is halfway between their numbers of cubes. In the example, one student with six cubes will be left standing, so the *median* of the data set is six.

- Tell each student to find a student with a different number of cubes from them: at least two more or two fewer than their number of cubes. The student with more cubes should give one cube to the student with fewer cubes. Repeat until all students have six cubes. Explain that the *mean* of a data set is the total value divided equally among the number of elements in the data set. Since each student now has six cubes and the total number of cubes is the same as it was in the original data set, the *mean* of the data set is six.
- Have students return to their seats. Explain how to compute the mean, median, and mode of a data set.

Modifications/Adaptations Students who have difficulty standing can raise or lower their hands instead of standing or sitting. If the class contains students with limited physical mobility, lines and groups may form near that student's seat.

Extensions Repeat the activity with an unusual data set. For example, all students could have either three cubes or nine cubes, or most students could have one cube while a few students have many. For a different extension, use the data set from the activity to show how computations of mean, median, and mode are performed. The answers will be same, helping students connect the concrete context to the computation of *mean*, *median*, and *mode*.

Algebra

Algebra is one of the major cornerstones of mathematics. Strong algebra skills are essential to enable students to succeed in higher mathematics. In spite of its importance, algebra is all too often considered an abstract and difficult subject that is mostly taught to upper middle and high school students (NCTM, 2000). However, algebraic thinking begins at a very young age. *Principles and Standards for School Mathematics* (NCTM, 2000) identifies four major themes in this strand: (1) understanding patterns, relations, and functions; (2) representing and analyzing mathematical situations; (3) using mathematical models to represent and understand quantitative relationships; and (4) analyzing change in various contexts. All of these themes are relevant for elementary students and these foundational ideas of algebra need to be emphasized to foster a deep understanding of future algebraic concepts (Russell, Schifter, & Bastable, 2006). Young children think algebraically by observing and exploring patterns; describing, sorting, and classifying those patterns; and re-creating and identifying missing items.

Kinesthetic movement helps provide a connection to support algebraic thinking. Noble (2003) conducted a case study using motion detectors to assist students in understanding graphs. The experience of interacting kinesthetically with the graph allowed the students to make the connection between the visual features of the graph and the physical reality it represented. Later, one of the students even used gestures reminiscent of his interactions with the motion detector when describing graphs and was able to make conjectures and understand unusual graphs.

Another case study showed that the use of a physical activity, such as a water wheel, helped develop skills in using mathematical symbols (Nemirovsky & Rasmussen, 2005). In this study, college mathematics students were given a rotating device with flowing water which displayed complicated patterns of movement. The students used the motion of the water wheel to develop an understanding of the motion, including the notation used in a differential equation describing it. The study illustrates how kinesthetic experiences can help make connections between symbol manipulation and understanding of physical phenomena. The two activities in this section provide ways of integrating movement with the fundamental algebra skills of drawing graphs and solving equations.

Activity 1: Walk the Line

Suggested Grade Level: 5

Standards
TEKS: Grade 5
5.4 (C) The student is expected to generate a numerical pattern when given a rule in the form $y = ax$ or $y = x + a$ and graph.

Goals Students will review and reinforce the concept of graphing linear equations in slope–intercept form.

Objective Students will be able to create human lines given slope and y-intercept.

Suggested time frame	15–20 min
Equipment/technology	Tarps with a marked coordinate plane, popsicle sticks with y-intercept and slope numbers, a string or rope for every 3–4 students
Start/stop signals	Use a computer to play a chime to begin the activity Play the chime again to end the activity
Skill cues	"Stand straight and still"—students should be careful to stand still in a straight line
	"Work together"—students should discuss graphing using slope and y-intercept and work together to graph the function
Safety cues	Remind students to be mindful of other students, so they do not bump into them. Tell them to take turns to be the y-intercept so that each students gets a chance to start the line
Teaching style	Demonstration (one example), guided discovery, cooperative learning
Assessments of content through the activity	Observe and actively monitor the student groups throughout the activity. Use questioning such as, "What does the slope mean?", "How did you make this line?", and "If there needs to be another point on the line, how would you show it?"
Transition activity	The students transition to their seats to graph one of the equations they created on graph paper

Description of Walk the Line Activity In this activity, the students review graphing linear equations by creating human lines for the given slope and y-intercept. This activity is done in two phases. In phase one, the teacher demonstrates the activity using one group of students as an example and in the second phase the students practice graphing linear equations within their groups.

Preparation:

- For every three to four students, prepare a tarp with a coordinate plane. Use masking tape to mark squares on the tarp and use a permanent marker to write numbers (see Fig. 10.12). Students should be able to stand at the grid points on the graph with enough space not to touch each other.
- Prepare popsicle sticks with possible slopes and y-intercept numbers for the lines students will make. The simplest activity will have sticks marked 0, 1, 2, and 3 in each category. Depending on students' level of familiarity with linear equations, negative numbers may be used for one or both categories and fractional slopes such as 1/2, 1/3, and 2/3 may be added.

Introduction:

- During the activity, students will review drawing graphs of lines given a slope and y-intercept. Begin by reminding students that the y-intercept is the point where the graph crosses the y-axis; that the slope of the line tells how many units *up* the line represents for every unit *right*; and that in a line with equation $y = mx + b$, the slope is m and the y-intercept is $(0, b)$.

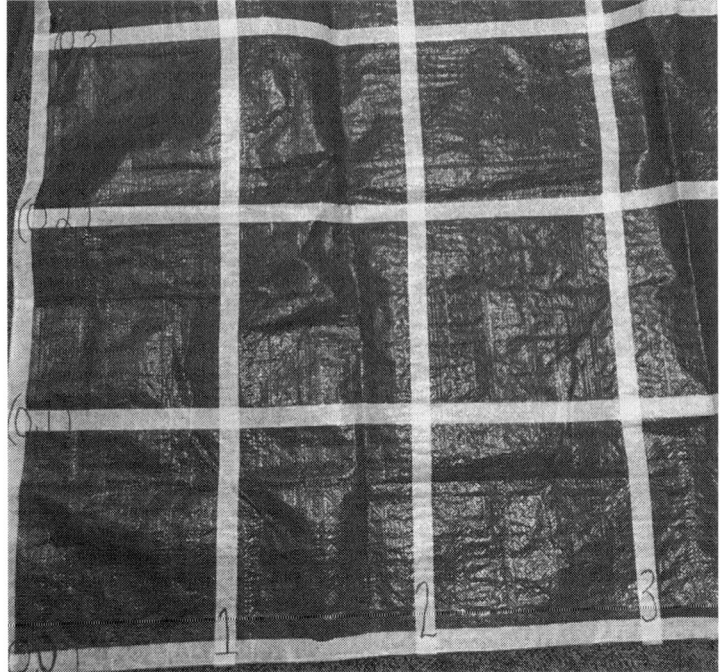

Fig. 10.12 Sample of a tarp for "walk the line"

Activity:

- Divide the students into groups of three to four and give each group one coordinate plane drawn on a tarp.
- Choose one group to demonstrate the activity. Tell the class this group will be drawing a line with a slope of 2 and y-intercept of 1.
- Discuss the y-intercept with the students. Ask, **Where is the y-intercept on this coordinate plane?** Students may respond with the number 1 or the ordered pair (0, 1) or they may move directly to finding the correct point on their coordinate plane tarp. Once a student has identified the correct location, have that student stand on the point, representing the y-intercept of the line.
- Remind the students that the slope of a line is rise over run and that the line the group is graphing has a slope of two. Ask the students to explain the rise and the run of their line. They should identify a rise of two with a run of one, since 2 can be written in fraction form as 2/1.
- Ask the students in the group to identify a second point on the line using the slope. Since the rise is two and the run is one, the students will identify the next point by starting at the y-intercept and moving two units up and one unit across: $(0 + 1, 1 + 2) = (1, 3)$. Have a student stand on that point.

Fig. 10.13 Students stand on a tarp to form a line

Fig. 10.14 Students hold a rope to show the line through the points they stand on. Some students are marking the estimated positions of points not on the tarp

- The group continues finding points on the coordinate plane by moving up two units and right one unit (as the slope is 2/1) until all students are standing on the tarp (see Fig. 10.13). If the tarp does not include enough points, students can estimate the positions of points not marked (see Fig. 10.14).
- Once all students are standing on the tarp, give the students a string or rope so that they can see that their points form a straight line (see Fig. 10.14).
- In the second phase, the students practice within their groups. Give each group a number for y-intercept and a number for slope. Let the students work together to make linear equations and place themselves as points on the coordinate plane

depicting the linear equations. To make the linear graph more clearly visible, students can hold a string to represent all points on the line.

Modifications/Adaptations Students with limited physical mobility may need assistance moving to the tarp. They may need to represent the y-intercept in order to allow enough space. If they are unable to move to the tarp, place a grid on the desk or board and let them mark the points with something sticky.

Extension The activity can be extended by adding slopes and y-intercepts that are negative or fractions. The activity can also be extended by having two groups of students work on one tarp. Giving both groups lines with the same slope will help students develop the idea of parallel lines. If the lines intersect on the tarp, one student will be part of both lines, helping students understand that the intersection of two lines is the point that lies on both lines.

Activity 2: I Have/You Have Equations

Suggested Grade Level: 1–2

Standards
CCSS.Math. Content. 1.OA.D.8: Determine the unknown whole number in an addition or subtraction equation relating three whole numbers. For example, determine the unknown number that makes the equation true in each of the equations $8 + ? = 11, 5 = ? - 3, 6 + 6 = ?$

Goals Students will practice finding missing numbers in equations. Students will apply knowledge of number operations to balance equations.

Objectives Students will able to solve equations with missing numbers using number appropriate operations.

Suggested time frame	15–20 min
Equipment/technology	Cards with an equation on one side and a number on the other, soft ball for every 8–10 students: use a ball size appropriate for the space and throwing ability of the students
Start/stop signals	Begin the activity by blowing a whistle End the activity by blowing the whistle twice
Skill cues	"Keep your eye on the ball"—remind students to keep their eyes on the ball, catch with two hands, and to follow through to their target Check with the physical education teacher to determine if you should use underhand or overhand throwing with the students, depending on their skill levels
Safety cues	Remind students to pay attention to the ball. Tell students to make sure the target person is making eye contact before throwing. Tell them not to play with or throw the balls except as needed for the activity

Teaching style	Guided practice, cooperative learning
Assessments of content through the activity	Note which students have difficulty identifying missing addends or sums
Transition activity	Have students stand by their seats. Ask them to take two deep breaths, then three deep breaths. Ask how many breaths they have taken, then ask them to be seated

Description of I Have/You Have Equations Activity In this activity, students will solve equations and throw a ball to a student with the solution. This will allow them to practice balancing equations.

Preparation:

- Prepare a card for each student with a missing-addend or missing-sum expression on the back and a number on the front. The cards should be large enough to be visible from several feet away.
- The answer to each problem should appear on another student's card. Students will work in groups of eight to ten, so the cards should form groups of those sizes. Some examples appear in Fig. 10.15. Make each group of cards with a different color to help students find their groups.
- If you are unsure of how many students will participate, make some cards where the number on the front is the answer to the question on the back, and that number is a duplicate of another number in the group (in Fig. 10.15, these are the last two cards in each column). These cards can be omitted without breaking the chain of numbers needed to keep the activity continuous. Choosing a student with one of these cards for the starting student will prevent the situation where a student holding the answer to her own problem is the only student left with a card.

Introduction:

- During this activity, students will apply appropriate number operations to find missing numbers in equations and balance them. Introduce the activity by showing the students the word problem, "Amy has six books about helicopters and some books about trains. Amy has eleven books in total. How many books about trains does Amy have?" Discuss ways to solve this problem. Then discuss the importance of missing factor-problems.

Activity:

- Give each student a card with a number on one side and a missing-addend or missing-sum expression on the other side. Tell students to form groups where all students have the same color card and stand in a circle. There should be 8–10 students in each group. Tell students to hold their cards so that the rest of their group can see the number side.

Group A		Group B		Group C	
Front	Back	Front	Back	Front	Back
4	2 + __ = 11	15	8 + __ = 14	11	4 + __ = 9
9	2 + 6 = __	6	6 + 7 = __	5	5 + 7 = __
8	__ + 4 = 7	13	__ + 2 = 9	12	__ + 2 = 6
3	3 + __ = 9	7	4 + __ = 8	4	7 + __ = 13
6	5 + 6 = __	4	3 + 9 = __	6	4 + 6 = __
11	__ + 8 = 15	12	__ + 4 = 7	10	__ + 5 = 8
7	6 + __ = 7	3	2 + __ = 11	3	7 + __ = 12
1	3 + 1 = __	9	9 + 6 = __	5	6 + 5 = __
7	__ + 2 = 9	3	__ + 5 = 8	4	8 + __ = 12
8	3 + __ = 11	6	__ + 4 = 10	6	__ + 3 = 9

Fig. 10.15 These are possible groups of cards that can be used in the activity. The last two cards in each column may be omitted to allow for smaller groups of students. Mark the last card used in each group as the START card

- The student that has the "START" equation is the starter. The starter shows the missing-addend or missing-sum expression to all the other students. Give that student a ball and ask what addend or sum is missing from the number on their card.
- Once the starter has found the missing sum or addend, ask them to identify a classmate whose card has the solution on it and throw the ball to them. The starter should then turn their card around to show the number.
- The student holding the ball repeats the process of turning their card around to show the missing-addend or missing-sum expression, solving the equation, and throwing the ball to a classmate with the solution. Then they turn their card back around to show the number.
- Continue until each student has had a turn to solve the equation on their card. The ball should end up back at the starter.
- Give each student a new card if more practice is needed.

Modifications/Adaptations If a student cannot throw the ball, allow them to roll or push the ball with their hands or feet to the other students' feet. If needed the student can use a tool, such as a pool noodle or hockey stick, to assist with pushing.

Extensions Students can return to this activity later in the curriculum with subtraction, multiplication, and division facts. Students could work in small groups to create additional sets of cards for the activity.

Geometry

The geometry strand of the mathematics curriculum is about spatial sense and understanding defined as "an intuition about shapes and the relationships between shapes" (Van de Walle et al., 2013, p. 403). *Principles and Standards for School Mathematics* (NCTM, 2000) identifies five major themes for the geometry strand at the elementary level: (1) analyzing characteristics and properties of two-dimensional and three-dimensional geometric shapes; (2) developing mathematical arguments about geometric relationships; (3) specifying location and describing spatial relationships using coordinate geometry and other representational systems; (4) applying transformations and using symmetry to analyze mathematical situations; (5) and using visualization, spatial reasoning, and geometric modeling to solve problems.

Geometry is the study of physical attributes of the environment and can be learned by directly interacting with the environment (Howse & Howse, 2014). As students build, sort, manipulate, model, trace, measure, and construct, they begin to develop spatial reasoning skills (Howse & Howse, 2014; NCTM, 2000). Clements and Burns (2000), while designing enrichment activities for fourth grade students on angles and rotation, found that integrating physical rotations, such as students rotating their own bodies, helped students develop physical intuition about turning. This physical intuition helped students reason about both direction (left or right) and size of turn. Results suggest the integration of physical motion can help solidify the abstract concepts in a geometry curriculum. During the activities in this chapter, students will use movement to practice specifying points in a plane using ordered pairs and to review different geometric concepts.

Activity 1: Coordinate Darts—Practice/Review

Suggested Grade Level: 5

Standards

CCSS.Math.Content.5.G.A.1

Use a pair of perpendicular number lines, called axes, to define a coordinate system, with the intersection of the lines (the origin) arranged to coincide with the 0 on each line and a given point in the plane located by using an ordered pair of numbers, called its coordinates. Understand that the first number indicates how far to travel from the origin in the direction of one axis, and the second number indicates how far to travel in the direction of the second axis, with the convention that the names of the two axes and the coordinates correspond (e.g., x-axis and x-coordinate, y-axis and y-coordinate).

Goals Students will practice finding ordered pairs on the coordinate plane. Students will also calculate x- and y-axis distances.

Objective Using dart guns, the students will choose ordered pairs as a target.

Suggested time frame	25–30 min
Equipment/technology	Projector, activity sheet, dart guns, darts that stick to white board, pencils
Start/stop signals	Teacher gives the ordered pair and says "shoot" to start the activity Teacher says "done" to end the activity
Skill cues	"Aim with your whole arm"—students should practice careful aim. Remind them to stretch their arms out straight to improve accuracy
Safety cues	Remind students not to aim the dart gun at peers or at anything other than the white board. Tell students to be respectful of everyone and to wait patiently for their turns
Teaching style	Hands-on, guided, cooperative learning, and competition
Assessments of content through the activity	Actively monitor students as they identify the landing dart ordered pair and the distance from the target-ordered pair. Collect activity sheet to gauge student understanding of writing ordered pairs and calculation of the "x" and "y" distances
Transition activity	Once all students have shot a dart for an ordered pair, have them return to their seats. Teacher can have students give the teacher an ordered pair and the teacher tries to shoot the dart. As a whole class, they discuss the landing ordered pair, and review the "x" and "y" distances. Teacher can also lead the class to Pythagorean theorem (as described in the extension)

Description of Coordinate Darts Activity In this activity the students practice and review locating ordered pairs on a coordinate plane by aiming dart guns at points specified by ordered pairs. They will also be able to compare the target with the impact point to describe the distance in terms of x- and y-axes.

Preparation:

- Have 1–2 dart guns ready with darts that stick to the white board. Project a coordinate plane on the whiteboard. Use masking tape to mark the point where students will stand to shoot the dart. Make sure there is enough space for two students to stand and take aim at the coordinate plane at the same time.

Introduction:

- Talk to students about aiming. Ask students if they have ever been to a shooting range. Ask if anyone has played the game at a carnival in which they shot darts at a target. Engage them in a small discussion.
- Tell them that today's lesson focuses on reviewing ordered pairs using dart guns and calculating the difference between the target-ordered pair and actual ordered pair hit by the dart in terms of the distances on the x- and y-axis.

Activity:

- Divide students into groups of three to four and have each group choose someone to be the first shooter. Ask the shooter from the first group to step forward to the marked line and aim at the point (4, 5) (see Fig. 10.16). If more than one dart gun is available, have two students from different groups shoot at the same time (see Fig. 10.17). Repeat the process until the selected shooter from each group has had

Fig. 10.16 Students aiming at target-ordered pairs using dart guns

Fig. 10.17 Two students getting ready to aim at the same time

a chance to shoot at the ordered pair. The student whose dart lands closest to the
target-ordered pair earns a point for his or her team.

- Once students have shot the dart, they determine the ordered pair of the dart's
  actual location. They then calculate the distance from the given ordered pair in
  the x- and y-directions and record in the "Coordinate Dart" activity sheet (see
  Appendix C).
- Repeat the process until all students have had a chance to shoot the dart gun.

Modifications/Adaptations Students struggling with the concept can get peer
help. Target-ordered pairs may be marked on the whiteboard to help students
calculate distances. Students can be moved closer or farther from the board
depending on ability level.

Extensions The teacher can incorporate the Pythagorean Theorem in the lesson by
having students use $a^2 + b^2 = c^2$ to find the hypotenuse of the right triangle made
by the original given ordered pair and the landing dart ordered pair.

Activity 2: Twist and Learn

Suggested Grade Level: Any

Standards

CCSS.Math.Content.1.G.A.1

Distinguish between defining attributes (e.g., triangles are closed and three-sided) versus non-defining attributes (e.g., color, orientation, overall size); build and draw shapes to possess defining attributes.

CCSS.Math.Content.2.G.A.1

Recognize and draw shapes having specified attributes, such as a given number of angles or a given number of equal faces. Identify triangles, quadrilaterals, pentagons, hexagons, and cubes.

CCSS.Math.Content.4.G.A.1

Draw points, lines, line segments, rays, angles (right, acute, obtuse), and perpendicular and parallel lines. Identify these in two-dimensional figures.

Goals Students' prior knowledge of different geometric shapes will be activated and they will be ready for learning.

Objectives Using a Twister™-like game, the students will be able to identify and recognize different geometrical shapes.

Suggested time frame	15–20 min
Equipment/technology	Tarps prepared according to the needs and level of students, popsicle sticks with body parts, popsicle sticks with geometric words or definitions
Start/stop signals	Teacher calls a body part and geometric definition or word and says "go" to start the game Each round of the game stops when there is one person left balancing on the tarp The activity ends when teacher says, "return to your seats"
Skill cues	Remind students to "stretch" to reach some squares, to "distribute their weight" in order to hold themselves up, and to "find their balance" so they are less likely to fall
Safety cues	Ask students to wear comfortable clothes the previous day. Let students know that they need to be respectful and not shove or push while playing
Teaching style	Competition, student-centered
Assessments of content through the activity	Observe students as they choose the geometric words or figures. Correct misconceptions and review geometric
	vocabulary as the game progresses. An observational checklist can be used to make notes about students' understanding of geometric words and figures. See Appendix C for a sample checklist
Transition activity	Teacher says "back to your seats" to transition students. Once the students are in their seats, they draw and label four shapes from the activity in their notebooks

Fig. 10.18 A prepared tarp with angles

Fig. 10.19 A prepared tarp with written geometry terms

Description of Twist and Learn Activity This activity is aimed toward getting students to review different geometrical concepts in a fun, exciting way. This activity can be done before starting a lesson to review geometrical concepts, the activity can be done as practice during the lesson to bring excitement and interest into the lesson, or the activity can be done after the lesson as a reinforcing activity.

Fig. 10.20 A prepared tarp with figures from plane geometry

Preparation:

- Prepare tarp(s) with figures or words as needed for the lesson. (One tarp should be prepared for each group of 3–4 students.) Words or figures can be drawn on construction paper and then taped using clear tape. For example, a tarp with different types of angles can be prepared to review angles (see Fig. 10.18). A tarp with different words or figures can be prepared to reinforce definitions or practice identifying different geometrical shapes (see Figs. 10.19, 10.20, and Fig. 10.21). Geometric figures or words should be repeated several times on the game board. The figures or words chosen should be appropriate to the grade level of the students and relevant to the lesson. (Instead, the teacher could ask students to prepare the shapes, angles, or names of figures as a review or introduction to the activity.)
- Additionally prepare two sets of popsicle sticks. One set will have 4 popsicle sticks with "left arm", left leg", "right arm", and "right leg" written on it. The second set either has geometric words or definitions on them (see Fig. 10.22). Some possible game setups are:

  – Tarp has vocabulary words and popsicle sticks have definitions
  – Tarp has 2-D figures and popsicle sticks have definitions or names of the figures

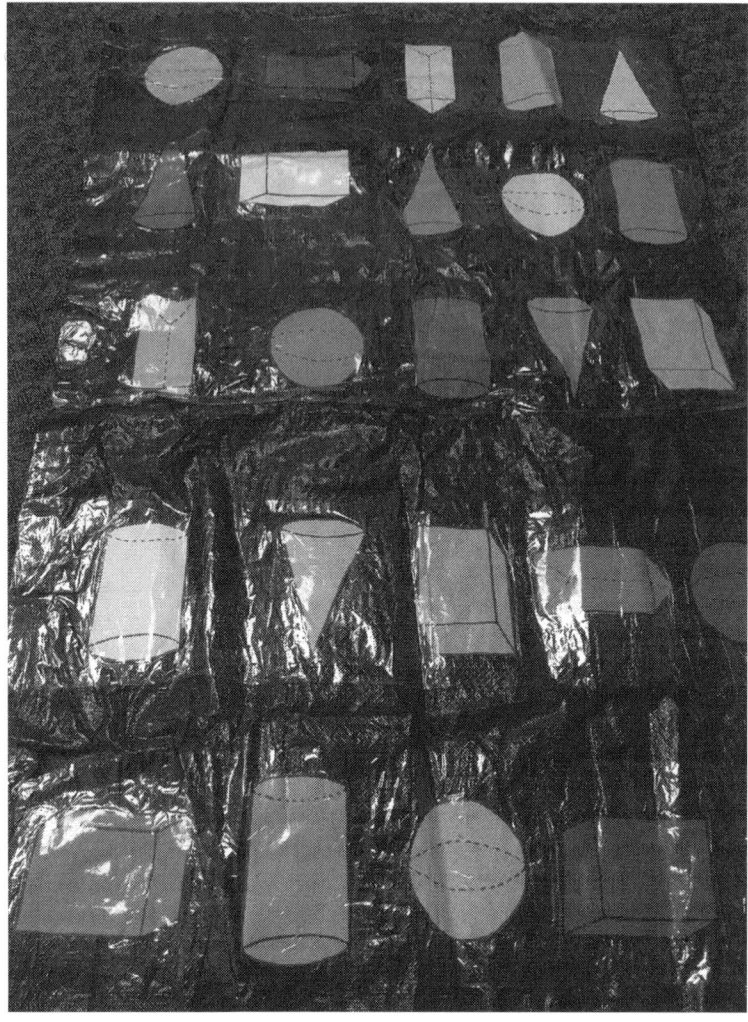

Fig. 10.21 A prepared tarp with figures from 3D geometry

- Tarp has drawings of 3D shapes and the popsicle sticks have definitions or names of the figures
- Tarp has angles drawn and the popsicle sticks have the corresponding mathematical terminology.

Introduction:

- Ask students if they have played the game Twister. Tell them that they are going to play a Twister-like game and review geometrical concepts.

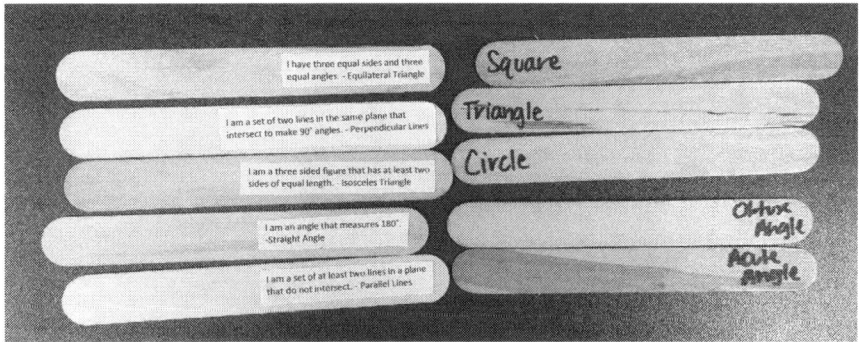

Fig. 10.22 Popsicle Sticks for the Twister Game with definitions or words

Fig. 10.23 Students playing Geometric Twister

Activity:

Divide the class into groups of 3–4 and have the first group come to the tarp. *The teacher should have enough tarps prepared, so that groups of 3–4 students can participate in the activity at the same time.*

- Explain the rules of the game to the students:

  - The teacher draws a body part popsicle stick and a vocabulary popsicle stick and reads both sticks aloud. Next, the students choose the figure corresponding to the word or definition and place the required hand or foot on it. Since each word or figure appears several times, students will have a choice of where to place their hands or feet.
  - The teacher draws another pair of popsicle sticks and students twist to get their hand or leg on that word or figure (see Fig. 10.23).
  - The goal is to balance on the tarp; any student who falls is out of the game. The round continues until there is one person left balanced on the tarp. Play music during the game to create more excitement.

- Once the first group has modeled the activity, have all groups go to their assigned tarps to begin the activity. Give all groups adequate time to finish a round of play. Then let the winners from each group play against each other. To create more excitement, students, instead of the teacher, can take turns calling the body part and the word or figure.
- During the game, the teacher can use an observational checklist to make note of any students who have misunderstandings of geometric vocabulary and/or figures.

Modifications/Adaptations For students with physical impairments, the teacher can place a Twister-like board at a level they can reach (e.g., on the table, on the wall, in their lap). The student can choose the figure corresponding to the word or definition either using their hands only or an object or implement (e.g., a pointer, a pool noodle, or other marker).

Extension The teacher can have students identify three vocabulary words and describe them or talk about the figures that confused them.

References

Adams-Blair, H., & Oliver, G. (2011). Daily classroom movement: Physical activity integration into the classroom. *International Journal of Health, Wellness and Society, 1*(3), 147–154.

American Alliance for Health, Physical Education, Recreation and Dance. (2013). *Comprehensive school physical activity programs: Helping students achieve 60 minutes of physical activity each day [position statement]*. Reston, VA: Author.

Azrin, N. H., Ehle, C. T., & Beaumont, A. L. (2006). Physical exercise as a reinforcer to promote calmness of an ADHD child. *Behavior Modification, 30*(5), 564–570.

Baroody, A. J., & Dowker, A. (2003). *The development of arithmetic concepts and skills: Constructing adaptive expertise*. Mahwah, NJ: Erlbaum.

Beaudoin, C. R., & Johnston, P. (2011). The impact of purposeful movement in algebra instruction. *Education, 132*(1), 82.

Block, C. C., Parris, S. R., & Whiteley, C. S. (2008). CPMs: A kinesthetic comprehension strategy. *Reading Teacher, 61*(6), 460–470.

Bragg, P. & Outhred, L. (2000a). What is taught a versus what is learned learnt: The case of linear measurement. In *Mathematics Beyond 2000. Proceedings of the 23rd annual conference of mathematics education research group of Australia, Fremantle* (Vol. 1, pp. 112–118).

Bragg, P. & Outhred, L. (2000b). Students' knowledge of length units: Do they know more than rules about rulers? In T. Nakahara & M. Koyama (Eds.), *Proceedings of the 24th annual conference of the international group for the psychology of mathematics education* (Vol. 2, pp. 97–104).

Carpenter, T. P., Lindquist, M. M., Brown, C., Kouba, V. L., Silver, E. A., & Swafford, J. O. (1988). Results of the fourth NAEP assessment of mathematics: Trends and conclusions. *Arithmetic Teacher, 36*, 38–41.

Caterino, M. C., & Polak, E. D. (1999). Effects of two types of activity on the performance of second-, third-, and fourth-grade students on a test of concentration. *Perceptual and Motor Skills, 89*(1), 245–248.

Centers for Disease Control and Prevention (CDC). (2013). *Comprehensive physical activity programs: A guide for schools.* Atlanta, GA: U.S. Department of Health and Human Services.

Clements, D. H., & Burns, B. A. (2000). Students' development of strategies for turn and angle measure. *Educational Studies in Mathematics, 41*(1), 31–45.

Coe, D. P., Pivarnik, J. M., Womack, C. J., Reeves, M. J., & Malina, R. M. (2006). Effect of physical education and activity levels on academic achievement in children. *Medicine and Science in Sports and Exercise, 38*(8), 1515.

Cook, C. D. (2008). I scream, you scream: Data analysis with kindergartners. *Teaching Children Mathematics, 14*(9), 538–540.

DeFrancesco, C., & Casas, B. (2004). Elementary physical education and math skill development. *Strategies, 18*(2), 21–23.

Erwin, H., Fedewa, A., & Ahn, S. (2013). Student academic performance outcomes of a classroom physical activity intervention: A pilot study. *International Electronic Journal of Elementary Education, 5*(2), 109–124.

Erwin, H. E., Abel, M. G., Beighle, A., & Beets, M. W. (2011). Promoting children's health through physically active math classes: A pilot study. *Health Promotion Practice, 12*(2), 244–251.

Hall, E. M. (2007). Integration: Helping to get our kids moving and learning. *Physical Educator, 64*(3), 123–128.

Hannaford, C. (1995). *Smart moves: Why learning is not all in your head.* Arlington, VA: Great Ocean Publishers Inc.

Hart, K. (1989). Volume of a cuboid. In K. Hart, D. Johnson, M. Brown, L. Dickson, & R. Clarkson (Eds.), *Children's mathematical frameworks 8–13: A study of classroom teaching* (pp. 126–150). London: NFER-Nelson.

Hourigan, M., & Leavy, A. (2016). Practical problems: Using literature to teach statistics. *Teaching Children Mathematics, 22*(5), 282–291.

Howse, T. D., & Howse, M. E. (2014). Linking the Van Hiele theory to instruction. *Teaching Children Mathematics, 21*(5), 304–313.

Jones, J. C. (2011). *Visualizing elementary and middle school mathematics methods.* Hoboken, NJ: Wiley.

Lynch, P. (2007). Making meaning many ways: An exploratory look at integrating the arts with classroom curriculum. *Art Education, 60*(4), 33–38.

Mahar, M. T., Murphy, S. K., Rowe, D. A., Golden, J., Shields, A. T., & Raedeke, T. D. (2006). Effects of a classroom-based program on physical activity and on-task behavior. *Medicine and Science in Sports and Exercise, 38*(12), 2086.

National Council of Teachers of Mathematics. (2000). *Principles and standards for school mathematics.* Reston, VA: NCTM.

Nemirovsky, R., & Rasmussen, C. (2005). A case study of how kinesthetic experiences can participate in and transfer to work with equations. *International Group for the Psychology of Mathematics Education, 4*, 9–16.

Noble, T. (2003). Gesture and the mathematics of motion. Retrieved from http://files.eric.ed.gov/fulltext/ED478190.pdf.

Norris, E., Shelton, N., Dunsmuir, S., Duke-Williams, O., & Stamatakis, E. (2015). Physically active lessons as physical activity and educational interventions: A systematic review of methods and results. *Preventive Medicine, 72,* 116–125.

Outhred, L. N., & McPhail, D. (2000). A framework for teaching early measurement. In J. Bana & A. Chapman (Eds.), *Proceedings of the 23rd Annual Conference of the Mathematics Education Research Group of Australasia, Fermantle, Australia* (pp. 487–494). Sydney: MERGA.

Outhred, L. N., Mitchelmore, M. C., McPhail, D., & Gould, P. (2003). Count me into measurement: A program for the early elementary school. In D. H. Clement & G. Bright (Eds.), *NCTM 2003 yearbook: Learning and teaching measurement* (pp. 81–99). Reston, VA: National Council of Teacher of Mathematics.

Riley, N., Lubans, D. R., Holmes, K., & Morgan, P. J. (2014). Rationale and study protocol of the EASY minds (encouraging activity to stimulate young minds) program: Cluster randomized controlled trial of a primary school-based physical activity integration program for mathematics. *BMC Public Health, 14*(1), 1.

Rittle-Johnson, B., & Schneider, M. (2014). Developing conceptual and procedural knowledge of mathematics. In *Oxford handbook of numerical cognition.* Oxford: Oxford University Press.

Rittle-Johnson, B., & Star, J. R. (2007). Does comparing solution methods facilitate conceptual and procedural knowledge? An experimental study on learning to solve equations. *Journal of Educational Psychology, 99*(3), 561.

Russell, S. J., Schifter, D., & Bastable, V. (2006). Is it 2 more or 2 less? Algebra in the elementary classroom. *Connect Magazine, 19*(3), 1–3.

Schwartz, S. L. (1995). Developing power in linear measurement. *Teaching Children Mathematics, 1*(7), 412–417.

Shaughnessy, J. M. (2007). Research on statistics learning and reasoning. In F. K. Lester Jr. (Ed.), *Second handbook of research on mathematics teaching and learning* (pp. 957–1009). Charlotte, NC: Information Age Publishing.

Skoning, S. (2010). Dancing the curriculum. *Kappa Delta Pi Record, 46*(4), 170–174.

Stalvey, S., & Brasell, H. (2006). Using stress balls to focus the attention of sixth-grade learners. *Journal of At-Risk Issues, 12*(2), 7–16.

Star, J. R., & Seifert, C. (2006). The development of flexibility in equation solving. *Contemporary Educational Psychology, 31*(3), 280–300.

Stephan, M., & Clements, D. H. (2003). Linear, area, and time measurement in prekindergarten to grade 2. In D. H. Clement & G. Bright (Eds.), *NCTM 2003 Yearbook: Learning and Teaching Measurement* (pp. 3–16). Reston, VA: National Council of Teacher of Mathematics.

Theodorakou, K., & Zervas, Y. (2003). The effects of the creative movement teaching method and the traditional teaching method on elementary school children's self-esteem. *Sport, Education and Society, 8*(1), 91–104.

Van de Walle, J. A., Karp, K. S., & Williams, J. M. B. (2013). *Elementary and middle school mathematics. Teaching developmentally* (8th ed.). Boston: Pearson.

Vazou, S., Gavrilou, P., Mamalaki, E., Papanastasiou, A., & Sioumala, N. (2012). Does integrating physical activity in the elementary school classroom influence academic motivation? *International Journal of Sport and Exercise Psychology, 10*(4), 251–263.

Verschaffel, L., Luwel, K., Torbeyns, J., & Van Dooren, W. (2009). Conceptualizing, investigating, and enhancing adaptive expertise in elementary mathematics education. *European Journal of Psychology of Education, 24,* 335–359. doi:10.1007/BF03174765.

Wade, M. (2016). Math and movement: Practical ways to incorporate math into physical education. *Strategies, 29*(1), 10–15. doi:10.1080/08924562.2015.1111788.

Chapter 11
Lesson Plans for Movement in the Mathematics Classroom

Dittika Gupta, Sarah Cobb, Shelby Butler and Mary Brady

Abstract This chapter features four full-length lesson plans designed to address the main strands of mathematics as highlighted in the *Common Core State Standards* (CCSS) for Mathematics and in the *Principles and Standards for School Mathematics* (NCTM 2000). The lessons and activities presented in this chapter aim to develop understanding in data analysis, numbers and operations, algebraic thinking, and geometric concepts.

The first lesson, "*Search, Collect, and Conquer,*" develops the concepts of data collection, sorting, graphing, and interpreting data. The lesson includes accommodations to scaffold the activity for different grade levels. The second lesson, "*Show me the Number!*" is geared toward developing flexibility in thinking about numbers and operations for students in the lower elementary grades. The third lesson, "*I like to Move it!!!*" is for upper elementary grades and focuses on developing understanding of unit rates. The fourth lesson, "*Shape Seek*" is for upper elementary grades and is aimed at helping students identify geometric figures in everyday contexts. Through this lesson, students discover different geometric figures in the real world.

All lesson plans and activities can be adjusted to accommodate needs and development levels of the students. Possible extension activities are also provided with each lesson as springboards for modifying the lesson to fit the needs of specific student populations.

D. Gupta (✉) · S. Cobb · S. Butler · M. Brady
Midwestern State University, Wichita Falls, TX, USA
e-mail: dittika.gupta@mwsu.edu

S. Cobb
e-mail: sarah.cobb@mwsu.edu

S. Butler
e-mail: shelby.butler@burkburnettisd.org

M. Brady
e-mail: marybrdy@gmail.com

© Springer Nature Singapore Pte Ltd. 2018   247
S.C. Miller and S.F. Lindt (eds.), *Moving INTO the Classroom*,
Springer Texts in Education, DOI 10.1007/978-981-10-6424-1_11

Lesson Plan: Search, Collect, and Conquer

Suggested Grade Level: Kindergarten-3rd

Lesson Overview

Engagement and Instructional Input (15 min) *Search, Collect, and Conquer!!!*

Cooperative Learning (15–20 min) Students will work in groups of 2–3. They will sort the collected leaves, pebbles, acorns, and sticks, then make bar graphs of the data.

Whole Class Sharing (10–15 min): Students will share and explain graphs.

Closure (2 min) Students will answer questions on sorting and graphing posed by teacher.

CCSS	CCSS.Math.Content.K.MD.B.3 Classify objects into given categories; count the numbers of objects in each category and sort the categories by count CCSS.Math.Content.1.MD.C.4 Organize, represent, and interpret data with up to three categories; ask and answer questions about the total number of data points, how many in each category, and how many more or less are in one category than in another CCSS.Math.Content.2.MD.D.10 Draw a picture graph and a bar graph (with single-unit scale) to represent a dataset with up to four categories. Solve simple put-together, take-apart, and compare problems using information presented in a bar graph CCSS.Math.Content.3.MD.B.3 Draw a scaled picture graph and a scaled bar graph to represent a data set with several categories. Solve one- and two step "how many more" and "how many less" problems using information presented in scaled bar graphs. *For example, draw a bar graph in which each square in the bar graph might represent 5 pets*

NCTM	• In grades Pre-K-2, all students should be able to formulate questions that can be addressed with data and collect, organize, and display relevant data to answer them
	  – Pose questions and gather data about themselves and their surroundings
	  – Sort and classify objects according to their attributes and organize data about the objects
	  – Represent data using concrete objects, pictures, and graphs

Goals	Students will use the collected leaves, pebbles, acorns, and sticks to understand the concepts of data. Students will sort and graph the collected items found in everyday life
Objectives	The students will sort and classify the leaves, pebbles, acorns, and sticks in different categories. Students will represent the collected items in a bar graph and make interpretations from the graph

Description of Search, Collect, and Conquer! Activity

In this activity, the students will use collected real-world objects to develop concepts of data, sorting, and graphing. The students will sort leaves, pebbles, acorns, and sticks, represent them in graphs or pictures, and answer questions about the categories.

Engagement and Instructional Input: Search, Collect, and Conquer! Activity

Activity Preparation

Make sure each student has a plastic bag and is appropriately dressed for walking outdoors. Make sure an area has been designated for the walk and a copy of activity sheet is printed for each student. Each student will collect the materials and groups will be made after the walk.

Introduction

- Introduce the lesson by talking about nature and what students notice outside.
- Give each student a plastic bag and explain that the class will be going outside to collect leaves, small rocks (pebbles), sticks, acorns, or other small objects they find in nature and put them in their bag.
- **We will be going outside to collect small objects such as leaves, pebbles, acorns, and small sticks. Each one of you will have about 10–15 min to collect the objects. No running, shoving, or pushing is allowed. Each one of you will collect your own objects and in the marked areas. I will blow the whistle once to start the collecting and when the whistle is blown twice, you will stop collecting. Walk around and collect things carefully.**
- Reinforce the nonacceptable movements for the activity such as shoving, pushing, bumping, or racing. Ask if there are any questions and then take the students outside in the marked areas.

Activity Instructions

- Take students on a nature walk to collect leaves, pebbles (small stones), acorns, and sticks.
- Blow whistle to have them start collecting the real-world objects. After 10–15 min, blow the whistle to tell them it is time to stop collecting.

Cooperative Learning

- After the nature walk, divide the class into groups of 2 or 3 students. Each group will work together to sort all the objects collected by individual students in the group. Give each student an activity sheet.

- **You will be working as a group to sort the objects collected by everyone in the group together. Work together but fill in your own activity sheet**.

  - Students in Kindergarten and 1st grade will count the various collected items, sort them, and discuss ways they are the same. They can make pictures to represent the number of items in each group. As students work, the teacher should ask them questions, such as:

- **How many items did you collect?**
- **Why are they in the same group?**
- **How are they similar?**
- **How many more leaves are there than pebbles?**
- **How many items are in each category?**

  Next, they will compare the various items found and fill in the Activity sheet (see Appendix C).

  - Students in 2nd grade will not only organize the collected items but also represent them through bar graphs. They will make graphs for leaves, pebbles, acorns, and sticks (see Appendix C). They will also combine categories such as pebbles and sticks and represent them on the graph. Discuss and answer questions on comparing categories, putting together, and taking apart categories such as:

    How many items did you collect?
    Why are they in the same group? How are they similar?
    What does the graph show you?
    Which category has the fewest objects? How can you tell?
    What does the bar on the leaves tell you?
    How many objects are there that come from trees? How did you know that?

  - Students in 3rd grade will also represent data as bar graphs but they further sort the objects by color, shape, type, size, or length. For example, color or shape of leaves, type of pebble (smooth or rough), and size or length of stick. Once students have finished graphing in small groups, the whole class can work together to graph objects collected by the whole class. Introduce students to scale for graphs so that they are able to represent each square in the bar graph as 2 or 3 units. Ask questions such as:

    How many items did the class collect?
    How can you represent leaves collected by everyone on the graph?
    What does the graph show you?
    Which category has the fewest objects? How can you tell?
    What does the class bar graph tell you? How does it compare to your group bar graph?
    How many objects are there that come from trees? How did you know that?

Whole Class Sharing

- After each group has worked together for about 20–25 min, they should share their results. Each group will present and share about their sorted objects such as how are they similar, how many, how many more, which one was the least. They will also share their pictures and graphs and explain them. The teacher can ask questions to foster higher order thinking and developing mathematical communication.

Closure Teacher will ask groups to discuss and give one example where sorting and graphing can be used and how can it be used.

Suggested time frame	45–50 min
Equipment/technology	Sorting activity sheet Graphing activity sheet Pencils Plastic bags Whistle
Start/stop signals	Students start searching and collecting objects when the teacher blows the whistle once Students stop collecting when the teacher blows the whistle twice
Skill cues	"Be aware of your environment"—students should be aware and considerate of each other when selecting their leaves, pebbles, acorns, and sticks. Students should meet expectations of being outside
Safety cues	Mark areas with cones or other clear markers to indicate the appropriate places that the students can collect
Teaching style	Cooperative learning, guided practice
Assessments of content through the activity	Actively monitor and observe as students sort and organize the leaves, pebbles, acorns, and sticks. Ask questions about the sorting. Use their activity sheet and graphs or pictures to check for understanding about sorting and organizing objects
Transition activity	After the students return from the nature walk, they should get into groups to work on sorting their objects and graphing the data

Extensions Teacher can have four corners of the room represent four different types of candy, four seasons, four TV shows, or four superheroes and have students move to their favorite spot. More discussions on sorting, graphing, and even frequency table can be conducted.

Modifications/Accommodations Students with physical impairments limiting lower body movement can work with a partner and point in the direction of items to be collected.

Lesson Plan: Show Me the Number

Suggested Grade Level: Kindergarten-3rd

Engagement (3 min): The teacher introduces the lesson and gives number necklaces to the students.

Demonstration and Guided Practice (15 min): *Show me the Number!!!* The teacher explains that they will be using operations to make different numbers and demonstrates ways to make the number 10.

Cooperative Learning (15–20 min): Students work as a whole group to make the target number chosen by the teacher.

Whole Class Discussion (10–15 min): Students share and explain different ways and strategies used to make the number.

Closure (2 min): Students will answer questions about making different numbers.

CCSS	CCSS.Math.Content.K.OA.A.3 Decompose numbers less than or equal to 10 into pairs in more than one way, e.g., by using objects or drawings, and record each decomposition by a drawing or equation (e.g., $5 = 2 + 3$ and $5 = 4 + 1$) CCSS.Math.Content.K.OA.A.4 For any number from 1 to 9, find the number that makes 10 when added to the given number, e.g., by using objects or drawings, and record the answer with a drawing or equation CCSS.Math.Content.1.OA.C.6 Add and subtract within 20, demonstrating fluency for addition and subtraction within 10. Use strategies such as counting on; making 10 (e.g., $8 + 6 = 8 + 2 + 4 = 10 + 4 = 14$); decomposing a number leading to 10 (e.g., $13 - 4 = 13 - 3 - 1 = 10 - 1 = 9$) CCSS.Math.Content.2.OA.B.2 Fluently add and subtract within 20 using mental strategies. By end of Grade 2, know from memory all sums of two 1-digit numbers CCSS.Math.Content.3.OA.A.4 Determine the unknown whole number in a multiplication or division equation relating three whole numbers • In grades Pre-K-2, all students should be able to understand numbers, ways of representing numbers, relationships among numbers, and number systems – Develop a sense of whole numbers and represent and use them in flexible ways, including relating, composing, and decomposing numbers
NCTM	• In grades Pre-K-2, all students should be able to understand meanings of operations and how they relate to one another – Understand the effects of adding and subtracting whole numbers • In grades 3–5, all students should be able to understand meanings of operations and how they relate to one another – Understand the effects of multiplying and dividing whole numbers – Identify and use relationships between operations, such as division as the inverse of multiplication, to solve problems

(continued)

(continued)

Goals	Students will develop flexibility and understanding of decomposing different numbers. Students will develop fluency in number operations, especially addition and subtraction
Objectives	The students will illustrate a number by decomposing it using number necklaces. Students will create a given number using number operations

Description of Show Me the Number Activity

Engage

Introduce the lesson by asking about number operations. Show students the number necklaces and tell them that they will be playing a game with numbers.

Demonstration and Guided Practice

Activity Preparation

- Make a number necklace for each student. Write a number between 0 and 9 on an index card and tie a string to the top corners of the index card (see Fig. 11.1). Repeat numbers if needed.
- Make sure there is enough space for students to move around.

Activity Instructions

- In this activity, each student is given a number on a necklace (see Fig. 11.1). The teacher will choose a target number and the students in small groups will use arithmetic operations to combine the numbers on their necklaces to make the target number.
- Ask for five volunteers. Give them any five number necklaces. Discuss the different ways 10 can be made. Have students move to make 10. For example, if

Fig. 11.1 Sample number necklace

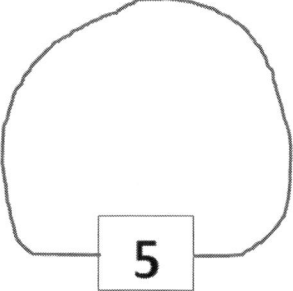

the five students are given number necklaces as 2, 3, 4, 5, 6, students can make 10 as 6 + 4=10, 5 + 3 + 2 = 10, 5 × 2 = 10, or 3 × 4 − 2 = 10.

- Have students pose their bodies to indicate the operation being used: arms outstretched to form a plus sign when the operation is addition; arms at sides to form a straight line when the operation is subtraction; arms and legs forming an X to for multiplication; arms forming circles to indicate division.
- Ask for input from students as you form the groups:

  - **What two numbers add to 10?**
  - **We can add three numbers to make 10, what are those?**
  - **This student has a 5. What number would we multiply by 5 to get 10?**
  - **These two numbers multiplied together make 12. How can we make 10? Is there a number we can subtract to make 10?**

- Discuss other ways to form number 10 if digits 0 to 9 are given.

  - For kinder and 1st grade, students can use addition to make 10. Some possible groups are:

    $9 + 1 = 10$
    $7 + 3 = 10$
    $8 + 2 = 10$
    $4 + 6 = 10$
    $4 + 3 + 3 = 10$
    $7 + 1 + 2 = 10$
    $5 + 3 + 2 = 10$
    $2 + 3 + 4 + 1 = 10$
    The number 0 can go with any of the groups

  - For students in 2nd and 3rd grade, students can use addition, subtraction, multiplication, and division to make 10. A few possible groups are:

    $5 × 2 = 10$
    $3 × 3 + 1 = 10$
    $8 + 4 + 1 − 3 = 10$
    $5 × 4 ÷ 2 = 10$
    The number 0 can go with any of the groups using addition or subtraction
    The number 1 can go with any of the groups using multiplication or division as well as any of the addition groups above.

Cooperative Learning

- After the demonstration and discussion, give all students number necklaces and have them stand up.
- Give class different target numbers such as 5, 6, 7, 8, or 9 and two-digit numbers between 10 and 20, depending on the level of the students. Students make

smaller groups representing the target number, posing to indicate the operation being used. If there are students left that cannot make the given number, have them combine into groups as close to the target number as possible.

- As shown in the demonstration, have students pose their bodies to indicate the operation being used: arms outstretched to form a plus sign when the operation is addition; arms at sides to form a straight line when the operation is subtraction; arms and legs forming an $\times$ to for multiplication; arms forming circles to indicate division.

Whole Class Discussion

- Have the students return to their seats and lead them in a discussion of the activity. Ask questions like:

  - **Which number was the toughest to make? Why was it difficult?**
  - **Which numbers were the hardest to fit into groups? Why was it difficult?**
  - **Which numbers were the easiest to fit into groups?**
  - **How can we make the number 7? How can we make the number 9? How can we make the number 12?**

Closure

- End the lesson by asking students to choose one of the target numbers and write down five ways to make it. Encourage them to use a variety of operations and numbers.

Suggested time frame	25–30 min
Equipment/technology	Number necklaces
Start/stop signals	To start the activity, the teacher announces the target number and says, "Go" Students are done when the teacher says, "Stop"
Skill cues	Remind students to be aware and considerate of each other when making groups Have the students use their hands and bodies to indicate the operation being used: arms outstretched to form a plus sign when the operation is addition; arms at sides to form a straight line when the operation is subtraction; arms and legs forming an $\times$ to for multiplication; arms forming circles to indicate division
Safety cues	Student should not shout or yell at their classmates Remind students that there should be no running while making groups

(continued)

(continued)

Teaching style	Cooperative learning, student centered
Assessments of content through the activity	Actively monitor and observe as students as they make groups and discuss the different number operations Observational checklist can be used or notes can be taken about students' understanding
Transition activity	After the students are done with creating numbers, they return to the seats to work on combining two-digit numbers

Extension Use negative numbers in the activity or give students negative target numbers. The activity could also be extended by pointing out that the numbers 0 and 1 can be added to any group without changing the value. Discuss the ideas of additive and multiplicative identities.

Modifications/Accommodations Students with physical impairment limiting lower body movement can have other students move to their location. The number can be displayed and also written and spoken in Spanish for English Language Learners.

Lesson Plan: I like to Move It!!!

Suggested Grade Level: 5–6

Lesson Overview

Engagement (10–12 min): "*I like to Move it*" Unit rates movement activity.

Transition Group up by working with an elbow partner.

Instructional Input (15–20 min): Modeling of unit rates and group discussion.

Cooperative Learning and Practice (15–20 min): Students will convert their rates for the four different movements to unit rates with an elbow partner.

Closure (3 min): Review unit rates and relate how the different types of movements influenced their walking rate.

CCSS	CCSS.Math.Content.6.RP.A.2 Understand the concept of a unit rate a/b associated with a ratio $a{:}b$ with $b \neq 0$, and use rate language in the context of a ratio relationship
NCTM	• In grades 3–5 all students should analyze change in various context – Investigate how a change in one variable relates to a change in a second variable

(continued)

(continued)

	– Identify and describe situations with constant or varying rates of change and compare them • In grades 6–8, all students should be able to understand numbers, ways of representing numbers, relationships between numbers, and number systems – Understand and use ratios and proportions to represent quantitative relationships
Goals	Students will compute rates associated with several movements and convert the rates to unit rates. The movement will help students understand the difference between a rate and a unit rate. The students will create the rate itself by performing four different movements
Objectives	The student will be able to apply rates and unit rates to everyday problem solving and use quantitative reasoning to solve real-world problems using rates. The students will be able to relate rates and unit rates through the different movements enacted in the class

Description of I like to Move It Activity

Activity Preparation

- Have a copy of the activity sheet ready for each student. Queue up appropriate music on a computer or audio system. Make sure there is enough space in the middle or front of the room for students to walk. The teacher will choose a song or songs to play during the activity. (Any songs can be used because the music will be used to provide the students with a beat to move.) Song suggestions are listed in Fig. 11.3.

Engage

- To hook the students, have them get out of their seats and move all the desks and chairs to the sides of the classroom.
- **Get out of your seats and stand in the middle of the classroom. Make sure to keep your hands and feet to yourself. Also, make sure you are not touching anyone else and have room to freely move around.**
- Hand out the "Unit Rate Activity Sheet" (see Appendix C).
- The students will perform a series of movements (see Fig. 11.2) as instructed by the teacher. Music should be used as a start/stop signal for the movements (see Fig. 11.3 for some suggested musical selections). When the music starts, the students start to do one of the movements in Fig. 11.2 and count the number of steps they take. After 30 s, stop the music. Students freeze in place. Then they record how many steps they took on the chart on their activity sheet (see Appendix C).
- **Music will be your start/stop signal for this activity today. You will hear music play and that means to start walking around the room in a certain**

- Mud Walk: students walk like they are stuck in mud. They move slowly, taking big steps as though pulling their feet out of the sticky mud
- Mouse Walk. Students should take very tiny steps. Demonstrate the movement and start the music.
- The third movement is the gorilla walk: flex arms, shoulders back, and walk with bent knees. Demonstrate the movement and start the music.
- Skipping: The last movement is skipping. Students should step and hop. Demonstrate the movement and start the music.

Fig. 11.2 Movements for "I Like to Move It!!!"

- "Happy" by Pharrell Williams
- "Stronger" by Kelly Clarkson
- "Best Day of My Life" by American Authors

Fig. 11.3 Suggested music for the "I Like to Move It!!!" activity

way, which I will tell you more about in a few minutes, and as soon as the music stops you will freeze. As you are walking around the room, I want you to count the number of steps you are taking. You will do a series of four different movements.

Activity Instructions

- In this activity, students will develop a concrete understanding of unit rates by walking with various kinds of movements and calculating the number of steps per second they take during each movement. Different kinds of movements change the number of steps they take in a given amount of time, giving the students a contextual physical model for the abstract idea of unit rates.
- Make sure that the students know the expectations of the activity. For example, keeping hands, feet, and objects to themselves; to start when music starts and to stop when the music stops. *The music should be played for 30 s for each movement.*
- **Your first movement is a mud walk. Walk as though you are stuck in mud. Move slowly, taking big steps like you are pulling your feet out of the mud. Make sure to count your steps as you move around the room.**
- **Remember to count your steps! Make sure to fill in the number of steps on your recording sheet after each movement. You will calculate unit rate after we have completed the four movements.**
- Once students have completed the mud walk and recorded the number of steps, repeat the activity for the other three movements. Before each movement, remind students to count their steps and after the movement have them record the number of steps they took during each movement.

Transition

- Have students return to their seats and discuss the activity with an elbow partner (or person sitting next to the student).
- **Look at your elbow partner's recording sheet. Compare their number of steps for each activity to yours. During which movement did your elbow partner take the most steps? Was it the same as the one during which you took the most steps?**

Instructional Input

- Have several students share with the class how many steps they took for each movement.
- Explain to students that a *rate* is a special type of ratio that compares quantities with unlike units. Often the second unit is a unit of time, such as seconds or minutes. Demonstrate on the board to students that if they took x steps during the 30 s activity, their rate would be x steps/30 s. For example, if the mud walk had 15 steps in 30 s, then their rate is 15 steps/30 s.
- Explain that *unit rates* are rates when compared to one unit. A student who has a rate of 15 steps/30 s has a unit rate of 0.5 steps/s. The word "per" is often used in unit rates, so this rate can also be expressed as 0.5 steps/s. Unit rates are useful for measure many things, such as heart rate (beats per minute) and speed (miles per hour). The difference between *rate* and *unit rate* is that in *unit rate*, the denominator is one. For example, the number of students in three buses is the rate but number of students in one bus is the unit rate.
- The teacher should facilitate a class discussion and students should be prepared to answer the questions about unit rates. Teacher can facilitate discussion using a scenario (e.g., If you traveled 7 km in 4 min, this would be your rate, but the unit rate would be compared to 1 min instead of 4 min)

  - How would you convert 7 km/4 min. to km over 1 min?
  - Wait until students mention dividing, and/or relate to simplifying fractions.
  - Show on the board 7/4 and 4/4 to get x km over 1 min.

- Compare *rates* and *unit rates* to something that is relatable to students. For example, *unit rates* can be used in something as simple as the number of classes they attend per day. Other examples that might be mentioned by students are that rates can help us know how fast or slow we are driving a car, distance traveled by a car, plane, train, in an hour, walking up or down the hill, and how much gas mileage we get in a car.

Be prepared to discuss the following with the class:

- When could you use a rate?
- What are some examples of rates and unit rates to describe things you do in your life?
- Why do you think rates are important to understand?
- Why do you think we use rates and unit rates?

Cooperative Learning and Practice

- Explain the activity sheet to the students.
- **In the Number of Steps column, you recorded the number of steps for each movement.**
- **In the Time column, record the amount of time you spent taking those steps. This was 30 s for each movement.**
- **In the Rate column, express your rate in ratio form. For example, if you took 15 steps in 30 s during the mud walk, then your rate is 15 steps/30 s.**
- **To fill in the unit rate column, find your unit rate for each movement. Remember that the unit rate is the number of steps in 1 s.**
- When students have finished filling in their sheet, have them check their answers with their elbow partner. Remind them that they can determine whether two ratios are equivalent by using the cross-product.

Closure

- End the lesson by reviewing the content. Ask:
  - **What is a rate?** (a ratio that compares measurements with unlike units)
  - **What is a unit rate?** (a rate when compared to *one* unit)
  - **What are some situations where you can use unit rates?** (Many possible examples. Students might mention speed of a car or bicycle, heart rate, or growth rates.)

Suggested time frame	50 min
Equipment/technology	Pencils (one for each student) Activity sheet (one for each student) Whiteboard Dry erase marker Computer Music
Start/stop signals	Students begin walking when the music starts Students stop walking and freeze in place when the music stops
Skill cues	Mud walk: move slowly, take big steps like you are pulling your feet out of the mud Mouse walk: take quick, tiny steps. Move quietly like a mouse Gorilla walk: flex arms, shoulders back, and take slow, heavy steps with bent knees. Pretend your legs are very heavy Skipping: Step and hop. Count each foot movement separately
Safety cues	During the preparation and lesson, make sure that each student has plenty of room to walk around and is not too close to another student. Tell students to hold out their arms and make sure that they are at least an arm's width apart from each other to avoid collisions with each other. They are also told to not bump into each other or the activity will be stopped

(continued)

(continued)

	The teacher should push any hazardous objects to the perimeter of the room to avoid students tripping or hitting themselves on anything
Teaching style	Direct instruction, cooperative learning
Assessments of content through the activity	Check for understanding about the activity by asking random students to repeat the expectations Use random calling to answer questions related to rate Monitor actively while students are doing the activity sheet Activity sheet: students will complete the movement activity chart individually or with elbow partner
Transition activity	Following the skipping movement, have students freeze in place at the stop signal. Direct the students to record the number of steps in the correct column on the activity sheet (Appendix C) and compare the number of steps for each movement with their elbow partners. If the desks need to be rearranged, give students 5 min to rearrange them

Extension Have students compute the number of steps they would take in 1 min. Discuss the relationship between unit rates in seconds and in minutes.

Modifications/Accommodations
Students with physical impairments limiting lower body movements can move their hands or fingers across their desk using the same kinds of movements described.

Lesson Plan: Shape Seek

Suggested Grade Levels: 3rd–4th

Lesson Overview

Engagement (3 min): *Shape Seek*—Teacher will introduce the activity.

Instructional Input (10 min): Teacher will explain directions and expectations for the activity.

Cooperative Learning (20–30 min): Students will work in groups of two to three students to find real-life examples of mathematical shapes.

Group Presentations (25–45 min): Students will prepare and present their pictures of the real-life shapes to their classmates.

Closure (2 min): Review the many shapes that can be found in the students' everyday lives.

CCSS	CCSS.Math.Content.3.G.A.1
	Understand that shapes in different categories (e.g., rhombuses, rectangles, and others) may share attributes (e.g., having four sides), and that the shared attributes can define a larger category (e.g., quadrilaterals). Recognize rhombuses, rectangles, and squares as examples of quadrilaterals, and draw examples of quadrilaterals that do not belong to any of these subcategories
	CCSS.Math.Content.4.G.A.2
	Classify two-dimensional figures based on the presence or absence of parallel or perpendicular lines, or the presence or absence of angles of a specified size. Recognize right triangles as a category, and identify right triangles
	CCSS.Math.Content.4.G.A.3
	Recognize a line of symmetry for a two-dimensional figure as a line across the figure such that the figure can be folded along the line into matching parts. Identify line-symmetric figures and draw lines of symmetry
NCTM	• In grades 3–5, all students should be able to use analyze characteristics and properties of two- and three-dimensional geometric shapes and develop mathematical arguments about geometric relationships
	– Identify, compare, and analyze attributes of two- and three-dimensional shapes and develop vocabulary to describe the attributes
	• In grades 3–5, all students should be able to use visualization, spatial reasoning, and geometric modeling to solve problems
	– Recognize geometric ideas and relationships and apply them to other disciplines and to problems that arise in the classroom or in the everyday life
Goals	Students will use movement to help them find various types of geometric figures and shapes in real-world surroundings. Students will summarize their findings of different types of geometric figures in everyday life through a presentation or poster
Objectives	The students will recognize and identify different types of geometric figures in everyday life settings while using locomotors movement. Students will be able to draw and identify characteristics of different geometric figures

Description of Shape Seek Activity

Engagement

Introduce the lesson by talking about different shapes and figures found in real-life. Ask students to give some examples. Then introduce the lesson by stating that **we will find these figures or shapes today in groups**.

Activity Preparation

- The teacher will need to decide if the activity will be done inside the school building, outside on the school campus, or in the classroom.
- If students will be leaving the school building, prepare maps the activity area, clearly marking the areas students are allowed to search in and those that are off-limits. Maps can be hand drawn by the teacher or can be mapped already in existence.

- Provide one camera per group if the students are taking pictures and one activity sheet (see Appendix C). Clipboards may be provided if the students are going outside the classroom.
- Prepare one timer per group by setting it for the length of the activity.

Instructional Input

- Hand out the "Geometry Scavenger Hunt Activity Sheet."
- Divide the class into groups of 2 or 3.
- Explain that the students will work within their groups to find objects around the school that match the definitions on the activity sheet. If it is not possible to go around the school or outside, use the classroom (To increase movement for this activity, students can penguin walk, tip-toe, or skip to find each object.).
- Use the first definition as an example to explain the activity sheet. The first definition says, "I am a round object. All of my points are an equal distance from the center of me. What am I?" (see Appendix C).

  – Ask students **what shape does that definition describe?** Once the students identify the figure as a circle, explain that they would write "circle" in the second column.
  – Next, students would find a real-life example of a circle around the school. Ask, **What examples of circles do you see in the classroom?** They may mention a clock, a pencil eraser, a trash can, or other round items. They can write the name or draw a picture of the example in the third column. If you have provided cameras, they can take a picture of the circle to use in their PowerPoint presentation later.
  – Once they find an example, they will write at least two things they notice about the shape in the fourth column. Ask students **what are some things you notice about a circle?** They might say that it is curved, that it is round, that it has no corners, or that it looks the same no matter how it is rotated.

Cooperative Learning

- Explain the rules of the activity:

  – **Work in your groups to figure out the vocabulary word for the definition.**
  – **When you are done with definitions, go outside and find objects that match the definitions on the activity sheet.**
  – Give each group a timer set for the length of the activity.
  – **You have x minutes (suggested 20–30) minutes to complete the activity. When the instructions are done, start your timer. Make sure you are back in the classroom before it reaches zero.**
  – **Find a different object for each definition. If an object fits more than one definition, decide which one it fits best.**
  – **Use acceptable movements and behaviors as you go on your hunt.**

Explain that nonacceptable movements will include shoving, bumping, or racing.

Acceptable movements will be:

In a room—penguin walk (heels down toes up, arms down hands out or tip-toe (small steps on their toes)

In the school—walking (toes straightforward, heel-toe, opposite arm, and leg swing), tip-toe (small steps on their toes), cloud walk (very large, gentle steps, as though trying not to break through a cloud)

Outside the school—walking (toes straightforward, heel-toe, opposite arm, and leg swing) or skipping (step and hop)

- Once instructions have been given, let the students work together to find shapes.
- **You should stay with your group for the whole activity. Take turns writing, drawing, and taking pictures.**

Group Presentations

After students come back to the classroom, they create a PowerPoint presentation or poster to display the pictures of the examples they found and present to the class. The presentations will be done in the next class. They can use photos taken during the activity or draw sketches of the shapes.

- Lead discussion during student presentations by asking questions such as:

  - **What shapes were you surprised to find around the school?**
  - **What objects were difficult to find? Why?**
  - **What objects were especially easy to find in many places around the school? Why do you think that is?**
  - **Which shape was your favorite? Why?**
  - **What did you notice about …?**

Closure

- To close the lesson, students work with the person sitting next to them to identify and draw three geometric shapes they can see from their desks.

Suggested time frame	50 min
Equipment/technology	Geometry Scavenger hunt activity sheets, geometry Scavenger hunt activity sheet key
	Map (if necessary)
	Pencils
	Clipboards (for activity sheet)
	Cameras (if taking pictures) and cords to transfer pictures on computer
	Computers (if making PowerPoint presentations) or poster boards and markers
	timer for each group

(continued)

(continued)

Start/stop signals	When instructions for the activity are done, say "Go!" to start the activity After 25–30 min, signal students to return to the classroom. Use a whistle if outside or three claps inside the classroom Students should use a timer to keep track of their time to know when to return to class
Skill cues	In a room—penguin walk (heels down toes up, arms down hands out or tip-toe (small steps on their toes) In the school—walking (toes straightforward, heel-toe, opposite arm and leg swing), tip-toe (small steps on their toes), cloud walk (very large, gentle steps, as though trying not to break through a cloud) Outside the school—walking (toes straightforward, heel-toe, opposite arm, and leg swing) or skipping (step and hop)
Safety cues	Discuss nonacceptable movements such as shoving, bumping, or racing Make sure students stay in the boundaries and follow the map, reminding them when necessary Students are to return to the classroom in 25–30 min
Teaching style	Direct instruction/cooperative learning
Assessments of content through the activity	Geometry activity sheet: check that students have the correct names of the shapes and/or figures for each definition. Check that the students can name correct attributes for each shape and/or figure Presentation: the presentation of the pictures and attributes of each real-life example will show the students' understanding of geometric shapes and their attributes
Transition activity	After the students return from the scavenger hunt, they get into their groups to work on the presentation and complete the attributes noticed on their geometry Scavenger hunt activity sheet

Extension Students can create a room, holiday scene, market, or shopping store using the different geometric shapes they found while doing the activity.

Modifications/Accommodations Make sure all spaces included in the searchable areas are accessible for all students. Mark areas with cones or other clear markers to indicate the appropriate places that the students can search. Provide word bank if needed.

References

Anehall, K. (n.d.). *Locomotor movement—Animal walks*. PE Scholars. Retrieved from http://peteacher4.tripod.com/pe_curriculum/locomotor_movement.htm.

Appendix A
Language Arts Resource

Y and I Endings—Read the rules and then using your cards glue an example.

Rule: "y" often ends a word which has no other vowel such as "my" or "why."

Rule: "y" ends words of more than one syllable such as "puppy."

Rule: "y" immediately follows another vowel such as "monkey."

Rule: If the word ends in a vowel (a,e,i,o,u) + y then just add s.

Rule: If the word ends in a consonant + y then y changes to –ies

© Springer Nature Singapore Pte Ltd. 2018
S.C. Miller and S.F. Lindt (eds.), *Moving INTO the Classroom*,
Springer Texts in Education, DOI 10.1007/978-981-10-6424-1

Alphabetize It
Observational Checklist
Observe students as they work independently and/or in groups and record your observations. Place a check if students are able to alphabetize.

Group number/names	Alphabetize to 2nd letter	Alphabetize to 3rd letter	Additional notes
Group 1			
Group 2			
Group 3			
Group 4			
Group 5			
Group 6			
Whole class observation			

Appendix B
Science Resources

3-2-1 Exit Ticket: Busy Bees

Exit Slip	
3	Things I Learned Today …
2	Questions I Still Have …
1	Opinion about the Lesson …

© Springer Nature Singapore Pte Ltd. 2018
S.C. Miller and S.F. Lindt (eds.), *Moving INTO the Classroom*,
Springer Texts in Education, DOI 10.1007/978-981-10-6424-1

My Weather Forecast

Fill in the square next to the weather condition observed each day.
After the chart is complete, make a forecast.

		Yesterday	Today	Tomorrow
	Sunny			
	Cloudy			
	Windy			
	Rainy			

Based on my data, tomorrow's forecast is _____ .

Name_____

LIGHT LAB

Name of Object	Prediction What do you think will happen when you shine a flashlight on this object	Results What happened when you shined the flashlight?	What kind of material is it? Translucent, transparent or opaque

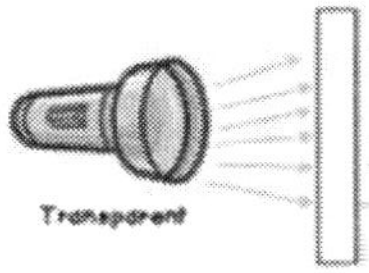

ALL light passes through

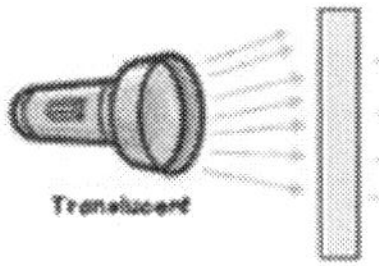

Transparent

SOME light passes through

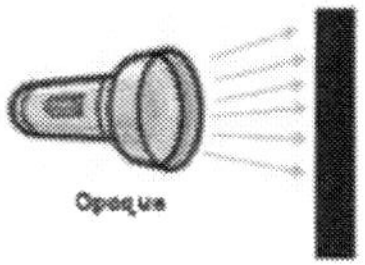

Translucent

NO light passes through

Opaque

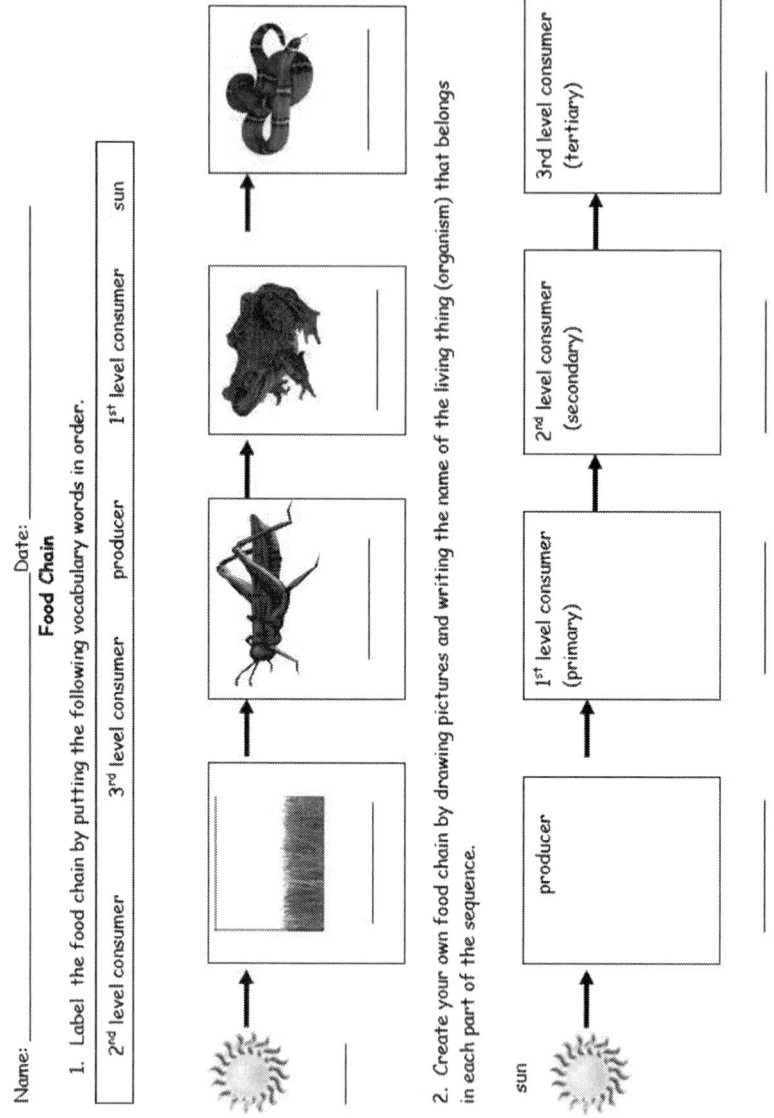

Name: _____ Date: _____

Food Chain

1. Label the food chain by putting the following vocabulary words in order.

| 2nd level consumer | 3rd level consumer | producer | 1st level consumer | sun |

2. Create your own food chain by drawing pictures and writing the name of the living thing (organism) that belongs in each part of the sequence.

sun → producer → 1st level consumer (primary) → 2nd level consumer (secondary) → 3rd level consumer (tertiary)

Name_____

Puff Mobiles

Challenge: Your TASK is to create a vehicle that can go the furthest with five seconds of blowing on it.

Materials:

4 wheels   10 straws   1 piece of paper   tape   scissors

You MUST use ALL your materials.

STEP ONE: Design your car here and name it.

Name of our car_____

Sketch of the car:

STEP TWO: Test your car

Estimated distance _____   Actual distance Trial One   _____
                                     Actual distance Trial Two   _____
                                     Actual distance Trial Three_____

STEP THREE: Re-design your car here. Sketch of the modified car:

STEP FOUR: Test your car again

Estimated distance _____   **Actual distance Trial One** _____
                                        Actual distance Trial Two _____
                                        Actual distance Trial Three_____

Time to Reflect and Write

1) How did you change/modify your car for the second trial?

_____
_____
_____

2) What would you do differently if you had a chance to do a third trial?

_____
_____
_____

Date of Observation: _____Time of Observation: _____

Observer: _____ Class Activity/Concept Taught: _____

Observation Checklist: Metamorphosis Activity

The teacher needs to know whether or not students understand the concept of metamorphosis through their participation in and study of the life cycle of a butterfly.

An *observation checklist* is a helpful formative assessment tool to assist the teacher in analyzing how well students are engaged in the lesson, are grasping the science concept being studied and to assist the teacher to facilitate class and/or group discussions during the activity. Teachers can utilize the observation checklist to monitor student behavior and performance toward the stated goals of the activity.

Teacher Instructions:

Observe students as they work independently and/or in groups and record your observations. Place a check or an 'X' in the appropriate box.

	Observed	Needs improvement	Not observed
Listening			
Student is able to follow simple instructions			
Student is able to answer simple questions			
Student is able to perform a task when explained by the teacher			
Speaking			
Student can express herself/himself clearly			
Student can articulate the appropriate terminology/language with correct pronunciation (e.g., *metamorphosis, larvae stage*, etc.)			
Student can express herself/himself clearly in song along with the whole group			
Reading/writing			
Student can read the selected material (card sort/illustrations) with correct comprehension			
Student is able to write a summary of activity using the learned terminology/language			
Movement			
Student is able to model appropriate use of terminology/language when instructed to do so			
Student is creative in her/his overall physical interpretation/modeling of the life cycle of a butterfly			
Student is able to appropriately model the *egg* stage of the butterfly life cycle			
Student is able to appropriately model the *larvae/caterpillar* stage of the butterfly life cycle			
Student is able to appropriately model the *pupa/cocoon* stage of the butterfly life cycle			

(continued)

(continued)

	Observed	Needs improvement	Not observed
Student is able to appropriately model the *butterfly* stage of the butterfly life cycle			
Student is able to appropriately model the life cycle of a butterfly in the correct sequence or order			

Appendix C
Mathematics Resources

Measuring with everybody		
Name_____		
Measuring unit	Student #1 measurement	Student #2 measurement
Student heights		
Forearms		
Foot lengths		
Fingers		

Stretch it till you break it!!!

Name_____

Measurement of original tootsie roll	Measurement of the stretched tootsie roll	How much longer?	Convert the difference to...... units	Convert the difference to...... units

© Springer Nature Singapore Pte Ltd. 2018
S.C. Miller and S.F. Lindt (eds.), *Moving INTO the Classroom*,
Springer Texts in Education, DOI 10.1007/978-981-10-6424-1

Coordinate Dart			
Name_____			
Target ordered pair	**Impact ordered pair**	**Distance in x-direction from target**	**Distance in y-direction from target**

Sorting activity sheet
Name_____

Item	Quantity

BAR GRAPH AND TALLY SHEET

NAME
OF
OBJECT

TALLY

Note This is a sample bar graph activity sheet. Students can fill in the names of the objects, or the teacher can fill it in ahead of time. An additional column is given in case students find something outside the listed categories. *Source* http://vnzgames.com/bar-graph-template/.

"*I like to Move it*"
Let's Understand Unit Rates!!!
Name_____

Type of walk	Number of steps	Time (30 s)	Rate	Unit rate
Mud walk				
Mouse walk				
Gorilla walk				
Skipping				

Can You Find Me?
Geometry Scavenger Hunt
Directions: Work with your partner to figure out the geometry words from the definitions in the chart below. Find at least one example of each word as you tour the school. Write and draw the example you find for each geometry word. Write at least **two** features you notice for each example. Take a picture when you find an example of a geometry word.

Definition	Word	Name the object or draw it	What do you notice? (Write two sentences)
1. Two lines meet at a common point. What do they form?			
2. I am round and I have no sides? What am I?			
3. A geometric solid with a circular base and curved surface that meets at a point What am I?			
4. A solid figure with six square faces. What am I?			
5. A geometric solid with 2 circular bases and a curved surface. What am I?			
6. The place where two flat surfaces of a solid figure meet. What is it?			
7. Half of a circle. What is it?			
8. A closed figure with 6 straight sides. What am I?			
9. A closed figure with 5 straight sides. What am I?			
10. Figures that are the exact same shape but different sizes. What are they?			
11. A closed figure with 4 sides and 4 square corners and my opposite sides are equal. What am I?			
12. A geometric solid with a curved surface. What am I?			
13. A closed figure with 4 sides that are the same length and 4 right angles. What am I?			
14. A closed figure with 3 straight sides. What am I?			
15. A line segment from the center of a circle to any point on the circle. What is it?			
16. I am a dot. What am I?			
17. A line that splits the figure so that both parts are exactly same. What is it?			

(continued)

(continued)

Definition	Word	Name the object or draw it	What do you notice? (Write two sentences)
18. The point where sides of a shape or angle meet. What am I?			
19. I am a type of angle that measures exactly 90°. What am I?			
20. I am a type of angle that measures less than 90°. What am I? What am I?			

Can You Find Me?
Geometry Scavenger Hunt Key

Directions: Work with your partner to figure out the geometry words from the definitions in the chart below. Find at least one example of each word as you tour the MSU campus. Write and draw the example you find for each geometry word. Write at least **two** features you notice for each example. Take a picture when you find an example of a geometry word.

Definition	Word
1. Two lines meet at a common point. What do they form?	Angle
2. I am round and I have no sides? What am I?	Circle
3. A geometric solid with a circular base and curved surface that meets at a point What am I?	Cone
4. A solid figure with six square faces. What am I?	Cube
5. A geometric solid with 2 circular bases and a curved surface. What am I?	Cylinder
6. The place where two flat surfaces of a solid figure meet. What is it?	Edge
7. Half of a circle. What is it?	Semicircle
8. A closed figure with 6 straight sides. What am I?	Hexagon
9. A closed figure with 5 straight sides. What am I?	Pentagon
10. Figures that are the exact same shape but different sizes. What are they?	Similar figures
11. A closed figure with 4 sides and 4 square corners and my opposite sides are equal. What am I?	Rectangle
12. A geometric solid with a curved surface. What am I?	Sphere
13. A closed figure with 4 sides that are the same length and 4 right angles. What am I?	Square
14. A closed figure with 3 straight sides. What am I?	Triangle
15. A line segment from the center of a circle to any point on the circle. What is it?	Radius
16. I am a dot. What am I?	Point
17. A line that splits the figure so that both parts are exactly same. What is it?	

(continued)

(continued)

Definition	Word
	Line of symmetry
18. The point where sides of a shape or angle meet. What am I?	Vertex
19. I am a type of angle that measures exactly 90°. What am I?	Right angle
20. I am a type of angle that measures less than 90°. What am I?	Acute angle

Observational Checklist—Twist and Learn Activity

The labels of the checklist (horizontal columns) can be repeated as many times as needed, based on the number of figures learned, or the teacher may also keep marking in a single column for multiple shapes. The comments column may be used for the teacher to make note of any "aha" or "misconceptions" for reteach purposes.

Student Name	Recognize/identify the Figure	Able to say the name of the figure	Describe the vocabulary word	Recognize/identify the Figure	Able to say the name of the figure	Describe the vocabulary word	Comments

Appendix D
Social Studies Resources

Torch Journey Mapping Checklist

As student groups arrive, review map routes and ask for group supervisor input regarding group success in following the route. The teacher will check that each group stopped where they were supposed to, then he/she should place a check under each correct stop.

	Map stop 1	Map stop 2	Map stop 3	Map stop 4	Map stop 5
Group 1					
Group 2					
Group 3					
Group 4					
Group 5					

© Springer Nature Singapore Pte Ltd. 2018
S.C. Miller and S.F. Lindt (eds.), *Moving INTO the Classroom*,
Springer Texts in Education, DOI 10.1007/978-981-10-6424-1

Printed in Great Britain
by Amazon

61651236R00169